THE TEAPOT DOME SCANDAL

HOW BIG OIL BOUGHT

THE HARDING WHITE HOUSE

AND TRIED TO STEAL

THE COUNTRY

RANDOM HOUSE
NEW YORK

THE
TEAPOT
DOME
SCANDAL

LATON McCARTNEY

Published in the United States by Random House,
an imprint of The Random House Publishing Group,
a division of Random House, Inc., New York.

RANDOM HOUSE and colophon are registered trademarks of
Random House, Inc.

Grateful acknowledgment is made to Alfred A. Knopf, a division of Random House,
Inc., and Ed Victor Ltd. on behalf of the Estate of Raymond Chandler for permission
to reprint an excerpt from *The High Window* by Raymond Chandler, copyright © 1942
by Raymond Chandler and copyright renewed 1970 by Helga Greene, Executrix of the
Estate of Raymond Chandler. Rights in the United Kingdom are administered by Ed
Victor Ltd. Reprinted by the kind permission of Alfred A. Knopf, a division of Random House, Inc., and Ed Victor Ltd on behalf of the Estate of Raymond Chandler.

LIBRARY OF CONGRESS CATALOGING-IN-PUBLICATION DATA
McCartney, Laton.
The Teapot Dome scandal: how big oil bought the Harding White House and tried
to steal the country / Laton McCartney.
p. cm.
Includes bibliographical references and index.
ISBN 978-1-4000-6316-1
1. Teapot Dome Scandal, 1921–1924.   I. Title.
E785.M38 2008   973.91'4—dc22   2007024396

Printed in the United States of America on acid-free paper

www.atrandom.com

4 6 8 9 7 5 3

Book design by Mary A. Wirth

FOR RY RYAN

CONTENTS

THE INVESTIGATION

CONTINENTAL TRADING

RECKONINGS

AUTHOR'S NOTE

In the interest of full disclosure, I should mention that my family benefited from some of the ill-gotten gains accumulated from the Teapot Dome affair. In 1935, my father, Frederick Laton McCartney, then going into his senior year at Yale, spent the summer in Europe.

By the time he got to Paris in late August, my father was flat broke. Desperate, he called the only person he knew in the city, Harry M. Blackmer, one of the chief participants in the oil swindle, and asked for a loan, explaining that he was Fred McCartney's son. At the time, Blackmer was living in exile in Paris with a $10 million Teapot windfall and his mistress and later second wife, a Norwegian opera singer named Eide Norena. A former resident of Denver, Blackmer had often played golf with my grandfather, but as a wanted man, he was leery that my father might be an FBI agent or a journalist. "If you're Fred McCartney's son," he asked, "how would your father play the thirteenth hole at the Denver Country Club?"

My grandfather was a champion amateur golfer and the designer of the golf course in question. He was also left-handed, which meant that his game, and in particular his strategy in playing the thirteenth hole, differed from that of right-handed players such as Blackmer. After my father, a golfer himself, explained how Fred Sr. typically played the thirteenth, Blackmer gave him his address and asked him to come right over to his apartment. There, my father enjoyed a lavish dinner and drank champagne with the old rogue and his Norwegian ingenue while Blackmer pumped him for news from home and later presented him with $150. That was a sizable sum in 1935, more than enough to sustain my father until his ship departed a few days later.

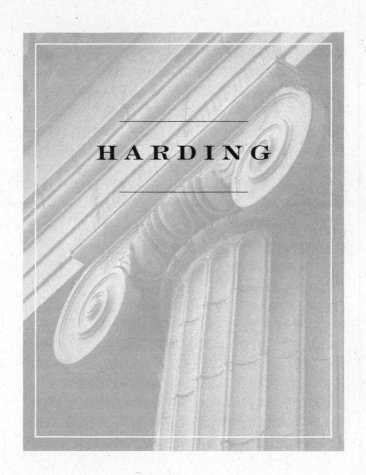

HARDING

1

A REVERSAL OF FORTUNE

The Oil King of Oklahoma" came back to the Randal Hotel and flopped down on the bed in room 28 without undressing. It was just after 6:00 p.m. Jake Hamon had been drinking most of the afternoon. He needed a nap if he was going to make supper.

Clara Hamon was in the adjoining room when Jake came in. She listened as he dropped his keys and change on the bureau and collapsed on the bed. She and Jake had been together ten years. They shared the Hamon name but were neither married nor related. A few months after they met, Jake had paid his nephew Frank Hamon $10,000 to marry Clara and then sent him off on the first train to California. The marriage had been a "blind." Jake wanted Clara for himself. Sharing the Hamon name made it easier for them to travel together, registering in hotels as Jake and Clara Hamon.

Jake had left his wife and two children for Clara. A clerk in a dry goods store, Clara had been seventeen at the time, eighteen years Jake's junior. With her wavy brown hair modestly done up, her deep blue eyes, and her reluctance to wear rouge, she looked more like an attractive young schoolteacher than Jake Hamon's mistress. After they met, Jake offered her a job, sent her to stenography school, and took her out to the oil fields with him when he'd been wildcatting on the Osage and up on the Panhandle. Clara was smart and every bit as ambitious as Jake. For the past few years, she'd been acting as his business partner and adviser. "He was . . . a masterful man," Clara said. "He dominated me from the first time I looked into his eyes and noted the strange glint in them."

· Now Jake had hit the big time, the jackpot of all jackpots. Not even in his wildest dreams could he have imagined the good fortune that had recently befallen him. Until six months ago, Jake had been a big fish in a pond that was far too small to accommodate his vast ambitions. "The Oil King of Oklahoma," the newspapers called him. The raucous, hard-drinking Hamon had graduated from the Law Department of the University of Kansas, then set off for Indian Territory (present-day Oklahoma), where he clerked in a store in Newkirk. When the Kiowa-Comanche country opened up to settlement, Jake went in with the first rush of new settlers to Lawton, then an Indian town. Over the next few years, he had been named Lawton's first city attorney and chairman of the Oklahoma Republican Territorial Committee; made money building a railroad with John Ringling, the circus impresario; and then got into oil, where the real money was.

With the 1920 presidential election coming up, Jake decided to gamble almost everything he had on backing a long shot in the 1920 Republican presidential convention, Senator Warren G. Harding from Ohio. Hamon borrowed nearly $1 million from the National City Bank of New York (today's Citibank), using his substantial oil holdings as collateral. He took his bankroll to Chicago and spread his money around where it counted, buying delegates and influencing the people who needed influencing. Working in tandem with Harding's campaign manager, Harry Micajah Daugherty, Hamon got Warren Harding the Republican presidential nomination.

Six months later, Warren Harding was elected president of the United States. Going into the convention, Harding had been a forty-to-one shot. Hamon agreed to back him on the condition that if he was nominated—and made it to the White House—Harding would appoint Hamon secretary of the interior. That would give Hamon control of the Teapot Dome Naval Reserve in Wyoming, an oil supply potentially worth several hundred million dollars—1920 dollars—a bonanza so rich that it was almost beyond comprehension. Of course, Jake wasn't going to pocket it all. He agreed to lease out the government fields to some of his friends in the oil business, who in turn would kick back a third of the take to Jake.

Hamon had a fortune within his grasp that could put him in the same league as old John D. Rockefeller, the richest man in America. And Jake already knew what he was going to do with a big chunk of the money—make his son president of the United States. If Hamon and Big Oil could get an empty suit like Harding elected, putting a bright, ambitious kid like Jake Jr. in the White House would be a breeze when the time came. Of course, there was a caveat regarding the Interior post. Initially, Jake hadn't thought the matter would prove a problem, but he'd been badly mistaken. When Hamon and Harding first met in New York before the convention, they discovered to their mutual amazement that their wives were related—second cousins, in fact. This, of course, had given Jake a big "in" with Harding, but it also presented a problem. Once "the Duchess," as Harding called his wife, Florence, got the low-down on Jake and Clara, she insisted that Jake get back with his wife before coming to Washington. Florence Harding wasn't going to allow her cousin's husband to come to Washington accompanied by some twenty-seven-year-old floozy.

Clara had to go.

Harding spelled out the demands in a letter Jake had brought back from the Chicago convention, packed in his trunk. It stated unequivocally that Hamon had to resume his legal marital relations before he could be considered for an appointment. Not that Harding cared one way or another. He chased anything in a skirt; that was no secret. But Florence was a tough old bird. There was no getting around her.

Of course, Jake waited until after Harding won the election to break the bad news to Clara. No point in getting her all riled up until he was sure Harding had the job. Clara wasn't the kind of woman you wanted to give up unless you had a good reason, and Jake had two of the best— money and power. Jake would be generous in settling with her, of course. He'd already given Clara a couple of oil wells from which she received small royalties. He'd instructed his business manager, Frank Ketch, to work out a reasonable agreement. Clara would walk away from their ten-year relationship a well-to-do woman with enough to put her younger brother, Jimmy, through college and take care of her ailing father, J. T. Smith, down in El Paso. Back a decade or so ago, J.T.

had come after Jake with a pistol for having absconded with poor innocent Clara. Fortunately, the sheriff managed to disarm him before he could do any damage.

Old J.T. had a nasty temper, but then so did Clara, though she had seemed calm enough when Jake told her that he had to leave her, that he was going back to his wife. Icy calm, in fact. He broke the news on November 7 and gave Clara three weeks to clear out, explaining that his wife and family would be arriving at the end of the month in Ardmore.

God knows, Jake told Clara, he hadn't wanted it to end this way, not after ten years, didn't know what he'd do without her. Jake wanted nothing more than to bring Clara with him to Washington, take her to black-tie dinners at the White House and formal balls, have her meet heads of state, even royalty, but the president-elect of the United States had insisted. Either get back with his wife or forget about the Interior job. What choice did he have?

The day after Jake broke the news, Clara went out and bought a .25-caliber pistol. That, Jake hadn't known. What he knew was that Clara had started packing and seemed resigned to the breakup. It was only a matter of a few days now before she'd be off. In fact, when he got back to the hotel on the evening of November 21, he half expected that she would have already gone. Instead, she came into Jake's room from the adjoining room, her room, after he toppled onto the bed. He was awake, if a little woozy from the whiskey. It was nearly dark. Clara came over to the bed and put her left hand on Jake's forehead as if to stroke it and with her right shot him in the chest with the .25-caliber pistol. *Pop*—one shot that pierced his ribs and lodged in his liver.

Jake jumped up from the bed, knocked the gun from Clara's hand before she could get off a second round, and then began crawling around the floor on his hands and knees, clutching the chest wound with one hand and looking for the tiny pistol with the other in the near darkness. Finally he retrieved the gun, put it in his pocket, and staggered to his feet to confront Clara.

"Clara, you hit me," Jake said, looking at the blood that had begun to soak through his vest and now covered his hand.

Clara would later claim that she pleaded with Jake to lie back down on the bed. She wanted to call for Dr. Walter Hardy, the town doctor, but Jake was determined to walk to the nearby Hardy Sanitarium himself. "Let's call it an accident," he said as he staggered out the door. That suited Clara just fine. She wanted Jake Hamon dead, and she wanted it to appear as if he'd shot himself while cleaning his pistol. She told her driver so the following day.

Clara didn't offer to accompany Jake the few blocks to the sanitarium. Instead, she waited until he was gone, opened his trunk, and took out the letter from the president-elect of the United States, Warren Harding, stipulating that Jake must reunite with his wife if he wanted the cabinet. The letter was Clara's insurance policy. As long as she had possession of the letter, she'd never go to the electric chair for shooting Jake Hamon.

Five days later, Jake Hamon died. By that time, Clara was safely across the border into Old Mexico. "What a wonderful fellow he was," Warren Harding said when he heard the news, tears streaming down his cheeks. "Too bad he had to be taken out. Too bad he had that one fault—that admiration for women."

Florence Harding had a less sympathetic reaction when a reporter told her the news. "Was there a woman involved?" she asked.

2

BREAKFAST OF CHAMPIONS

Prior to Warren Harding's election, the Democrats under President Woodrow Wilson had been in power nearly eight years. Wilson had led the country through the Great War, but in 1920 he lay incapacitated in the White House after suffering a severe stroke the previous year. In the interim, the president's wife, Edith, had been acting as her husband's steward. The White House was in limbo. Even some of the Democrats, including thirty-six-year-old Eleanor Roosevelt, complained that the country was rudderless.

Meanwhile, America was beginning to cut loose after a prolonged interval of wartime self-sacrifice. The country was rushing pell-mell into "the Roaring Twenties," a period of permissiveness, greed, and change. Bessie Smith, Duke Ellington, and Louis Armstrong ushered in the Jazz Age. F. Scott Fitzgerald published his first novel in 1920, *This Side of Paradise*. Eugene O'Neill's first play, *Beyond the Horizon*, opened on Broadway, winning the Pulitzer Prize. The robber barons slipped their political constraints. There was money to be made, piles of it.

If there had been a cultural seismograph at the time, Chicago would have registered as the era's epicenter. It was here that "the 'Black Sox' scandal" had come to light after the 1919 World Series; here that the trial of "Shoeless Joe" Jackson and the other Chicago players who'd thrown the series to Cincinnati would commence in September 1920. The 1919 Volstead Act, which led to Prohibition, was received enthusiastically by Chicago's lawless elements. Chicago soon boasted ten thousand speakeasies and served as the headquarters of a bootlegging and rum-running cartel whose reach extended all the way to southern Florida. Al Capone had moved from Brooklyn to Chicago's South Side in 1919. It was his kind of town.

In June 1920, the Republicans were coming to Chicago for their national convention. Sensing the White House was theirs for the taking, a record eighteen candidates were seeking the nomination, among them General Leonard Wood, Governor Frank Lowden of Illinois, Herbert Hoover, and an obscure senator from Ohio, Warren G. Harding.

Harding's campaign manager was a fleshy, balding, partially blind Scottish Irishman with one blue eye and one brown named Harry Micajah Daugherty. In April 1920, nearly eight months before Jake Hamon was murdered and two months before the Republican convention was scheduled to convene, Daugherty and Jake Hamon had breakfast together in Washington, D.C. With the million dollars he had borrowed from the National City Bank of New York, Hamon was shopping for a candidate he could put in the White House. Daugherty intended to pitch the Oil King on Harding.

Hamon had been introduced to Harding not long before in New York, learning then that his estranged wife, Ruth Hamon, was Florence Harding's second cousin. He'd never met Daugherty before their breakfast. The sixty-one-year-old Daugherty ranked as one of the shrewder, more seasoned and successful political operatives in a state where back-office politics was a game played with brass knuckles and hard cash. Always fastidiously dressed in a well-tailored three-piece, a pearl stickpin in his necktie, he had been born in the small town of Washington Court House, Ohio, just as the Civil War began. His father died when he was a boy, leaving his family penniless. Working in a grocery store, Daugherty put himself through high school, going on to the University of Michigan Law School, where he earned a law degree in 1881. On graduating, he went into politics, served briefly in the state legislature, but soon found his true métier working behind the scenes as a fixer and political deal maker. Mark Hanna, the legendary political kingmaker and Daugherty's onetime boss, was among his mentors. Daugherty was tough, smart, and determined—a mover and shaker. In Ohio, if you needed an arm twisted, a corner cut, a wire pulled, or a pocket lined, Daugherty was your man.

No question he was qualified to run Harding's campaign, having helped McKinley gain the Republican nomination twice. He'd also been instrumental in putting Teddy Roosevelt in the White House and managed Taft's last campaign in Ohio. "For more than a quarter of a century I had played a responsible role in every Republican National Convention and knew the job to which I had set my hand," he said. In those earlier campaigns, however, the Ohioan had been a hired gun. Daugherty had a far more vested interest in Harding, whom he had known twenty years. Harry Daugherty viewed Harding as his creation. "When I met him, he was like a turtle sitting on a log," Daugherty said of Harding. "I pushed him in the water."

Now he intended to push Harding all the way to the White House.

A mutual friend of Hamon and Daugherty's, circus impresario John Ringling, had brokered the breakfast meeting. Ringling and Hamon had built a railroad together in Oklahoma in 1913. It wasn't much of a railroad, running from Ardmore to nearby Healdton, but both men made money on the deal and had stayed in touch. Hamon went on to make his real fortune in the oil fields.

From Ringling, an Ohioan like Daugherty, Daugherty had learned that Hamon was looking to back a presidential candidate and had the deep pockets needed to put his man in the winner's circle. Daugherty immediately began badgering Ringling to set up a meeting in Washington. "I finally told him if he didn't bring Hamon to see me, I'd slip into his circus enclosure some dark night and kill every elephant he had," Daugherty later wrote.

At breakfast in the Oklahoman's Washington hotel, Hamon ordered the hungry man breakfast, three eggs, ham—the works. Normally a tea-and-dry-toast man, Daugherty ordered the same, earning Hamon's immediate approval. "You live among the tenderfeet, but you know how to order a real breakfast," Hamon said.

The forty-seven-year-old Hamon was a prototype of the high-rolling, risk-taking, winner-take-all corporate buccaneers who would be much admired in the 1920s. He was powerfully built, with features that had been weathered by years in the oil fields and a lifetime of hard drinking and high living. Daugherty described him as "a real he-man."

For Hamon, politics was largely a means to an end, the end inevitably having to do with oil and money. The Oklahoman was always looking to develop new oil fields. "All I want to do is make money, and I don't care much how I make it," he once said. In building a fortune, he had made a practice of buying politicians. It was a rare legislator in Oklahoma and Hamon's native state, Kansas, who hadn't benefited from the oilman's under-the-table largesse. Of course, there were always a few fuddy-duddies who wouldn't play the game. In 1910, Hamon had offered the blind U.S. senator from Oklahoma, Democrat Thomas P. Gore, $50,000 to assist him in swindling the Choctaw and Chickasaw out of their reservation land. Gore not only turned Hamon down, but went to the press with the allegations of the bribe attempt. Hamon, of course, denied the incident, his word against Gore's.

More recently, Hamon had done his best to convince President Wilson's interior secretary, Franklin K. Lane, to grant him permission to drill on as yet unallotted sections of the oil-rich Osage Reservation. When Lane refused, Hamon vowed to replace him with an interior secretary who was simpatico to Big Oil, a Republican. And Jake had just the man in mind—himself.

Coming into the Republican convention, Jake had spent $120,000 to get Oklahoma's eighteen delegates in his pocket and bragged openly about controlling another thirty delegates from other states. He was also spending an equivalent sum to get elected national committeeman from Oklahoma. His rival James J. McGraw, the current committeeman, supported General Leonard Wood for the presidency. Early on, Hamon had committed to Frank Lowden, governor of Illinois. Hamon had financed Lowden's defeat of Wood in the Oklahoma primary and was now after McGraw's scalp as well.

As Harding's campaign manager, Harry Daugherty seemingly was backing a loser. Political pundits at the time first coined the term *dark horse* to characterize the less promising of the Republican presidential hopefuls. Harding was as dark a horse as there was in the race. In the respected *Literary Digest* poll that came out prior to the convention, Harding ranked a distant sixth behind the three leaders—Wood, Lowden, and Senator Hiram Johnson from California—as well as Herbert Hoover and Charles Evans Hughes, who had unsuccessfully opposed Woodrow Wilson in the 1916 election. *The Wall Street Journal* listed Harding as an eight-to-one shot to win the nomination. Sportswriter

Ring Lardner, who was covering the convention for several New York papers, put Harding's odds at two hundred to one, only slightly worse than the tongue-in-cheek odds Lardner gave himself.

With two months to go before the convention, the Harding campaign was in dire need of cash. Harding had attracted little early enthusiasm among the delegates who would soon be heading for Chicago. This was understandable, given that Harding's six-year record in the U.S. Senate was largely undistinguished; he wasn't much known outside Ohio and in fact didn't really want the presidency, much preferring the lower-key, less scrutinized life in the U.S. Senate. As a senator he could lead a reasonably normal life, pursue his various extracurricular interests, notably women, poker, and golf. He lacked ambition, discipline, and self-esteem in equal measure. Outside of Daugherty, Harding's ambitious wife, Florence (the Duchess), and some of his political cronies in Ohio, no one seemingly took the Harding campaign seriously.

Daugherty thus far had accumulated a campaign fund of a little over $100,000, most of it made up of relatively modest donations. Daugherty himself was one of the biggest backers, with a contribution of $9,000. Most of the other contenders had amassed significantly larger war chests. Wood's forces, in fact, would end up spending $1.7 million on the record and likely far more off the books. Lowden's funding came to $414,984, most of it his wife's money. The governor was married to the Pullman car heiress.

Going into the convention, the delegate tally was equally bleak. Of the 984 voting delegates, 125 had pledged to Wood, 112 to Johnson, and 72 to Lowden. Harding had mustered only 39. Not even the Ohio delegation was lined up entirely behind him, being split between Harding and Wood.

For Daugherty, gaining Hamon's support was critical, but he had no intention of asking the Oklahoman to abandon Lowden. At least not right away. "I did not care at the time who his first choice was," Daugherty said. "Our whole plan of campaigning was centered on second-choice votes."

During their initial meeting, Daugherty proposed that the Harding forces and the Hamon-supported Lowden camp team up to take Wood out of contention. "The farmer's friend," Lowden, was just the man to beat the seemingly stern, intensely nationalistic Wood, Daugherty asserted. And if Lowden later faltered, Daugherty wanted Hamon's assurance that he would commit entirely to Harding.

It was an offer that could only better Hamon's chances of gaining the coveted secretary of the interior post, a classic "win-win" situation. "Hamon spent the day with me, and when he left, I'd won him," Daugherty later recalled. "He promised that if the time came that Harding had a chance for the nomination and Lowden could not win, he would support Harding."

3

CONVENTION

After his initial meeting with Harry Daugherty in Washington, Jake Hamon had visited the Harding campaign headquarters in Indianapolis. He'd also met with Jess Smith and Howard Mannington at the Deshler Hotel in Columbus, Ohio. There, both Smith, the brilliantined, small-town dandy who served as Daugherty's man Friday, and Mannington, one of the campaign's main fund-raisers, collected a check from Hamon for $25,000 to cover the entire cost of Harding's Chicago campaign headquarters at the Congress Hotel. The Oil King later would brag that he had "signed the check" that resulted in the nomination of Warren Harding, but it would end up costing him far more than $25,000 to get Harding nominated.

The Republican National Convention was scheduled to run from June 8 to June 12 at the immense Chicago Coliseum. Hamon arrived in town early, on Thursday, June 3, establishing his headquarters on the twelfth floor of the William Holabird–designed La Salle Hotel. When Daugherty got in later the same day, he contacted Hamon, who asked him to come immediately to the La Salle. The Oklahoman had delivered on his part of the bargain that had been struck in Washington. Now it was Daugherty's turn.

"He insisted on my seeing Governor Lowden," Daugherty recalled. "I wanted to get to our headquarters, but . . . I agreed to see Lowden first."

As soon as Daugherty arrived from the train station, Hamon called Lowden, who he discovered was sick. The governor couldn't see anyone, not even Hamon, doctor's orders. Before Daugherty could get away, Hamon made another call, this one to Louis Emmerson, Lowden's campaign manager. Summoned by Hamon, Emmerson appeared soon after. "We'll do our best, Mr. Emmerson, to put Harding over," Daugherty told Emmerson after they'd been introduced. "We know Governor Lowden has a large following. But we believe our man can win."

"But you'll give Lowden a chance to land the nomination first?" Emmerson asked.

"That's exactly what I was going to tell you. General Wood must be beaten first. And Lowden's the man to beat him. . . . We'll loan you every vote we can until you pass Wood. The minute you do this, Wood is out of the race and all friendship on the floor of the convention ceases between us—you understand that?"

"Certainly," Emmerson said. "You couldn't make a fairer proposition."

Hamon gave Lowden news of the agreement he'd brokered the following evening in the governor's suite in the Blackstone Hotel. "Frank, you haven't got a Chinaman's chance for the nomination, but I am going to stick with you for a while to give you a chance," Hamon explained with his usual bluntness. "Then we go for Warren Harding."

WARREN HARDING HAD hoped to arrive in Chicago on Saturday in order to see his twenty-three-year-old mistress, Nan Britton, before the convention got under way. Nan and her baby daughter, Elizabeth Ann, whom Harding had fathered, had recently moved to Chicago to live with Nan's sister. Harding had planned to spend Saturday evening with Nan, who had her sister's apartment on Woodlawn Avenue all to herself for the weekend, but the Duchess put the kibosh on the long-planned rendezvous, sensing that her philandering husband was up to no good. Much to Harding's chagrin, she insisted on traveling with him rather than take a later train from Washington that would get her into Chicago on Sunday.

They arrived together aboard the *Republican Special* at Union Station. In a *Chicago Daily News* photo, the usually robust Harding seems frazzled from the sweltering heat that would linger for the duration of the convention. He was fifty-five, stood slightly over six feet, and had classically handsome features that wouldn't be out of place on Mount Rushmore or, in profile, on a Roman coin. One political wag characterized him as the only man in America who could get away with wearing a toga. "Like everyone else I instantly perceived that this man, who talked like somebody invented by Sinclair Lewis, looked more like a president than any president who ever lived with the possible exception of George Washington," noted Bruce Bliven, who interviewed Harding for the *New York Globe* in Chicago prior to the convention. From his exasperated expression in the *News* photograph, Harding gives the impression that he would rather be almost anywhere than at the convention—on a golf course, say, or between the sheets with nubile young Nan. He was a reluctant candidate, had threatened to quit the race on a number of occasions. Daugherty kept pumping him up, telling Harding he could win, all evidence to the contrary. Harding had shown poorly in the Indiana primary. More recently in his home state, Ohio, he'd won but had come away with a split delegation—thirty-nine delegates for Harding, nine for General Wood.

"Well, it looks like we're done for," he told Daugherty when the Ohio results were in.

Not at all, Daugherty reassured him. It was often a badge of honor to go into the convention with a split delegation. He reminded Harding that Grover Cleveland had failed to gain the full backing of the New York delegation because of Tammany Hall opposition and had still come away with the 1884 nomination, going on to win the presidency. In fact, Daugherty was so confident Harding would be the next Republican presidential candidate that he boasted to reporters: "At the proper time after the Republican National Convention meets, some fifteen men, bleary-eyed with a loss of sleep and perspiring profusely with the excessive heat, will sit down in seclusion around a big table. I will be with them and will present the name of Senator Harding to them, and before we get through they will put him over."

In view of what ensued in Chicago, Harry Daugherty was either extraordinarily prescient or was privy to some inside information about how the next Republican presidential candidate was going to be selected.

He and Will Hays, the jug-eared, whippet-thin Republican National Committee (RNC) chairman, were among those who were at Union Station to meet the train and escort the Hardings back to campaign headquarters at the Congress Hotel. En route, Daugherty briefed the Hardings on the campaign strategy. This was a moment Daugherty had been preparing for since he'd first met Harding twenty years earlier after a political rally in rural Ohio. In the rear of a backwater hotel, they'd shared a wad of chewing tobacco and chatted for a few minutes. "Gee," Daugherty thought to himself as the then publisher of the *Marion* (Ohio) *Star* walked away, "what a great-looking president he'd make."

In Chicago, Daugherty seemingly had thought of everything. He had handpicked a staff of more than five hundred men from Harding's former headquarters in Columbus, and from Washington, D.C., New York, and Indianapolis. "They had proven their loyalty and ability in the primary struggle," he later said. "There wasn't a traitor among them." Another fifteen hundred volunteers had been recruited to help out as well. Harding's people would meet every train, greeting the delegates as they arrived, and make appointments to see them. Round-the-clock lookouts had already been posted in every hotel in Chicago. The campaign staff knew the names of all 984 delegates, their hotels, and the room numbers at which they were registered. Daugherty had also placed Harding people in each of the opposing candidates' headquarters. He had arranged for the seventy-five-man Columbus Glee Club to be brought up to Chicago. Hourly, the glee club, which still listed Harding as an honorary member, serenaded the delegates with such toe tappers as "A Great Big Man from a Great Big State" and "We'll Nominate Harding in the Morning."

The Hardings were staying in the La Salle, Hamon's hotel, but the Harding campaign headquarters was at the Congress in the ornate Florentine Room. There the Hardings wooed delegates and made themselves available to journalists. Normally, the wives of candidates remained in the background at political gatherings of this sort, but it was largely Florence Harding who held court in the Florentine Room.

In some early accounts of the Harding era, the Duchess was characterized unfairly as a social-climbing shrew who was capable of almost anything, even poisoning her husband. Although she was not quite five years Warren's senior, Florence could have passed as his mother. There was an autumnal, postmenopausal aura about her, but when she spoke, her features became animated with a lively intelligence. In interviews she was unpretentious, candid, and well-informed. The press found her refreshing, accessible, and always quotable.

Daugherty admired her enormously. He viewed Florence as his most important ally in getting Harding elected president, though she was considerably less enthusiastic about the prospect than Daugherty, having had a premonition that Warren was going to be assassinated in office. In this, the first year women won the right to vote, Daugherty was shrewd enough to put Florence front and center in Chicago. "I . . . gave Mrs. Harding a free hand in talking to anybody she pleased," he said. "I could trust absolutely her keen intuitions and her straightforward, honest thinking. . . . She made friends with every reporter who talked to her. She disarmed criticism by her frank declaration that she only wished Harding's success because he wanted it. Personally she had always opposed his running."

In contrast, Daugherty told Harding to make no predictions or statements, smile amiably, and look presidential. Florence would do the talking for both of them. This suited Harding fine. At the first opportunity, he slipped away to see Nan at her sister's apartment.

WITH HIS $1 MILLION piggybank, Jake Hamon wasn't the only oilman in Chicago shopping for a president. Harry Ford Sinclair, president of the Sinclair Consolidated Oil Corporation, and William Boyce Thompson, one of Sinclair's directors and largest stockholders, were in the market as well. Several months before the convention, Sinclair—"Sinco" to his friends—and Thompson had, like Hamon, come up with funding for the convention and the ensuing election. Using Sinclair stock as collateral, Sinclair and Thompson, a New York banker who was treasurer of the Republican Party and a delegate to the convention, borrowed $3 million that Sinclair intended to use incrementally to underwrite the Republican campaign. This, investigators would later claim, was a dummy loan, a way of enabling Sinclair and his associates to pass along money to the RNC without it showing up as an individual contribution.

Conveniently, the chairman of the Republican National Committee, Will Hays, was also a director of one of Sinclair's companies, a Sinclair stockholder, and an attorney who counted Sinclair among his most important clients. Prior to the convention, the Indiana-born Hays, a Presbyterian elder, had decreed that he would accept no campaign contributions larger than $1,000. This put Sinclair potentially $2,999,000 over the limit, but Hays apparently was willing to cut his boss a little slack. Besides, even in pre–electronic media 1920, running a national presidential campaign was an expensive proposition. Sinclair's largesse would go a long way toward covering those costs.

In return, Sinclair wanted the Republicans to handpick a presidential candidate who would put a compliant interior secretary in office—namely, Jake Hamon. Sinclair knew Hamon from the Oklahoma oil fields. Prior to the convention, Sinclair and Hamon had agreed that once Hamon took over Interior, he would lease the Wyoming Teapot reserves to Sinclair in return for one-third of the earnings. Going into Chicago, though, the two oil titans differed as to which candidate they intended to back. Initially a Wood supporter, Hamon had a falling-out with some of Wood's top people and switched his allegiance to Lowden. Thanks to Daugherty's persuasiveness, however, he was leaning heavily toward Harding when the convention finally got under way.

In contrast, Sinclair was an early and unwavering supporter of Wood's. The general, a friend and protégé of Teddy Roosevelt's and America's proconsul in Cuba and later the Philippines, had attracted the backing of much of Wall Street and many of the nation's big moneymen. George F. Baker, Vincent Astor, T. Coleman du Pont, Horace Havemeyer, John D. Rockefeller Jr., Marshall Field, Andrew Mellon, and William Boyce Thompson (who had made his fortune in the copper business) had all contributed to Wood's coffers. By the convention, though, Wood's star had lost some of its luster. The Republican old guard, led by Henry Cabot Lodge, had come to view the general as a little too independent for the party's good. Also, it was becoming clear that Wood's persistent warnings about the need for military preparedness weren't resonating among war-weary voters.

Coming into the convention, Sinclair developed reservations about Wood as well. While Hamon had gotten a verbal agreement from the Harding camp about securing the Interior post, Wood had agreed to nothing. In fact, the general boasted he was his own man, a candidate unencumbered by ties to special interest groups and what he called "shady business." Such posturing was to be expected from a presidential candidate, of course, but some of the higher-ups in the GOP ranks were beginning to think Wood actually *meant* what he was saying. One alarming indication: Wood had recently distanced himself publicly from the support of the party's top political boss, Pennsylvania's Boies Penrose, going so far as to fire John T. King, an associate of Penrose's who had been the general's campaign manager.

Wood's holier-than-thou attitude was a big reason Hamon had originally switched to Lowden and was now leaning toward Harding. Harding was the consummate "go along to get along man." He'd shown that repeatedly in his six years in the U.S. Senate. Still, Sinclair—initially, at least—had largely written Harding off. Simply to hedge his bets, Sinclair had *loaned*, not given, Harding's campaign $7,500. Now, at Hamon's urging, however, Sinclair was willing to take a second look.

At the start of the convention, he and Thompson arranged to meet the Hardings at the Sinclairs' suite in the Blackstone Hotel. There, Sinclair had taken out an entire floor of the hotel at the cost of $400,000 to entertain delegates, politicians, and journalists round the clock for the duration of the convention. The meeting gave Sinclair a chance to check out Harding in person, get a first-person "read" on the man whom Jake Hamon was now touting as a nominee.

Though brief, the meeting apparently went well. Like Sinclair, Harding was a "man's man": an inveterate poker player who liked his whiskey, Prohibition notwithstanding; a small-town boy who had pulled himself up by the bootstraps, becoming publisher and owner of his hometown paper, the *Marion Star*. Harding was a man with whom you could do business, not some straight-backed general exuding Victorian rectitude. Still, Wood remained the clear favorite. The delegates, it was rumored, were merely waiting for the second ballot before throwing their votes to the general. Sinclair had no cause to pull his support as long as Wood agreed to put the right man in the secretary of the interior job.

THE CONVENTION FINALLY got under way Tuesday morning. Some 984 delegates plus 30,000 guests crowded into the Chicago Coliseum. This was the first convention in history to include women delegates—27 of them—and also the first time reporters were allowed into the convention hall. By 11:00 a.m., the scheduled time of the opening, it was already ninety degrees. This, of course, was well before air-conditioning. The women in the balconies were already fanning themselves with their programs. The band played "Columbia, the Gem of the Ocean" and then "Dixie." From the floor came wiseacre requests for "How Dry I Am." On Monday, the U.S. Supreme Court had ruled in favor of both the contested Eighteenth Amendment (for Prohibition) and the Volstead Act.

At 11:34, RNC chairman Hays strode down the flying bridge to the speaker's podium, rapped for order with an oversize chairman's gavel that was hewn from a rafter in Philadelphia's Freedom Hall, and announced that the Republican National Convention of 1920 had officially commenced. The delegates roared their approval. For the Republicans, the new decade had begun.

The permanent convention chairman, Henry Cabot Lodge—"the Puritan aristocrat," Daugherty called him—gave the opening speech, lambasting Woodrow Wilson and the president's efforts to gain United States entry into the League of Nations, the precursor to the United Nations. For an hour and a half, Lodge went on. Listless attendees glanced at their watches and mopped their foreheads with linen handkerchiefs.

The nominating speeches followed. Wood, the war hero; Lowden, who'd slashed taxes as the governor of Illinois; the hard-charging, humorless reformer Johnson. Hamon had arranged for the Oklahoma delegates to nominate the state's favorite son—none other than Jake Hamon. Nathan L. Miller of New York nominated Herbert Hoover. Governor Calvin Coolidge of Massachusetts joined the list of candidates. It was said that "Silent Cal" had once opened his mouth and a moth flew out. He had gained national prominence after breaking a police strike in Boston. Put the micks in their place. The oddsmakers quoted him as an eight-to-one shot, the same odds that were currently being offered for Harding.

Daugherty purposely held off the nominating speech for Harding until late in the day, by which time the delegates and their guests were wondering if they were going to be able to get a cold beer when they got back to their hotels, given the untimely advent of Prohibition and an equally untimely waiters' strike. With a rousing endorsement of Harding, Frank B. Willis, governor of Ohio, managed to stir up a little excitement. "The members began to sit up and take notice," Daugherty said.

"Boys and girls, come on now and give us your votes—to nominate Senator Harding," Willis thundered. That set off ten minutes of cheers and foot stomping, especially among the first-time women voters. Some of the attendees turned to smile at Florence Harding, who was seated in a guest box belonging to Fred W. Upham, a Harding supporter and the RNC treasurer. High above her in the visitors' gallery, Nan Britton jumped up and down with the unrestrained enthusiasm of a cheerleader whose boyfriend had just scored a winning touchdown. Harding had given her a visitor's pass for the entire convention.

The balloting began Friday with no surprises. In the first go-around, Wood received 287 votes, well short of the 484 votes needed to gain the nomination; Lowden, 211; Johnson, 133. Harding placed seventh with 65 votes. By the end of the day, and three more ballots, Harding's total had dropped to 61, but with Daugherty's help, Lowden had moved up to 289, only 25 fewer than Wood's 314. Daugherty's strategy seemed to be working. "The Lord had been good to us," he said. "Our plans were working with the sure, soft power of a big Packard motor."

NOT QUITE. Unbeknownst to Daugherty, Hamon visited Wood's headquarters at the Elizabethan Room on the ground floor of the Congress Hotel after Friday's balloting. By now, Hamon had control of at least fifty delegates from the Southwest, most of them bought and paid for, and had been negotiating with John T. King in an attempt to secure the Pennsylvania delegation with its seventy-six delegates. King was a big, smooth-talking Irishman from Bridgeport, Connecticut. He'd made substantial money in the garbage business before becoming one of the sub-bosses of the GOP. Though he'd split from the Wood campaign, he remained in Chicago to look after the interests of Boies Penrose, the booze-bloated Harvard grad who was the Republicans' top deal maker.

Severely ill, Penrose hadn't come to Chicago but communicated with King almost hourly over both a private phone line and a telegraph line that he'd had installed between his sickbed and a suite in the Blackstone Hotel. The suite, it should be noted, was jointly occupied by RNC chairman Hays and Colonel George Harvey, a renegade Democrat with an almost pathological hatred of the severely ill president Wilson.

In the Elizabethan Room, Hamon told Wood and an old army colleague of the general's, Chauncey Baker, that he could deliver the southwestern votes as well as the Pennsylvania delegation. Hamon had also acquired the votes of the New York delegation at what he'd later complain was an exorbitant cost. Taken together, these delegates along with those already backing Wood would be enough to put the general over the 484 total needed to win. Hamon could make this happen if Wood allowed him to name the interior secretary and the ambassador to Mexico, where American oilmen had substantial interests.

Despite his rather fearsome visage, Wood, a graduate of Harvard Medical School who originally entered the army as a surgeon, was known as a comparatively temperate, fair-minded leader much beloved by his troops. At Hamon's proposal, however, he erupted. "I am an American soldier," he shouted at Jake. "I'll be damned if I betray my country. Get the hell out of here." Hamon fled before Wood went after him with the riding crop he almost always carried tucked under his arm. At least now Hamon and Sinclair knew where they stood with Wood. Harding alone, it seemed, held the key to Teapot.

The next twenty-four hours were frantic. Daugherty and his campaign workers went all out in their efforts to promote Harding. "Friday night was a memorable one," he recalled. "It was a night of wild excitement. Everybody who could be induced to do so was talking in favor of Harding." Meanwhile, Hamon, acting on behalf of Daugherty, approached King, who continued to act as the gatekeeper for Penrose. The Republicans had boasted that this was to be an "unbossed" convention, but the ailing sixty-one-year-old Penrose was still pulling strings, albeit from eight hundred miles away.

From King, Hamon learned that Penrose also had tried to make a side deal with Wood, ensuring him the nomination in exchange for being able to name three cabinet members. Penrose had called Wood's headquarters within minutes of Hamon's abrupt departure. Wood refused to speak to Penrose, instructing his personal secretary, John Latimore Himrod, to take a message. "You may say to General Wood if he were nominated tomorrow, would he give us three cabinet members?" Penrose said.

His hand over the receiver, Himrod relayed the message. Hearing Penrose's offer, General E. F. Glenn, one of Wood's campaign advisers, said to Wood: "Now, General, one word will make you president of the United States."

Wood shook his head. "Tell Senator Penrose that I made no promises and am making none," he responded.

Harding, or at least Daugherty, had no such scruples. In the next few hours, Hamon and Daugherty conferred and came to an understanding with King and Penrose. Daugherty promised King a lucrative position in the Harding administration. Penrose could have his cabinet posts as long as Hamon had "dibs" on the Interior slot. In addition, Hamon threw in a sweetener, $250,000, most of which was later found in Penrose's safe-deposit box. *This* was the check that won Harding the nomination. In return, King was to deliver Connecticut, his home state, to Harding. Penrose had been holding the Pennsylvania votes in reserve for Governor William Sproul. Once Wood went down, Penrose would release those delegates to Harding. By midnight, the Harding camp and the party bosses had a deal in place that would ensure Harding the nomination.

ON FRIDAY NIGHT, the party's old guard—Lodge, the eldest of the elders, and Senators Frank Brandegee of Connecticut, Charles Curtis of Kansas, and Reed Smoot of Utah, among others—had dinner and then retired to suite 404–406, the Hays-Harvey suite, for Cuban Perfecto cigars and brandy. Hays and the acerbic Colonel Harvey, an influential newspaper editor and the Republicans' resident Machiavelli, hosted this boozy, smoke-beclouded soiree, welcoming dozens of other senators and party leaders who dropped by. With the delegates increasingly out of sorts because of the unrelenting heat, the high cost of living in Chicago, and no resolution in sight, senior party members informally had come together to discuss the seemingly deadlocked convention. Or so the story goes.

This was the fabled "smoke-filled" room that Daugherty had uncannily prophesied several months earlier. According to traditional accounts, it was here that a junta of top Republicans—"bleary-eyed with a loss of sleep and perspiring profusely with the excessive heat"—sagely assessed the pros and cons of the various candidates, finally settling on Warren Harding as the man best suited to break the deadlock. And, yes, as he had predicted, Harry Daugherty was summoned before the afore-mentioned wise men to make the case for Brother Harding, though in his ghostwritten autobiography, Daugherty fails to mention he ever set foot in suite 404–406. "We were told afterwards that Colonel Harvey met his friends in a smoke-fogged room at the Blackstone Hotel, de-cided on a candidate and adjourned at two a.m.," he said. "We paid no attention to these meetings, but sought out and gripped the hands of the delegates who were to vote."

Between 1:00 and 2:00 a.m. Saturday morning, it was ordained that Warren Harding would be given the nomination, supposedly by Lodge and the other Republican leaders. In truth, it was Boies Penrose who or-dered the nomination of Harding from his deathbed in Philadelphia, the last power play of a dying man. A telegraph operator named John B. Alcorn was in the suite that night, working for the John King–led Pen-rose task force. He heard Harding's name being tapped out over Pen-rose's wire.

By the time Daugherty was summoned to the suite, Harding's se-lection was already a fait accompli. It had far less to do with Daugherty's masterful political strategizing than it did with Jake Hamon's check-book. Lodge, Colonel Harvey, and the others in the suite had simply summoned Daugherty to let him know the decision had been made. Find Harding and get him up here, Daugherty was told.

HARDING WAS DISCOVERED wandering the halls of the Congress Hotel, unshaven and hungover. He was marched up to the suite, where Colonel Harvey had decided to do a little last-minute due diligence on behalf of the party. Harvey asked Harding if he knew of any reason he could not be president of the United States. Harding was a little stunned by the question. He stepped out into the corridor for a few minutes of soul-searching. He had his young mistress, Nan Britton, and their illegitimate daughter stashed nearby. In fact, Harding had spent almost as much time these past few days with Nan as he had buttonhol-ing delegates. Another of his former mistresses, Carrie Phillips, the wife of a department store owner in Marion, was threatening to blackmail him. But the colonel, Harding suspected, wasn't interested primarily in his love life. For years, rumors had circulated that Harding had African American blood, and they'd resurfaced at the convention. His own father-in-law had spread rumors that Harding was, in his words, "a nigger" to dissuade Florence from marrying him. Harvey wanted to know if there was any truth to those rumors. Harvey had phrased the question diplomatically. Still, it came out the same: "Was he a nigger?"

It didn't take Harding long to come up with his answer. He might have been a serial philanderer, but he was as much a Caucasian as any man in the room. More so, in fact. Curtis, one of Harding's poker-playing buddies from the Senate, had Cherokee blood. "Gentlemen, there is no reason in the sight of God why I cannot be president of the United States," Harding announced when he returned to the suite.

Later the same day, with Florence Harding and Daugherty watching from the spectators' gallery and Nan Britton looking on from the balcony, Warren Harding won the presidential nomination with 674.7 ballots. Jake Hamon was the first to congratulate him. The oilman Hamon had delivered Oklahoma, Texas, Arizona, New York, Kentucky, and, through King and Penrose, Pennsylvania and Connecticut. Daugherty later acknowledged, "Jake Hamon . . . had more influence among the delegates than any other man in the convention."

A million dollars' worth.

4

THE PRIZE

Going into the 1920 presidential elections, the major oil companies had compiled a list of concessions they wanted from Washington if the Republicans gained power. Collectively and individually, they had been lobbying for these measures with little success throughout the eight years Woodrow Wilson was in the White House.

For petroleum interests, the stakes in 1920 were significantly higher than in past elections. During World War I, the demand for oil had increased markedly after both British and U.S. navies converted their ships from coal to oil. At war's end, restless and newly affluent Americans enthusiastically embraced automotive travel. "The transformation occurred with astonishing rapidity," wrote oil industry historian Daniel Yergin. ". . . With peacetime prosperity at hand . . . cars were rolling off the assembly lines in ever more staggering numbers."

In 1920, Ford and General Motors produced nearly 2.3 million automobiles. A Model T Ford cost $300. Drive-in gas stations were proliferating across the country almost as rapidly as speakeasies. Oil production kept pace, reaching 450 million barrels in the United States. Meanwhile, the price of crude soared to $3.40 a barrel.

Oil companies such as Sinclair Consolidated, Standard Oil of Indiana, Gulf, Standard Oil of New Jersey, and Texaco registered record profits, but already industry analysts were voicing concern that demand would soon exceed supply. "We have apparently used up to 40 percent of our oil supply," George Otis Smith, the director of the U.S. Geological Survey, warned in 1920. "There is a need for a countrywide thrift campaign looking to the saving of this essential resource."

Perhaps Smith envisioned millions of husbands around the country telling their spouses, "No, honey, we can't go for a drive this Sunday. There's an oil shortage." Not likely in an America where almost overnight the family car had become the ultimate status symbol, the Sunday afternoon drives a middle-class entitlement.

To deal with these perceived shortages, some American producers expanded internationally. Harry Sinclair was the most ambitious of his contemporaries in seeking to grow outside the United States. Both Sinclair and Edward Doheny, a Democrat whose petroleum holdings in Mexico dwarfed those of Sinclair and all the other American firms combined, had long been frustrated by what they perceived as President Wilson's failure to safeguard American oil interests south of the border. Not only had the Mexican government threatened to nationalize U.S. oil companies operating there, but Doheny and the other American producers were competing fiercely with British interests led by Lord Cowdray (aka Weetman Pearson). As one of his biographers noted, Pearson had the rare distinction of being both a robber baron and a real baron.

Instead of sending in the marines to secure American interests, Wilson adopted a "hands-off" policy toward Mexico, frustrating even Democratic supporters such as Ed Doheny. By 1918, Doheny had taken matters into his own hands, establishing a private six-thousand-man army to protect his extensive petroleum interests in the state of Tampico.

Domestically, the American Southwest, notably Texas, Oklahoma, and New Mexico, represented the most opportune area for new development. Unfortunately for the oil companies, the most promising of the undeveloped fields were situated on reservation land under the control and protection of the secretary of the interior. Hamon and Sinclair, among others, were counting on the Republicans to lift the leasing restriction on the reservations, notably on unallotted sections of the Osage Reservation and on Navajo land to the west.

At the top of the industry's wish list, however, were three fields that had been set aside as U.S. Naval Petroleum Reserves by the Taft and

Wilson administrations to provide the navy with oil in case of war or a national emergency. These included Naval Petroleum Reserve No. 1, a 38,969-acre field in Elk Hills, Kern County, California; Naval Petroleum Reserve No. 2, consisting of 29,341 acres at Buena Vista, also in Kern County; and Teapot Dome, some forty-five miles north of Casper, Wyoming. So named because of a teapotlike sandstone outcropping (the spout has long since disappeared, victim of a lightning strike) that marked the site, the latter reserve was smaller—9,481 acres in all—than its California counterparts but held an estimated 150 million barrels of oil, slightly more than both the California fields together.

Jake Hamon, Sinclair, Doheny, and Colonel Robert W. Stewart, chairman of Standard Oil of Indiana, were among the oil company heads who were hopeful that a new administration would open these reserves, especially Teapot, to commercial drilling. In fact, several operators including Doheny already had established mineral and mining claims on Teapot land in hopes that if drilling was allowed, the claims could be used to establish drilling rights. With oil prices rising along with demand, the naval reserves would generate revenues of several billion dollars in today's money to whichever producers won the contracts to develop them.

Even if Harding, the newly selected Republican candidate, won the election and appointed Hamon to head the Department of the Interior, however, Teapot, Buena Vista, and Elk Hills would remain under the control of the U.S. Navy. Before Hamon could open them up to commercial exploitation, they would have to be transferred to Interior, a move that could be made only with the approval of the president on the recommendation of the U.S. attorney general.

As the ever resourceful Daugherty envisioned how things would play out in the White House—the *Harding* White House—this likely wouldn't prove a problem. Flush from the victory in Chicago, Daugherty retreated to a cabin he owned outside Washington Court House, Ohio. Jake Hamon came along as well as Daugherty's guest, the two of them now bosom buddies in the glow of their shared triumph in Chicago. For three days, Hamon, Daugherty, and Jess Smith, Daugherty's housemate and constant companion, unwound, put their feet up on the porch overlooking Deer Creek, drank whiskey, smoked stogies, and rehashed the convention highlights. Mal Daugherty, Harry's brother, came over to join the celebration, as did Roxy Stinson, an at-

tractive redhead with a showgirl's figure who had been married briefly
to Jess. Roxy and her ex-husband remained close, though Daugherty
openly disliked her, was proprietary of Jess, and viewed Roxy as one cut
above white trash. No shrinking violet, Roxy held Daugherty in mutual
disregard and let him know it.

What we know about this little gathering comes from Roxy's later
testimony before a Senate subcommittee in late March 1924. Mostly,
she recalled Daugherty and Hamon bragging; Hamon was half-drunk
and trying to impress her, get her into bed maybe. He told Roxy how he
was going to be the next secretary of the interior. Daugherty went on
about how he'd gotten Harding the nomination and how he was "slated
for a big job" when Harding got in. Daugherty was going to Washington, and he was taking a lot of his Columbus cronies with him—the
"Ohio Gang," he called them. He was going to give them all plum jobs,
Jess Smith included, and he had a top spot all lined up for himself.
Harry Micajah Daugherty was going to be the next attorney general of
the United States.

5

A STAR OF A FELLOW

One of the first people Warren Harding wanted to see when he got back to Washington from Chicago was Albert Bacon Fall, the Republican senator from New Mexico. Politically and socially, Fall was as close to Harding as anyone in Washington. Elected to the Senate in 1912, when New Mexico was admitted to the Union, Fall had taken Harding under his wing after the Ohioan came to Washington three years later. They sat side by side in the Senate chamber, played poker three or four nights a week, usually at Fall's apartment in the Wardman Park Hotel on Connecticut Avenue or in the Hardings' comfortable home on Wyoming Avenue, drank whiskey and soda, and talked shop, always ending their game promptly at midnight.

Born in Frankfort, Kentucky, in November 1861 at the outset of the Civil War, Fall was six feet tall, mustached, and beginning to lose his wavy, graying hair. In photographs, he always looks a little angry and eyes the camera with an expression that reads: "Tread carefully, pal."

With his black slouch Stetson, an ever-present cheroot that Evalyn McLean, a wealthy friend of the Hardings, described "as being poisonous as a cobra," and the six-shooter he often carried as a sinister accessory, Fall was a living icon of a frontier that had all but vanished. He was smart, opinionated, outspoken, highly articulate, volatile, and, on occasion, a schoolyard bully, the schoolyard in this instance being the Senate floor. When debating there, he often aimed his index finger at an opponent as though he were holding his pistol and getting ready to pull the trigger. Even so, he was generally well liked and respected by many of his peers, including Henry Cabot Lodge and William E. "Lion of Idaho" Borah, as well as some Democrats such as Senator Marcus A. Smith of Arizona.

There was nothing neutral about Albert Fall. Vindictive in the extreme, he never forgave or forgot a slight. For the past few years, President Wilson and the First Lady, Edith Wilson, had topped his enemies list. Ostensibly, Fall, a strong advocate of protecting U.S. interests in Mexico, was angered that Wilson hadn't reacted militarily to the Mexican government seizing U.S. copper and oil holdings south of the border. This wasn't simply a partisan policy dispute, however. For Fall, it was a personal matter.

In 1918, Fall's thirty-two-year-old only son, Jack, and one of his daughters, Carrie, died in the so-called Spanish flu epidemic that killed more than fifty million people worldwide. Fall had planned for Jack to take over the ranching empire he'd built up over the years in southern New Mexico. "I built Three Rivers for my son," he said. "I molded my son for Three Rivers." Albert and Emma Fall were devastated by the loss of Jack and Carrie. Both left small children.

At the time, Fall was up for reelection in the Senate in a race that was viewed as critical in maintaining Republican control of the Senate. Only a few days after the Falls buried their children, President Wilson lashed out at Fall in a campaign speech. That the speech was political, not personal, made no difference to the bereaved father. Nor did it matter that Wilson likely hadn't known about Fall's loss. Fall never forgave the president for what he viewed as Wilson's callous insensitivity. Returning to the Senate—his victory in the 1918 Senate election gave the Republicans a one-seat majority—Fall lambasted Wilson at every turn and did his best to jeopardize every initiative that came out of the White House, especially the president's efforts to get the Treaty of Versailles approved after World War I.

He didn't let up even after Wilson suffered a major stroke in October 1919. After Mrs. Wilson appointed herself gatekeeper, keeping virtually everyone except the president's physician from the White House, Fall turned his sights on her. "We have a petticoat government!" he charged in a Senate speech. "Mrs. Wilson is president!"

She in turn dismissed Fall as a "provincial westerner of small intelligence."

A month after Wilson's stroke, the Venustiano Carranza government in Mexico announced it was dispatching troops to shut down American oil wells that were drilling without permits. Then, on December 3, 1919, a United States consular agent serving in Puebla, Mexico, was kidnapped. Fall, chair of the Foreign Relations Subcommittee on Mexican Affairs, had been warning about sinister Mexican plots against the United States for some time, one of them a plan to foment revolution in the American Southwest in order to regain land that had been ceded to the United States. Now, there had been a kidnapping. Mexican troops were capping American oil rigs. Clearly, this was an unfolding crisis that required the president's immediate attention.

Fall demanded an audience with Wilson. The president wasn't seeing even his own cabinet members at the time, but the bullheaded senator was not to be denied. "Fall entered the room like a regular Uriah Heep, washing his hands with invisible soap in imperceptible water," Edith Wilson later recalled. "I had taken the precaution to carry a pad and pencil so I would not have to shake hands with him."

Fall briefed the president, who lay in bed seemingly perfectly alert, on the situation in Mexico. The meeting was cut short, however, when Wilson's doctor interrupted with word from the secretary of state that the consul in Puebla had been released unharmed. The news seemed to deflate Fall's anger and certainly his sense of urgency. He departed somewhat sheepishly after expressing to Wilson his hope that their previous differences could be forgotten. On his way out the door, he told the president he was praying for him.

"Which way?" Wilson asked, meaning was Fall entreating the Lord to save him or summon him.

The Democrats would subsequently claim that the purpose of Fall's visit to the White House had been solely to prove that the president was too ill to conduct business and humiliate him. There were even reports that Fall had forcibly pulled down the covers to see if Wilson was paralyzed. There was probably some truth to the former charge, but the blanket story was entirely bogus. In fact, Fall told reporters after the meeting that Wilson seemed entirely fit to govern. Still, a number of Democrats had been angered by Fall's rude intrusion into the president's sickroom. It would come back to haunt Fall when he was subsequently tried for his role in the Teapot Dome scandal.

Both the hardings liked Fall, thought him, in Warren Harding's words, "a star of a fellow." The Duchess described him as "the real salt of the earth." What's more, Fall had been one of Harding's early backers for the presidency. During one of their poker evenings well before the convention, Fall even predicted that Warren Harding would win the Republican nomination. Harding was impressed by his friend's "political foresight," especially after Fall's prophecy came true. Believing that Fall might be "lucky" for him, Harding on his return from Chicago asked Fall to serve as a principal campaign adviser.

Despite his early prediction and public assertions that Harding was his personal choice to head the Republican ticket, Fall hadn't attended the convention or lifted a finger to swing New Mexico's electoral votes to Harding. For years, he'd run New Mexico like a private fiefdom, but now the political empire he'd long controlled was under attack from a group of Santa Fe–based Republican Progressives. Worse, his longtime political lieutenant Holm O. Bursum had emerged as one of the leaders of the revolt. Bursum had been wooed into the Wood camp even though he knew Fall was a Harding man. Rebuffed by his own party, Fall refused to serve as a delegate to the Chicago convention, instead staying behind in Washington. After nearly eight years in the U.S. Senate and another eighteen years serving in various offices in New Mexico, including as a member of the territorial council and as territorial attorney general, Fall had lost interest in politics. "I am more and more disgusted with politics as the game is played, and determined to get out of it as soon as my sense of duty will permit me to do so," he wrote his wife—"Miss Emma," he called her affectionately.

Still, Fall couldn't very well turn down Harding's request. He agreed to act as a campaign adviser on the condition that he would first return to New Mexico to see his family and tend to some ranch business. He also had several scores to settle, several new names at the top of his enemies list.

6

THE FRONT PORCH CAMPAIGN

Two weeks after Harding's nomination, the Democrats met in San Francisco to nominate the somber, hard-driving Ohio governor James M. Cox as their presidential candidate. For the vice presidential slot, the convention settled on the thirty-eight-year-old assistant secretary of the navy, Franklin Delano Roosevelt. Both were Wilson loyalists determined to further his progressive agenda and see the president's prized League of Nations come into existence.

While the Democrats settled on a candidate—a contentious process that ran from June 28 to July 6 and required forty-four ballots—the Republicans began converging on Marion, Ohio, Harding's hometown. Harding and his campaign people had decided that the candidate would run a so-called front porch campaign. Instead of barnstorming the country, Harding would hold forth on the front porch of the house he and Florence owned on Mount Vernon Avenue. Some Harding biographers claim it was he who came up with this strategy, but more likely Boies Penrose, who wanted to keep the candidate on a short leash, was its author. "Keep Warren at home," Penrose warned Hays and Daugherty. "Don't let him make any speeches. If he goes out on tour, somebody's sure to ask him questions, and Warren's just the sort of damned fool who will try to answer."

The Hardings arrived in Marion in early July, having motored back from Washington. Within an hour or so after they'd gotten back, several thousand inhabitants had gathered outside the house to welcome the hometown hero. Harding appeared on the porch to acknowledge the reception, flanked by Daugherty and Florence. He described her as "a good scout who knows all my faults and yet has stuck with me all the way." The crowd, of course, cheered wildly.

Actually, the real campaign was not scheduled to begin until August, with much of it being run out of Chicago, where both the RNC headquarters and its chairman, Will Hays, were based. The Presbyterian elder and Sunday school teacher came to Marion soon after the Hardings' arrival to attend church with the candidate and discuss strategy. This was their first meeting since Chicago. A week and a half later on July 23, Henry Cabot Lodge made a pilgrimage to Marion to officially notify Harding that he'd won the nomination. Party members from all over the state, including a trainload of two thousand Cleveland Republicans, poured into town to witness the ceremony. Every hotel and boardinghouse was filled to capacity. To preserve their yard from crowd damage, the Hardings had it covered with limestone. Again, the Columbus Glee Club was on hand to serenade visitors.

On his home turf, Harding came across as relaxed and confident in interviews with visiting reporters and editors such as William Allen White, nationally known editor of the *Emporia* (Kansas) *Gazette*. Harding was also effective in communicating with women, who found him attractive, attentive, and (on the surface, at least) reasonably attuned to their political agenda. Thanks to the Nineteenth Amendment, women could now vote for the first time in a presidential election. Harding's handlers did everything they could to pump up Harding's appeal to female voters, using the Duchess increasingly as the campaign went on. Since Jimmy Cox, Harding's opponent, was divorced, Florence would be the first woman in U.S. history to vote for her husband as president.

The front porch strategy was nothing new. Another Ohioan, William McKinley, had employed it in the 1896 presidential campaign. It had worked for McKinley, and it was clearly serving Harding well, showing off his best side. Behind the scenes, however, there were problems. Well before the campaign had gotten under way, Harding's handlers recognized they had several significant, largely anticipated obstacles to hurdle in selling their man to the American voters. True, Harding had a number of attractive attributes. He was a self-made man, publisher and owner of the local newspaper, the *Marion Star;* the organizer of the Citizens' Cornet Band ("I played every instrument but the slide trombone and the E-flat cornet," he once remarked); an Elk, a Moose, a Mason, a trustee of the Trinity Baptist Church. On and on. Warren Harding seemingly exemplified the Middle American values held near and dear. It is not simply a coincidence that seven U.S. presidents before Harding had hailed from Ohio. He was also strikingly handsome, usually impeccably tailored, had a vibrant speaking voice that reached the rear seats of the biggest auditoriums, and was as amiable as a Labrador retriever. But Harding had a long history of pursuing every comely female who came his way. And unlike some of his similarly inclined successors in the White House, Harding didn't view these liaisons simply as "slam, bam, thank you, ma'am" affairs. Harding would assiduously court each of his mistresses, write them gushing love letters, leaving a paper trail, and juggle multiple affairs concurrently.

Surely Daugherty knew about some of these liaisons beforehand. So did the Duchess, but with Harding's nomination the full extent of his prolific philandering became painfully evident. Less than three weeks after the nomination, the husband of one of Harding's mistresses appeared in the candidate's Senate office to demand blackmail. It would be the first of many such demands.

HAYS AND THE other campaign managers moved swiftly to deal with Harding's indiscretions, hiring Jim Sloan to serve as Harding's handler, bodyguard, and minder. In earlier studies of the Harding campaign, Sloan is portrayed as a U.S. Secret Service agent who was assigned to Harding. In fact, he had been in charge of the Secret Service presidential guard details but had been relieved of this work when Wilson became president. After heading up the St. Louis district for the agency, he requested a transfer to Chicago because of the higher pay but was about to resign after the transfer hadn't come about. At this juncture, Sloan was approached by Will Hays and another unidentified senior RNC man and offered a job at considerably more than the $9 a day he was getting as an employee of the U.S. Treasury Department. When he began working with Harding, Sloan was being paid by the RNC, not the U.S. Treasury Department. Will Hays was his paymaster. Sloan began his new job in Chicago at the start of the convention. There, for the first time, Sloan met Daugherty. Several days before the deciding votes had been cast, Daugherty told Sloan that Harding had already been decided upon as the nominee. Sloan's mission was to shadow the nominee at all times and try to keep him out of trouble. He even doled out Harding's spending money and paid Harding's expenses after the convention with money Hays gave him. The RNC had its presidential nominee on a tight leash.

Hays also hired Albert D. Lasker, head of the Chicago-based Lord & Thomas Company, an advertising and public relations firm. Lasker, the campaign cochairman, was a promotional genius and a Republican. He had worked with Hays in the past to their mutual advantage. Teddy Roosevelt had called him "the greatest advertiser in America." Lasker had made Quaker Oats, Lucky Strike cigarettes, and Kotex sanitary napkins much-in-demand household items. Now, Will Hays and Daugherty needed him to sanitize Harding's image and sell Warren to the American public.

Lasker's most immediate problem was to deal with the other women in Warren's past. Nan Britton wasn't perceived as an immediate concern because she wasn't making blackmail threats. The RNC couldn't stop Harding from seeing her, but one of Sloan's tasks was to ensure that Harding and Britton's trysts were discreet and as infrequent as possible. During the campaign and throughout Harding's presidency, Sloan also kept in close touch with Nan to ensure she wasn't going to tell the world about her love child with Harding, and he served as their go-between.

Far more immediate was the problem with one of Warren's former lady friends in Marion, the impetuous, outspoken Carrie Phillips, and her cuckolded and manifestly passive-aggressive husband, Jim. It had been Jim Phillips who had marched into Harding's Senate office after the convention to negotiate a payoff. With a few drinks in her, Carrie would open up about her fourteen-year affair with Harding to anyone within earshot. She also had kept hundreds of his letters, detailing their relationship. According to Carrie, Warren had been a passionate and impetuous lover whose libido rose in direct proportion to the risks he and his paramour took in their lovemaking. One afternoon, he'd made love to her on the Phillipses' kitchen table. They'd also had sex on the Phillipses' front porch, and on another occasion when the two couples had taken an ocean cruise together, Warren and Carrie went at it on the deck only a few feet from the cabin Warren shared with Florence.

Jim Phillips was understandably embittered by the affair, but not to the extent that he wasn't eager to make a few bucks when the opportunity presented itself. As a token of his resentment, he refused to hang buntings and decorations from the three-story office building he owned on Marion's main drag after Harding's nomination. His was the only business in town so unadorned, which caused visiting journalists to ask the kinds of questions that GOP leaders didn't want addressed. Moreover, on more than one occasion Carrie brazenly dropped by unannounced to greet Warren during the campaign, so aggravating the Duchess that she threw a piano stool at her far younger and more attractive rival. To get Carrie and John Phillips out of town pronto, Lasker met with them on July 27 and agreed to give Carrie and Jim $20,000 up front in "hush money," promised $2,000 monthly as long as Harding held public office, and sent them on a round-the-world, all-expenses-paid trip.

Lasker also silenced a pesky call girl in New York with a payoff and expunged Washington police records of a violent quarrel between Harding and another woman while he was in the Senate. Grace Cross, one of Harding's former secretaries, also let it be known through an intermediary that she had kept a batch of Warren's love letters. She claimed she could describe in great detail a birthmark on Harding's back. Having paid dearly for Carrie's silence, Lasker tried to stall Cross until after the election. In differentiating Harding and the man he hoped to succeed, knowing reporters joked that Harding frequented whorehouses in Columbus while the worldly Wilson, who also had a reputation as a ladies' man, frequented fancy bordellos in Paris.

Not the least of Lasker's challenges was the need to familiarize voters with a candidate who was generally unknown outside Ohio. Harding's six-year career in the U.S. Senate had been largely undistinguished. Nationally, he was a cipher. Of the 134 bills he had introduced, 122 had to do with local matters in Ohio.

Far ahead of his time in terms of understanding that political candidates could be sold like Ivory soap or Schlitz beer, Lasker orchestrated an ambitious national campaign using news clips, photos, and flyers to project Harding as a folksy, Main Street, pro-business candidate. Twice a week, under Lasker's supervision, eight thousand copies of photographs of Warren and Florence were dispatched nationwide. As a result, the Hardings were featured regularly on the front pages of almost every newspaper in America, Harding beaming at the cameras as he distributed surplus war supplies, played his cornet, or drove his father, still a practicing doctor, through the maple-shaded streets of Marion in a horse-drawn carriage as the old man made house calls. Pulling out all the stops, Lasker enlisted dozens of celebrities to come to Marion, including Al Jolson, Mary Pickford, and Lillian Gish, and pose with the candidate and his wife. The starstruck Duchess was delighted. At one point, the ad man even brought the Chicago Cubs, a team that he partially owned, to town to have Harding photographed with the players. Harding played golf, then considered an elitist sport. With the Cubs photograph, Lasker wanted to establish the senator's bona fides as a baseball fan.

During the campaign, the question of Harding having African American blood surfaced again, primarily through the efforts of an apparently unhinged political science professor named William Eastbrook Chancellor, who shadowed Harding's campaign, handing out flyers claiming that Harding's great-grandmother was a Negro and his father a mulatto. "We had been aware of the false propaganda campaign beginning immediately after his [Harding's] nomination," Will Hays said. "We paid little attention until the stories began to gain circulation outside Ohio, disseminated through underground channels difficult to trace."

Lasker dealt with the racial issue preemptively by having newspapers around the country run full-page photographs of Harding's ancestors. He had a historical society in Pennsylvania, where the Hardings had settled before migrating to Ohio, prepare extensive genealogies for reporters. "No family in the state has a clearer or more honorable record than the Hardings, a blue-eyed stock from New England and Pennsylvania, the finest pioneer blood, Anglo-Saxon, German, Scotch Irish, and Dutch," Harding's publicity people claimed when they distributed the genealogies to reporters.

DESPITE ITS NOSTALGIC, front porch trappings, the Republican campaign was a thoroughly modern effort that would serve as a model for many subsequent campaigns. It was also, for the time, extraordinarily expensive. In August, Harding's opponent, Governor James Cox, charged that the GOP had been working secretly to build a $15 million illegal slush fund, an unheard-of amount of money for a presidential campaign at the time. The purpose of the fund, Cox charged, was to "get an underhold" on the presidency.

Hays denied the charges, but Cox produced records from Republican national headquarters in Chicago showing that two days after Harding's nomination, the Republicans had dispatched teams of "money diggers" to begin seeking solicitations of at least $5,000 from party fat cats around the country. The RNC also established quotas for the fifty-one cities in twenty-one states. Cleveland's quota, for instance, was $400,000; Chicago's was $700,000. The fund-raising was overseen by an eight-man committee chaired by Hays. Fred W. Upham, from whose box at Chicago Florence Harding had watched as her husband received the nomination, was its treasurer. Daugherty and Jake Hamon were members, as was the former Republican senator from Massachusetts John W. Weeks, who had made a fortune in the brokerage business. With the campaign under way, the committee members gathered in Chicago to have their photograph taken. Amid these high rollers, Harding looks vaguely uncomfortable.

Cox's $15 million figure was high (later, it was established that the fund totaled $8.1 million). Still, Marion and the RNC headquarters were awash in money, much of it oil money. Harry Sinclair alone secretly added a cool million dollars to the slush fund, it was later learned. And there was more to come from Sinclair. Hamon, who had already anted up his million for Teapot during the convention, chipped in more, providing the payoff money for the Phillipses. Robert Stewart, chairman of Standard Oil of Indiana, was good for a few dollars, and even Democrat Ed Doheny, an old friend of Albert Fall's, contributed $25,000 to pay for the national ad campaign showing Harding's lily white lineage. As a measure of the vast sums flowing into the Harding camp, Jim Sloan later told Nan Britton, "During the presidential campaign of 1920, you could have had anything you wanted, and I myself could have gotten you anywhere from $200,000 to a million."

Some of this was legitimate campaign funding, but the bulk was so-called black money that went unreported by the RNC and was used largely for payoffs. After all, even slippery Will Hays couldn't very well write the Phillipses a check on the RNC account to cover their world travel expenses. According to Sloan, Florence Harding—perhaps rationalizing that if Carrie was collecting, why shouldn't she?—pocketed a sizable portion of these funds, as did many of the so-called Ohio Gang who gathered at Harding's Marion, Ohio, headquarters, eager to ride Harding's coattails to Washington. "The whole bunch out there is rotten," Sloan told Nan.

By mid-july, the odds favoring Harding had settled at two to one. Even so, Cox and young Roosevelt, as yet unencumbered by polio, toured the country relentlessly, often speaking several dozen times a day. By mid-August 1920, the Republicans had begun to get nervous. Jake Hamon urged Harding to come west. The West, he warned, was warming to Cox. Reversing himself, Boies Penrose, who would be dead in a few months, told Daugherty that Harding should exchange the front porch for the campaign stump. Cox and the energetic young FDR were gaining momentum.

Harding was well aware of his own shortcomings as a candidate. Foreign affairs was clearly among them. To date, he had expressed several vaguely defined and somewhat contradictory positions on the League of Nations, on occasion saying it should be approved but modified, on others nixing it altogether. If he was going to campaign nationally, Harding needed someone by his side with much needed expertise in these matters, someone he could trust. He also needed help in crafting speeches that set forth a cogent, well-defined foreign policy. As a speech maker, Harding could go on for hours. "The bloviator," he called himself with some pride. But his stentorian orations often lacked any real substance. Said Woodrow Wilson's secretary of the Treasury, William McAdoo: "[Harding's] speeches left the impression of an army of pompous phrases moving over a landscape in search of an idea. Sometimes these meandering words would actually capture a straggling thought and bear it off triumphantly, a prisoner in their midst, until it died of servitude and overwork."

With the national campaign tour imminent, Harding asked Fall to honor his promise to serve as a campaign adviser. Fall knew as much about foreign relations as any man in Congress. He was a member of the Foreign Relations Committee (so was Harding, but he rarely attended sessions) and a respected international lawyer. In the past year, Fall had made a number of speeches analyzing the League of Nations covenant Wilson had drawn up, often citing precedents in international law to make his case. Harding had been much impressed. He needed Fall's help to frame his campaign speeches, give them some cohesion and spine. On August 17, Harding wrote Fall, "Really, I very much need to be surrounded by some of the friends whom I trust most fully (especially) through some of the anxious moments of speech preparation and foreign policy. . . . I would like exceedingly much to have you here so that I may avail myself of your counsel and advice."

7

THE CAMPAIGN TRAIL

Despite Harding's entreaties, Fall delayed joining the campaign until late September. He'd been in ill health much of the summer and was struggling to retain control of the political machine in New Mexico that he and Holm O. Bursum had run unchallenged going back to territorial days. Now, Bursum and his newest ally, onetime chairman of the Republican National Committee Frank Hitchcock, were trying to take over the state themselves, doling out state campaign funds—most of which Fall had raised himself—to gain favors and win votes.

Fall had first encountered Bursum in 1905. At the time, the big, Iowa-born Norwegian had been accused of skimming off funds at the New Mexico state prison where he'd been superintendent. He and Fall had become friends and political allies, their names eventually becoming synonymous with Republican bossism. But when Bursum teamed up with Hitchcock before the convention, backing Leonard Wood, Fall felt he had been betrayed. Politically, Bursum had always followed Fall's lead. No longer. There was even talk Bursum would try to take Fall's place in the Senate when Fall's term expired in 1922. Before the boorish, often overbearing Bursum could go to Washington, Fall joked sarcastically, he'd have to learn to eat with a knife and fork so as not to embarrass himself in the Senate dining room.

Sensing the old man was losing his grip, Fall's enemies had come crawling out of the woodwork. State and local political hacks who until recently wouldn't have dared whisper an unfavorable word about Fall suddenly developed cojones. Even those who remained loyal noted Fall was imbibing heavily—or perhaps he just couldn't hold his liquor anymore—often seemed distracted, and was even more cantankerous than usual. Since Jack's and Carrie's deaths, he hadn't been himself. "Toward the end of his Senatorial tenure, colleagues and supporters began to sense changes in the Fall personality which might have foretold the debacle of the 1920s," one of his biographers noted.

On August 1, 1920, the *Deming* (New Mexico) *Headlight*, which in the past had treated Fall favorably, noted in an editorial:

> In the last election Senator A.B. Fall was returned to the United States Senate by a substantial majority. . . . And even some of the opposing political faith supported him in his race for reasons that seemed good to them at the time. It was widely maintained at the time that Senator Fall would make an excellent representative to Congress for New Mexico, for he was alleged to be a brainy man who would add to his already formidable reputation as a statesman in the present Congress. . . . But if there is one of the so-called leaders of the present Congress who has signally failed, it is Senator Fall. Everything that he has started has fallen flat and his reputation for sagacity has gone glimmering. Judging from what he has accomplished since his election, Senator Fall will end his present term . . . not as a statesman but as a broken and discredited political hack.

The most virulent of his critics, Carlton "Carl" Magee, was editor and publisher of the *Albuquerque Morning Journal*, a newspaper that Fall had co-owned until recently along with some of his long-term business partners and rich Republican friends. Among them were Cleveland industrialist Price McKinney, with whom Fall secretly owned copper mines in northern Mexico, and the wealthy former Massachusetts senator John W. Weeks.

A successful Oklahoma City lawyer, the forty-six-year-old Magee had moved to higher, drier New Mexico because his wife suffered from a lung ailment. Finding Albuquerque had all the lawyers it needed,

Magee decided to get into the newspaper business. In early 1920, he acquired the *Albuquerque Morning Journal* from Fall, who had purchased the paper three years earlier with some of his fellow Republicans. Not that Fall had any interest in the newspaper business. He needed the *Journal* to serve as a platform for his 1918 Senate campaign, which was vital to the Republicans' retaining control of the U.S. Senate. That may explain why Weeks, a senator from Massachusetts and one of the party's moneymen, had acquired a major interest in an Albuquerque newspaper, likely using RNC campaign dollars to fund the purchase.

To complete the deal, Fall asked Magee down to his sprawling Three Rivers ranch (so large, it was said, you could drive all day and still not get from one end to the other by sunset) in southern New Mexico. There, Fall conceded he was broke, land poor. He hadn't paid taxes on the Three Rivers spread in six years. With his $7,500-a-year salary as a U.S. senator, he couldn't afford the upkeep on the place. After dinner, he provided Magee with a rambling, bourbon-fueled discourse on New Mexico politics. In the course of this discussion, Fall gave Magee the names of those whose boots the newcomer should be careful not to tread on, number one on the list being Albert Bacon Fall.

Magee bought the paper for $115,000, invested an additional $20,000 in a new press, and hired an enterprising young reporter, Clinton P. Anderson, who years later would be elected U.S. senator from New Mexico and serve as secretary of agriculture under Truman. Together, Magee and Anderson began investigating political corruption in New Mexico, which soon led them to Fall and his ex-partner Bursum. "I found out in a little while that state officials went unchallenged," Magee recalled later. "They did what they pleased without criticism. Prisoners were cheated and starved of food. State institutions were run negligently. Public money was deposited in the banks, and state officials took the interest and put it into their own pockets."

By the time Fall returned to New Mexico in the summer of 1920, the *Journal* was lambasting him on a daily basis with stories that the state land office was rife with corruption and that money for public schools had been diverted instead to the Fall-Bursum–controlled political machine. Fall felt he had been blindsided. In his negotiations to buy the newspaper, Magee had claimed strong Republican loyalties (he was, in fact, a moderate Republican), but he had clearly been lying as far as Fall was concerned. Broke as he was, Fall would never have sold the

Journal to Magee had he known where the lawyer's real political sentiments lay. Here the newspaper he had owned only a few months earlier was pillorying him. Albert Fall was becoming a laughingstock in his home state.

Fall was determined to silence Magee. In the old days, he likely would have challenged him to a gunfight, called him out into the streets. After all, Fall had once disarmed the quick-triggered John Wesley Hardin in an El Paso saloon. Angry, he was as dangerous as a diamondback rattler. One of his old enemies, a rich rancher, Albert Fountain, and his young son both went missing one summer day in 1896 as they rode home on a buckboard, never to be seen again. Not hide, hair, nor bone. Though there never has been any proof of Fall's involvement, to this day the Fountain family believes that Fall was somehow responsible for the disappearance of father and son. "The bodies of Colonel Fountain and his little son were never found and the case was never tried," the former governor of New Mexico Territory, Miguel A. Otero, wrote Thomas J. Walsh on December 3, 1923. A Montana Democrat, Walsh took the lead in the Teapot investigation, which began in 1922.

Fall liked to boast that he had run any number of uncooperative newspapermen out of the state, even threatening to kill one editor if he ever mentioned Fall's name in his paper again. In midsummer of 1920, Fall marched into the *Journal*'s offices on Albuquerque's Gold Street to confront Magee man-to-man. "Lay off the land office, or I'll put you on the rack and break you!" Fall erupted after storming into the newspaper office.

Fall stood an even six feet and was still in reasonable fighting trim despite years of hard drinking and the sedentary life in Washington. The tall, lanky Magee wasn't especially intimidated, however. Fall was thirteen years his senior, a little long in the tooth to be pistol-whipping newspapermen. There was also something surreal about being threatened with the rack, a punishment much favored by Torquemada during the Inquisition. As Magee knew from his tour of the extensive Three Rivers library, Fall was a great reader. Perhaps the old man had been reading too much fifteenth-century Spanish history of late. At any rate, he told his visitor to go to hell, or words to that effect.

Very well. There was more than one way to run a man out of town.

Before returning east, Fall had a word with the two banks from which Magee had borrowed the money he'd used to buy the *Journal*.

ON SEPTEMBER 20, Fall wired Harding words of encouragement: YOU ARE ABSOLUTELY ON SAFE GROUND AT PRESENT TIME AND NOTHING BUT A MISTAKE OF THE REPUBLICAN PARTY CAN ADVERSELY AFFECT YOUR SUCCESS AT THE POLLS. A week later, Fall met with Harding at the Southern Hotel in Baltimore, modestly asserting to reporters that he would render "what service I could to him [Harding] quietly." He then continued on with Harding's campaign train, *Superb*, with Fall literally riding shotgun as the train headed west to Ohio. There had been rumors of a possible attempt to assassinate Harding en route, an ominous track-switching incident in West Virginia that much alarmed the nervous Duchess. At each whistle-stop, Fall got off the train along with Jim Sloan and Secret Service agent Walter Ferguson to scout the crowd for anyone who looked suspicious, his six-shooter at the ready.

In Marion, Fall provided talking points on the League of Nations issue and helped Harding draft several speeches, including one that called for the United States to close its borders to immigrants who weren't of Anglo-Saxon stock, another on the importance of developing water power in the southern and western states. He then continued west aboard the *Superb* for at least part of the campaign swing with the Hardings, Will Hays, Harry Daugherty, and Daugherty's sycophantic shadow, Jess Smith. Smith was a particular favorite of the Duchess's. He was funny, likely gay, seemed to know all the dirt on everyone, and relished dishing it out.

Ned and Evalyn McLean also joined the campaign train, attaching their private car, the *Enquirer*, to the *Superb*. A brief word of introduction here: Both in their early thirties, the McLeans would become emblematic of the excesses of the Jazz Age, Ned a dissolute rummy and womanizer—he used to attend the *Post* editorial meetings accompanied by his mistress du jour—who had inherited both *The Washington Post* and the *Cincinnati Enquirer* from his father. A silver mining heiress, Evalyn had a few peccadilloes of her own, including an addiction to morphine and expensive jewelry. The centerpiece of her collection, the fabled Hope diamond, had once belonged to Marie Antoinette. It supposedly brought bad luck to its owners. Ned had purchased it for her as a wedding present. Evalyn, however, was a good and loyal friend to the Duchess, though the two quarreled on several occasions during the campaign tour. "I stood beside her once as photographers prepared to take our pictures," Evalyn recalled. "I was engaged at the time in . . . one of the least compromising of my habits—I was smoking a cigarette. Suddenly, aware of the smoke, she [Florence] whirled on me and snatched the cigarette from my lips."

Later, Florence chided her wealthy friend for smoking in public and insisting on wearing her jewelry at the campaign gatherings, fearing the display might alienate voters and detract from the Hardings' carefully cultivated "just folks" image. When Evalyn responded that Warren also smoked, Florence snapped: "Not when he is having his picture taken."

The campaign train traversed Illinois, Iowa, and Kansas, passing endless corn and wheat fields shimmering in the heat and stopping at a mind-numbing succession of farm towns, one of them indistinguishable from another. From the *Superb*'s rear platform, Florence always said a few words first. "The boss's boss," was how she was introduced. That usually brought a knowing chuckle from the crowd.

Arriving in Oklahoma City on October 9, the Hardings received the most enthusiastic welcome of the whistle-stop tour. Jake Hamon had gone all out. There were cowboys and cowgirls on horseback, whooping and hollering, bronco busters, and even a herd of elephants borrowed from a visiting circus. Thousands lined the streets cheering as the Hardings passed in a motorcade. That night, Hamon hosted a banquet at the Huckins Hotel attended by party leaders, businessmen, their wives, and reporters. In a speech calculated to gladden the hearts of Jake Hamon and his pals in the oil business, the nominee's major benefactors, Harding talked entirely about the need to expand America's oil development internationally. Great Britain, he claimed, apparently pulling the grossly exaggerated figure out of the air, controlled 90 percent of the world's oil. For the British, oil represented a means of dominating "the commerce, trade, and industry of the twentieth-century world." And while the English were scrambling to seize global petroleum resources, Harding charged, the Wilson Democrats were preoccupied in getting the United States to join the League of Nations, a notion that was wildly unpopular in the heartland among those who feared that once America became a member of the League, it would lose its sovereignty.

"If the majority favors turning this government over to foreign powers," Harding warned, "I am going to favor turning the United States over to Oklahoma."

That brought the house down.

Was Clara in attendance? If so, the Duchess would have been much displeased. During dinner, both Florence and Warren repeatedly thanked Jake for all his hard work and support, while the Duchess quietly reminded him that he had to get back with his wife, her cousin, before coming to Washington. Clara had to go. "Our Jake," Florence called him. She was photographed standing over her host, a hand on his shoulder, while Jake looked up at her with what seemed a forced smile. Afterward, the Hardings, Hamon, and their guests proceeded in an old-fashioned torchlight parade to the state fairgrounds, where Harding spoke before a large, exuberant crowd. All in all, it was "the noisiest, gladdest, maddest day" the Republican Party had ever experienced in the state, reported the *Daily Oklahoman*.

The campaign train continued on through the South, then up the East Coast and back to Ohio, covering twenty states in all. Aside from several one-day excursions, the Hardings didn't leave Marion again until election day, November 2. By then, Harding was a ten-to-one favorite. On the morning of November 2, newspaper photographers snapped shots of Warren and the Duchess voting in their local polling station. Later, Warren changed into his knickers and his favorite red sweater and went off to Columbus with Harry Daugherty to play golf at the Scioto Country Club.

When the results were tallied, Harding and his vice president, Calvin Coolidge, carried thirty-seven of the forty-eight states, including Jake Hamon's Oklahoma, which voted Republican for the first time in its history. Some 26.7 million Americans voted, 16 million of them for Harding, a little over 9 million for Jimmy Cox. Harding received 60 percent of the national vote and 404 electoral votes; Cox took 34 percent of the national vote and 127 electoral votes. At the time, it was the largest margin of victory ever recorded in a presidential race.

8

FRIENDS OF JAKE HAMON

When Jake Hamon staggered into the Hardy Sanitarium on the night of November 21, he told Doc Hardy that he'd accidentally shot himself cleaning his pistol. The following morning when Frank Ketch, Jake's $1,000-a-week business manager, came to see him, Jake changed his story. "Frank, I'm never going to get well," Hamon told Ketch. It had been Clara who had shot him, he admitted, but he wanted it given out that he did it himself. And he wanted Clara gone. Out of the state and out of the country, if possible. Far enough away so that the scandal-mongering reporters couldn't get to her. He instructed Ketch to give her $5,000 and send her on her way.

Ketch went back to his office and summoned Clara. He and Bill Nichols, the former police chief of Oklahoma City and one of Hamon's top political associates, waited for her to arrive. When Clara walked in, Ketch said to her, "Clara, you've got to go. The parting of the ways has come. You're going away to stay."

"You think I shot Mr. Hamon?" Clara said. "I did not."

"I won't discuss that," Ketch said. He gave her the $5,000, had her trunks packed in the Randal, and told her to leave town. For the next four days, Ketch and Nichols, along with Hamon's wife, Ruth, who had arrived from Chicago with the Hamons' two children, Jake Jr. and Olive

Belle, stood watch, rarely leaving the sanitarium. Hamon was fading fast, but a cablegram from President-elect Harding, who was vacationing in Panama with Florence and Daugherty at the time, buoyed his spirits briefly. Nichols read it to him: DON'T WORRY. YOU WILL GET WELL AND WILL BE SECRETARY OF THE INTERIOR IF YOU WANT IT.

Two days before he died, Jake gave Nichols a sealed note addressed to Harding and begged him to deliver it as soon as possible. "Jake Hamon told me to go straight to Warren Harding and get some of his friends taken care of," Nichols later said. Presumably, he was speaking of Harry Sinclair and Robert Stewart of Standard Oil of Indiana.

With Hamon dead, Harding, Daugherty, and the RNC had to come up with a secretary of the interior who would accommodate Hamon's associates in the oil business. Even before Jake was shot, Harding had been looking at several candidates, including Fall, as a possible backup for secretary of the interior, largely because Florence feared Jake wouldn't give up Clara. She'd had a premonition that Jake's efforts to break off the affair might lead to trouble.

Only a few days before the shooting, Fall had driven over from his winter home in El Paso to meet with Harding in Brownsville, Texas, on the Gulf Coast. Prior to the election, Harding had announced that, if victorious, he planned to visit the Texas Gulf Coast for rest and some tarpon fishing, then sail to Panama. He invited Fall to accompany him. Fall declined but had business to discuss with the president-elect in Brownsville.

On November 3, only a day after the election, the oilman Ed Doheny wired Fall with a request. He wanted Fall to ask Harding if he would like to use his 375-foot oceangoing yacht, *Casiana* (named after the gusher in Mexico that had made Doheny one of the richest men in the United States), for his postelection vacation cruise. IT IS ONE OF THE BEST SEA BOATS AND MOST COMFORTABLE YACHTS AFLOAT WITH LUXURIOUS ACCOMMODATIONS FOR FROM TWELVE TO THIRTY PEOPLE, Doheny bragged in his message. IT IS PERFECTLY SAFE IN ANY KIND OF SEA WITH A SPLENDID CAPTAIN AND CREW. The oilman even volunteered to deliver the *Casiana* himself at Port Isabel, Texas, which, from Fall, he knew to be Harding's port of departure.

Of course, Doheny had a favor to ask in return, again using Fall as his intermediary. The new president of Mexico, Álvaro Obregón, was to be inaugurated in Mexico City on December 1. One of his predecessors, Venustiano Carranza, who had threatened to seize Doheny's wells in Mexico along with those of Harry Sinclair and other gringos, had been assassinated. The more conservative Obregón likely would be far more favorably disposed toward American oil interests, especially if Harding attended his inauguration, Fall suggested. Of course, Fall would go along as well. Doheny, Sinclair, and half a dozen big American oilmen also planned to show up.

Fall had driven over to Brownsville accompanied by Elias L. Torres, whom he introduced to Harding as Obregón's personal representative. Torres's boss, the Mexican assured Harding, would be honored to have the president-elect come to Mexico City for the inauguration ceremony, a move that would go far in smoothing over relations with Mexico and its neighbor to the north.

Harding regretfully declined Doheny's offer for the *Casiana*. He had already accepted use of the United Fruit yacht for the Panama cruise. "I . . . wish the circumstances were so I might accept, but we have already completed our arrangement," Harding told Fall to tell Doheny.

And it was too late to change his itinerary and come to Mexico City, much as he would have liked. As it developed, however, Obregón wasn't quite ready to extend a warm *abrazo* to industrialists from the north, especially Albert Fall. The Mexicans were so incensed by Fall's previous efforts to provoke armed intervention against their country that they wouldn't give him a visa when he tried to go to Obregón's inauguration on his own. For Fall, this was a slap in the face that resounded all the way to Los Angeles, where Doheny decided it would be prudent if he and his oil colleagues stayed clear of Mexico for a time as well.

In later years when Harry Daugherty was backpedaling from the Harding scandals, he claimed that Albert Fall had actively lobbied for the Interior post. Fall, he claimed, had even forged a letter to Harding in Daugherty's name, recommending himself for the job. This charge was entirely fallacious. Albert Fall had hoped to be Harding's secretary of state. In fact, at their meeting in Washington right after Harding's nomination, Harding told Fall, "I want you to be my secretary of state. I'm going to be elected." That changed, however, with Hamon's death. With Hamon gone, it was left to Harding, Hays, and Harry Daugherty to take care of Hamon's friends, notably Sinclair, whose money, along with Hamon's, had played an essential role in getting Harding nominated and elected—and was needed to help clear off an additional debt of $1.5 million the Republicans had incurred during the campaign.

Likely with input from others, including Hays and Weeks, Harding and Daugherty had decided Fall was the man for the job but reasoned he needed some persuading given his preference for State. In late January, Harding embarked on yet another vacation before taking office (at the time, U.S. presidents weren't inaugurated until March). Harding, Joseph Frelinghuysen (the Republican senator from New Jersey and a golfing buddy), Daugherty, Jess Smith, and Ned McLean planned to take a leisurely cruise up the Indian River aboard Frelinghuysen's houseboat, *Victoria*, starting in Miami. Florence had gone to New York, where she stayed at the Ritz-Carlton and spent a sizable amount on a new wardrobe suitable for the country's new First Lady.

That left "the boys" entirely free to pursue their fun and games: frequent stops along the way for golf, all-night poker parties, deep-sea fishing (Harding caught a hundred-pound sailfish and somehow snagged a giant turtle), and an abundance of wining and dining. In Palm Beach, where the McLeans had an oceanfront "cottage," Daugherty threw a big dinner party for the president-elect at the Everglades Club that was the highlight of the season.

Harding had asked Fall to come down from Washington and join the group. When Fall demurred initially, noting that he didn't play golf and wasn't a fisherman, Harding said he had some important business to discuss. He and Daugherty were going to decide on the cabinet. Harding wanted Fall's input as one of his official advisers. When he heard that, Fall boarded the next train south.

From January 31 to February 2 aboard the *Victoria*, Harding, Daugherty, Fall, and the others decided who would serve in Harding's cabinet. There's no record of these proceedings other than the fact that Harding spent considerable time and effort convincing Fall to take the Interior job. "He [Harding] thinks that the Interior Department is second only to the State Department," Fall wrote Emma after finally and somewhat reluctantly accepting the job on condition that he'd stay for only one year. "I am now trying to look on the bright side and see the compensations which may offer themselves in that position."

By February 3, the group had decided on six of the ten cabinet members. Despite strong opposition even from within the Republican Party, Daugherty was to be attorney general; Fall would be interior secretary; Will Hays, who had hoped to be secretary of commerce, was named postmaster general; for secretary of agriculture, Harding settled on Iowa newspaper editor and conservationist Henry C. Wallace; John Weeks, the wealthy Boston broker and former senator, was tapped for secretary of war; as part of the convention deal with Boies Penrose, Harding wanted Pittsburgh financier Andrew Mellon to serve as secretary of the Treasury. That left open four posts, Commerce, State, Navy, and Labor, though Harding already had candidates in mind for each job.

On the following day, Daugherty and Fall left the *Victoria* and returned immediately to Washington, traveling together by train. En route, one reporter noted that Fall had "the Harding cabinet slate tucked in his vest pocket." Harding didn't want the names to get out until he'd settled on all ten cabinet members. But even before Fall and Daugherty arrived, the press reported that Harry Daugherty would serve as Harding's attorney general and Albert Fall as secretary of the interior. Between them, they would set the gold standard for corruption in American politics.

9

ACQUITTAL

The murder trial of Clara Hamon began on March 10, 1921. It lasted only a week, during which time newspapers across the country displayed the sensational details of the case on their front pages. Reporters came to Ardmore from as far away as New York City and Washington. Clara herself penned a daily journal of the proceedings on behalf of United Press. "Back in the days of my early youth, a man came into my life, but I will skip over the story as it is well known to nearly everyone," she wrote in her first journalistic endeavor. "It is enough for you to know that I am today charged with murder and am fighting hard for freedom."

Five hundred people crowded into the Carter County Court House to hear Clara testify, while another five hundred or so gathered on the street outside. Clara's attorneys, "Wild Bill" McLean and "Sir" Walter Scott, claimed Clara had acted in self-defense and entered a plea of justifiable homicide. In testifying the first day, Clara told of being seduced and eventually abandoned by the much older and persistent Hamon. "I was seventeen—an unsophisticated clerk in a store," Clara recalled. "Jake Hamon came into the store time and again, under the pretexts of making purchases at my counter. Finally he lured me into his office by promise of a better position. How I hated him after that!

"For ten years I was dominated by him. But I came to love him. And I did everything possible to contribute to his success . . . but when he reached the apex of his power in business and politics, he told me I must go."

On the night of the shooting, Clara said that Jake had returned to the hotel drunk and angered because he thought she'd taken a drive with another man. He came into her room in a rage, beat her, cursed her, threatened to stab her but couldn't find his pocketknife, tried to strangle her, then collapsed into a chair after turning off the lights. At this point, Clara grabbed her pistol from the bureau drawer and shot Hamon as he was about to strike her with the chair. "I must have pulled the trigger," she conceded, "but I don't remember . . . my hand might have relaxed."

Hamon said, "Clara, you hit me." To which she responded, "Mr. Hamon, I couldn't have hit you. Lie down on your bed, and I will call Dr. Hardy." This explained, Clara's lawyers asserted, why Hamon's blood was found on his bed and not in Clara's room, where their client claimed the shooting had taken place. The prosecutor, Oklahoma attorney general S. P. Freeling, also got Clara to confess to a little white lie. She was twenty-nine, not twenty-seven as claimed, which meant she was nineteen when Jake seduced her. In Oklahoma in 1911, nineteen was middle-aged.

In cross-examination, Freeling asked Clara how she could tell Hamon was about to hit her with the chair, given that her room was dark. There was a little light coming through the transom, Clara explained. Freeling called Hamon's business manager, Frank Ketch; Bill Nichols, the former Oklahoma police chief; and Dr. Hardy to the stand. One by one, they testified that Hamon had initially said the shooting was an accident and then conceded that Clara had pulled the trigger. Doc Hardy asserted that after Clara had visited Hamon ever so briefly in the hospital, Hamon told him, "That's the woman that did the work. I was lying in the same position as I am now."

When Bill Nichols started talking about Hamon's ties to President Harding, Judge Thomas W. Champion ordered him to stop testifying altogether. This struck some reporters as a mite peculiar. Champion also seemed to be moving the trial along at such a breakneck pace that several seasoned crime reporters later claimed they'd never witnessed such an expedient murder trial.

Freeling's last witness was Ruth Hamon, who related how she and little Olive Belle had visited Jake and Clara's love nest at the Randal on several occasions during the decade she and Jake had been separated. On one of these occasions, she'd looked into Clara's closet and seen her beautiful clothes and fur coat. "After I had grown old—old before my time—she came along with her beauty and insulted me by parading my husband," she said, breaking into tears.

The jury was given the case at 4:30 on the afternoon of March 17. It took only forty minutes and one ballot to reach a decision. "Gentlemen, have you reached a verdict?" Judge Champion asked. F. C. Laughridge, the seventy-five-year-old foreman, responded affirmatively, "Not guilty." Clara gasped audibly and slumped forward in her seat, only to be caught and embraced by her younger brother, Jimmy. After tearfully thanking the jurors—"I am the happiest woman in the world," she said—Clara exited the courtroom from a private passage to escape the crowds that threatened to overwhelm her with congratulations. Ruth Hamon, who was on the verge of collapse, hadn't come to the courthouse and wasn't told of the acquittal until the next day for fear she'd have a complete breakdown.

Afterward, Clara and her attorneys, who now numbered half a dozen, said she was weighing several business opportunities. Clara had received offers from three movie companies as well as numerous book and magazine publishers. She also intended to seek a sizable share of Hamon's $3,143,903 estate, though he still owed $1 million off the top to National City Bank of New York. "Of course I can't say what I'm going to do," Clara said. "But I am not going to accept the one hundred proposals of marriage that have poured in during the trial."

There was one proposal, however, she did accept. In August, Clara married Hollywood director John Gorman, who was filming the story of her life, and moved to Los Angeles.

10

FATAL DISTRACTIONS

On a cold, windy March 4, 1921, inaugural day, President-elect Warren Harding picked up Woodrow Wilson at the White House. In an open Pierce-Arrow automobile, the soon-to-be twenty-ninth president of the United States and the outgoing Wilson, his body ravaged by illness, led a caravan of a dozen automobiles to the capital. There, Harding gave his inaugural address before thousands of onlookers who filled the broad plaza and surrounding streets. For once Harding was mercifully brief, but H. L. Mencken wasn't impressed. "It is rumble and bumble," he said of the speech. "It is flap and doodle. It is balder and dash. But I grow lyrical."

Proceeding soon after to the U.S. Senate chamber for an unexpected and unprecedented inaugural day visit, the new president, flanked on the rostrum by Vice President Calvin Coolidge, said he had come to present his cabinet in person. He began with Albert Bacon Fall, the first ever cabinet officer from New Mexico and the only Senate member selected. Fall's selection as secretary of the interior had been the worst-kept secret in Washington.

After an outburst of applause by the senators for one of their own, the president read off the rest of the names: Andrew Mellon, secretary of the Treasury; Will Hays, postmaster general; Harry Daugherty, attorney general; Charles Evans Hughes, secretary of state; Herbert Hoover, secretary of commerce; and on it went.

When Harding concluded, majority leader Henry Cabot Lodge, who had been aware in advance of Harding's visit and its purpose, asked for a confirmation vote on the entire cabinet. Caught by surprise, not a single senator objected to any of the nominations. This was Harding's moment, his first official act as president. Even those senators who had complained loudly about Harding's anticipated choices, especially Harry Daugherty, the unpopular Hoover, and Albert Fall, whom the conservationists viewed as an enemy, acquiesced.

In the space of ten minutes, Harding's entire cabinet had been confirmed.

To THE SURPRISE of some of his critics, Warren Harding started off his presidency with a sense of purpose and an energy that hadn't been evident during his tenure in the Senate. During his first months in office, Harding urged Congress to make formal peace with the imperial German government. Technically, the nation was still at war. In July, while on a golfing weekend in New Jersey, he signed the resolution officially putting an end to World War I. This likely was the only time in history that a treaty ending a major war had been signed by a world leader wearing golfing knickers.

He spoke out forcefully against the lynchings of African Americans that were rampant at the time in the Deep South. Concurrently, he pushed through new immigration laws that would restrict foreigners from entering the United States. In the prevailing mood of postwar nativism, immigrants were seen as taking jobs from Americans, many of whom were returning soldiers. He made good on a heartland promise to American farmers by signing an emergency tariff statute to protect them from being jeopardized by the resurgence of European agriculture.

To the public who glimpsed him in newsreels and newspaper photos, Harding seemed expansive, confident, accessible—especially in contrast with the remote Wilson—and entirely comfortable in his new role. But privately, Harding was having difficulty settling in. He had never really wanted to be president; he'd been pushed into it by Daugherty. "I am satisfied with being senator," he told Evalyn McLean before the election. "If I have to go on and live in the White House, I won't be able to call my soul my own. I don't want to be spied on every day."

At night, he paced the White House or sat alone playing solitaire. When he finally retired to his bed, the president couldn't lie flat but had to be propped up in a sitting position. Longtime White House chief usher Ike Hoover claimed Harding slept less than any president he had known. At times, he seemed bored or indifferent and chafed at what he viewed as Florence's matriarchal tyranny. In the Senate, Harding had hosted twice-a-week poker parties at his home on Wyoming Avenue. Once he took over as president, the venue for these gatherings became the White House study. At least the Duchess hadn't deprived him of this pleasure. In addition to the usual players—Daugherty, Ned McLean, Jess Smith, Secretary of War Weeks, and Fall—a number of out-of-town visitors would drop by, including Harry Sinclair. "Sinco" soon became such a favorite with the Hardings that he was often invited to stay over at the White House as a guest.

After attending one of these soirees with her congressman husband, Nicholas Longworth, Alice Roosevelt Longworth, her patrician nose pointed heavenward, wrote: "The study was filled with cronies, Daugherty, Jess Smith . . . and others, trays with bottles containing every imaginable brand of whiskey stood about, cards and poker chips ready at hand—a general atmosphere of waistcoats unbuttoned, feet on the desk, and spittoons alongside."

The Duchess, Harding believed, did her best to put the brakes on his having fun. She claimed it was unseemly for the president of the United States to chew tobacco. She wouldn't allow toothpicks on the buffet table. Toothpicks were vulgar. She refused to serve the guests wienerwurst and sauerkraut, a Harding favorite. Not in the White House. And God forbid he should ever smoke a cigarette within one thousand yards of a photographer. Florence would come swooping down on him like an avenging angel.

Sometimes he deliberately goaded her. One summer afternoon, he'd been playing bridge with Evalyn McLean, Secretary of War Weeks, and a stunningly attractive friend of Evalyn's named Nannie Duke. Angered that the president was flirting openly with Duke, Florence reminded Warren that they had to get back to Pennsylvania Avenue. There was a country to be run, important bills to be signed. He ignored her. "Warren, you really ought to be getting back to work," she said sharply a few minutes later. Evalyn recalled the president playing an ace with table-banging force. "I'm going to play all afternoon," he said, glowering at the Duchess across the table.

During the day, he'd frequently head off for a round of golf at the Chevy Chase Club or take in a Washington Senators game at Griffith Stadium. He also continued to see Nan Britton in Washington and New York. Two months after the inauguration, Harding had his body-guard and confidant, Jim Sloan, arrange to have Nan Britton brought to the White House on the sly. "I'm in jail, Nan, and can't get out," he told her after they had made love in the Oval Office.

Whenever possible after dinner, Harding slipped over to a house on H Street that Daugherty and Jess Smith had rented from the McLeans. Despite Prohibition, there was always plenty of booze there. Treasury trucks carrying cases of liquor that had been confiscated from bootleg-gers and rum-runners made deliveries every week. A poker game or two was usually in progress. Ned McLean frequently livened up the ongoing party by bringing call girls and showgirls down from New York. Daugh-erty and Jess Smith ran the place like a combination bordello, gambling den, and speakeasy at a cost of $50,000 a year. They employed a black butler, Walter De Marquis Miller, and a full-time cook.

At the H Street house, the president never had to look over his shoulder to see if the Duchess was giving him the evil eye. Only two blocks from the White House, a block from the Justice Department, and conveniently connected by an underground passage to the McLean mansion, it became Harding's home away from the White House—"the Love Nest," he called it. Always the generous hostess, Evalyn McLean sent food over to the H Street house while "[Harding] would be having a party there with these women and Florence would know it."

Florence valued Evalyn's friendship but quite rightly believed Ned was a bad influence on the president. Harding went on drinking binges with Ned, raced around town in one of Ned's sporty convertibles, lead-ing the Secret Service on a merry chase, or applauded the girlies with McLean from a specially concealed box at the Gayety Burlesque. Surely Harding recognized that his indiscretions might jeopardize his political career at its apex, but the president had a defiant, self-destructive streak that he brought with him to the White House. Harding made Daugh-erty his attorney general, his critics be damned. He continued to see Nan regardless of the risk of smuggling her into the White House under Florence's nose. He would tomcat with McLean, Washington's most dissolute playboy, and his other cronies even if it meant exposing himself to ruinous scandal.

One night at the H Street house, it had almost come to that. Ned McLean invited several chorus girls who were down from New York performing in a musical review to an after-theater supper at the house. Harding was there, along with Jess Smith and Daugherty. By 3:00 a.m., the guests were uproariously drunk. When someone suggested the dinner table be cleared so that the girls could dance on it, the guests obliged by throwing plates, glasses, bottles. One of the chorus girls was struck on the head by a water bottle and knocked unconscious. Smith immediately called Gaston Means, an agent for the Bureau of Investigation (the present-day FBI) and a "fixer" for Daugherty.

"This is Jess Smith," Means recalled Smith saying. "Say—come around to H Street quick as you can get here. There's a . . . little trouble."

When Means arrived soon after, the rooms were in wildest disorder. "Half drunken women . . . sprawled on couches and chairs—all of them now with terror painted on their faces," Means later wrote. A dazed Harding was leaning against a mantel with his bodyguards by his side, ready to hustle him back to the White House. No one had dared call a doctor or ambulance. Means said he carried the seemingly lifeless girl out to his car and took her himself to a nearby hospital. A few days later she died, but between them, Bureau of Investigation chief William "Billy" Burns and Daugherty hushed the matter up. Not that they had much to fear from the newspapers, certainly not from Ned McLean's *Washington Post*.

11

TROUBLE AHEAD

Like a number of his colleagues in the Senate and House, Albert Fall had little use for the American conservation movement. Understandably, then, Warren Harding's appointment of the New Mexico rancher as secretary of the interior triggered alarm among the nation's environmentalists. Some of the nation's leading conservationists such as Wisconsin's Progressive Republican senator Robert La Follette had, in fact, announced they intended to oppose Fall's nomination in Senate committee hearings. But Harding had managed to circumvent any hearings with his unprecedented inaugural day appearance on the Senate floor.

In 1921, the American conservation movement was going strong. Thanks largely to Teddy Roosevelt and his crusading forestry chief, Gifford Pinchot, much of the country's wilderness areas that had previously been open to exploitation had been placed under the protection of the federal government. An ardent outdoorsman and conservationist, Roosevelt set aside 230 million acres as national forests, national parks, bird and game reserves, and national monuments. Pinchot, "Sir Galahad of the Forests," had been the architect of much of this far-ranging program and is revered by many as the father of conservationism. The

United States Forest Service was his creation, the centerpiece of the preservation movement.

At the outset of his campaign, Harding had sent out a reassuring message to conservationists, stating in his acceptance speech at Chicago that the Republicans adhered to "that harmony of relationship between conservation and development which fittingly appraises our national resources and makes them available to developing America of today, and still holds to the conserving thought for America of tomorrow." Pinchot, like La Follette a Progressive Republican, was planning to run a second time for governor of Pennsylvania (he had lost on his first attempt in 1918 to Boies Penrose) and had supported the Republican ticket and Harding's views on conservation. The news of Fall's appointment caught him entirely off guard. HE [Fall] HAS BEEN WITH THE EXPLOITATION GANG, BUT NOT A LEADER, Pinchot wired a friend when news of the appointment first leaked out in late February. HE HAS LARGE PERSONAL HOLDINGS IN MINING AND OTHER RESOURCES IN THIS COUNTRY AND IN MEXICO. TROUBLE AHEAD.

To Harry Slattery, a conservation watchdog and Washington lawyer who had been Pinchot's right-hand man under Roosevelt, Fall was the fox given complete run of the henhouse. Fall's appointment "placed in the key conservation post one who for years had bitterly opposed the conservation program," he noted.

Whatever the conservationists' worst-case scenario, it fell well short of Albert Fall's audacious agenda. Once he was ensconced in his spacious redwood-paneled office at the Department of the Interior, Fall set out to bring all the nation's natural resources under his control and open them to exploitation. "He was determined to make Interior the Department of Natural Resources, the unchallenged federal agency for management and development of the national patrimony," one of his biographers noted.

This, of course, meant poaching from other agencies and departments, a power play Fall justified under a vaguely defined mandate issued by President Harding to reorganize, streamline, and downsize the federal government. Fall took this as license to try to co-opt the Forest Service, Pinchot's beloved creation, then part of the Department of Agriculture. At the same time, he planned to add the naval oil reserves at Teapot and Elk Hills, California, to his portfolio; open up Alaska's vast resources—primarily timber, oil, and coal—to development; and make the national parks and Indian reservations accessible to mining, cattle, and oil interests. In his campaign, Harding had promised "a return to normalcy" (he meant normality). Fall intended to do just that by turning back the clock twenty years and in the process summarily erasing all the gains the conservationists had achieved in the interim. And like any good poker player, he had no intention of showing his hand until he was ready to collect his winnings. At Interior, secrecy was the watchword of the new administration.

As a rancher, mine owner, and onetime prospector, Fall espoused the approach to natural resources that had long been prevalent on the western frontier: First come, first served. Take what you want, all you want. If there was nothing left for the next guy, tough. "I don't know how succeeding generations will do it—maybe they will use the energy of the sun or the sea wave—but they will live better than we do," he told one critic of his policies. "I stand for opening up every resource."

He was aware, as was just about everyone in Washington at this point, that the big oilmen couldn't wait to get their hands on the naval reserves, which were strictly off-limits as long as the navy controlled them. In 1921, oil prices were the highest in history. If Fall managed to bring Teapot and the California fields under him, the oil crowd would be lined up in front of the Department of the Interior building eager to bid for the drilling rights, their wallets bulging with cash. Fortunately, Harding had appointed a naval secretary, the bullet-headed Edwin Denby, a lawyer, former Michigan congressman, and U.S. Marines captain during World War I, who shared Fall's disdain for the conservationists. A protégé of John W. Weeks, Harding's ultraconservative secretary of war, and one of the Republicans' chief fund-raisers, Denby quickly proved amenable to just about anything Albert Fall wanted.

As for Fall's intended takeover of the U.S. Forest Service, that was personal, sweet retribution. Fall had never had any use for Pinchot, the Yale-educated, wealthy easterner who had built his exalted reputation telling westerners how to manage their resources and sticking his patrician nose where it didn't belong and wasn't wanted. Fall had been feuding with the Forest Service for years, beginning with an incident in 1911 when he had taken out a permit to graze two thousand sheep on the Alamo National Forest. A couple of wet-behind-the-ears forest rangers had come along and discovered that rancher Fall had twice his allotment, two thousand sheep under his name and another two thousand under an employee's name, growing fat on government land. The U.S. Forest Service promptly served notice that this practice would not be tolerated.

In high dudgeon, Fall had immediately written directly to Pinchot, warning that the Forest Service would "rue the day" its rangers had intervened and ominously promising "punishment."

After a decade, that day had finally come.

12

THE OHIO GANG

Daugherty was always on call if the president or the First Lady had a problem. Harding had a private line installed between the Justice Department and the White House. He was on the phone with his attorney general at least twice a day. Ever on the lookout to protect the Hardings' interests, Daugherty spent almost as much time in the White House as in the Justice Department, often staying over for the night. "I know Harding," Daugherty explained. "I know who the crooks are, and I want to stand between Harding and them."

Harry Daugherty did indeed know who the crooks were. He, in fact, was ringleader of what would later become known as the Ohio Gang. Once Warren Harding assumed office, this collection of swindlers, sharpies, con men, and extortionists descended on Washington like a pestilence, securing just about every job in the new administration that provided an opportunity for corruption.

Traditionally, the Ohio Gang has been depicted as a group of disparate crooks who came to Washington to capitalize on Harding's presidency. It was much more—a complex criminal enterprise that was run like a well-organized, well-coordinated business. If the Ohio Gang had an organization chart, Daugherty would have been listed as CEO and founder. He was the brains behind the outfit. The gang's enforcer, its

muscle, was none other than Daugherty's boyhood friend from Columbus, Ohio, freckle-faced, redheaded William "Billy" J. Burns, formerly
head of the famous detective agency that bore his name. In one of his
first acts as attorney general, Daugherty appointed Burns director of the
Bureau of Investigation, which later became the FBI. In turn, Burns ran
the Bureau as if it were a detective agency with one client—Harry
Daugherty.

Working out of Daugherty's hometown of Washington Court
House, Ohio, where he ran the local bank, Daugherty's brother Mal
acted as the gang's money launderer and banker. Harry Daugherty's
roommate and constant companion, Jess Smith, served as the organization's bagman, collection agent, and record keeper. "Jess Smith kept detailed accounts of every transaction," said Gaston Means, another
member of the gang and one of Burns's agents. Jess functioned as a de
facto assistant attorney general even though he had no official title or
brief and wasn't on the Justice Department payroll. At Justice, Jess's
desk was strategically situated just outside Daugherty's office. The message couldn't have been clearer if the Ohioans had handed out flyers: To
get to the attorney general, you had to go through Jess Smith. And
bring cash, lots of it.

Each of the organization's underbosses was given his own turf, usually as a reward for his campaign support. Although he was too distracted with the extraordinary demands of his new job and his
extracurricular activities to pay much attention to what was going on,
the president awarded many Daugherty lieutenants their jobs and frequently entertained them at the White House as members of his so-
called poker cabinet. For instance, Harding put Colonel Charles R.
Forbes in charge of the Veterans' Bureau. One of Harding's drinking
buddies, quick with a quip, and a ladies' man, Forbes had contributed
substantially to the Harding campaign. He'd entertained the Hardings
at his home in Hawaii during Harding's time in the Senate and helped
swing his native state, Washington, to the Republicans. The Duchess
was crazy for him, Forbes by one account having once made a pass at
her.

As director of the Veterans' Bureau, Forbes controlled a $500 mil-
lion budget as well as millions of dollars' worth of medical supplies—
everything from drugs and alcohol to unused pajamas, eighty-four

THE OHIO GANG · 71

thousand bedsheets, and more than a million towels—that had been stockpiled as part of the war effort. The colonel also had control over the construction of numerous new veterans' hospitals earmarked for disabled veterans. In Washington, Forbes promptly began soliciting kickbacks from contractors who wanted to build veterans' hospitals and surreptitiously sponsored a fire sale of surplus medical supplies. Sheets that had cost the government $1 each went for 20 cents, 54-cent towels sold for a nickel, and the profits all went to Forbes. Within a little more than a year, he had pocketed almost $1 million. When a disgruntled associate, Elias H. Mortimer, threatened to expose him, Forbes contacted Daugherty, who in turn had some of Burns's agents break into Mortimer's Wardman Park apartment twice and steal his papers. But Mortimer, who had discovered that Forbes had been bedding his attractive wife, wasn't easily silenced, not even after Forbes threatened that Daugherty was going to arrest him, have him flogged, and run him out of Washington.

Daugherty gave another Harding supporter, Colonel Thomas W. Miller, the job of alien property custodian. Miller had been eastern director of the RNC during the campaign. He wasn't from Ohio. Educated at Yale and Yale Law School, he boasted *Social Register*, Philadelphia Main Line bloodlines, which made him an oddity among the rough-and-tumble Ohioans. Still, Miller knew how to work a scam with the best of them. He and his associate, the smooth-talking John T. King, who had worked in tandem with Daugherty and Jake Hamon during the Chicago convention to get Harding nominated, began collecting bribes from German companies seeking to retrieve property taken from them during the war. Miller and King pocketed $200,000 from one company alone, taking their cut and passing along the rest to the Daughertys. Mal Daugherty banked the money in Ohio.

Daugherty kept the prime scams for himself. To an attorney general with a larcenous bent, the Volstead Act of 1919, which banned the sale or use of intoxicating liquor, was a godsend. The act had one major loophole: It stipulated that booze could still be sold if the seller received a permit indicating that it was to be used for medical purposes. These permits could be issued solely by the Justice Department. Using Smith as his front man, Daugherty began selling permits at $1.50 to $2.00 per case to bootleggers such as Cincinnati's George Remus. Known as "the

King of Bootleggers," Remus had his own distilleries, producing and selling more than one hundred thousand cases of whiskey annually. Most of his permits, he later testified, came from Smith, whom he'd meet every few months or so at New York's Plaza Hotel or at the Deshler in Columbus, Ohio. At these meeting, Remus would hand over payoffs of as much as $50,000.

Operating out of a town house at 963 16th Street, also known as "the House on K Street," the gang's undercover headquarters, Daugherty, Smith, and their associates openly sold pardons and paroles for convicted felons. After one of Ned McLean's employees, "Jap" Muma, showed a film at the McLeans' Washington mansion of the recent heavyweight championship fight between Jack Dempsey and Georges Carpentier, the French boxer, Daugherty arranged for Muma to play the film throughout the country despite a law against transporting films for interstate commerce. For this consideration, the attorney general and his associates received 50 percent of Muma's gross, a quick $180,000.

The money the gang collected was deposited on a weekly basis in an underground safe in the backyard of the 16th Street establishment. The house was overseen by the aforementioned Gaston B. Means, an unctuous North Carolinian who had somehow talked Burns into hiring him as a Bureau of Investigation agent even though he had spied for the Germans during the war and shot and killed a woman named Maude King in his hometown. Means estimated that at times the gang had as much as $500,000 stored in the headquarters safe.

Once a month or so, Smith would gather the accumulated earnings and take the money back to Mal Daugherty's bank in Washington Court House. During these trips, Smith always stopped off to see his ex-wife, Roxy Stinson. On these visits, Jess talked about how grand life was in Washington, about having dinner at the White House or attending a black-tie ball at the McLeans' fabulous Beaux Arts–style mansion. Jess, the small-town haberdasher, was listed in the *Social Register* now. He'd been asked to join the Metropolitan Club in Washington. Most of all, he talked about the deals he and Daugherty and the other boys were "putting over," the unbelievable amounts of money that were being banked.

Roxy was genuinely fond of Jess. He always brought her a present and often as much as $500 in cash, even though he didn't owe her a thing after the divorce. But Jess talked too much for his own good. Jess

Smith couldn't keep a secret if you sewed his lips shut. Roxy warned him he might be getting in too deep and had become too reliant on Daugherty. Daugherty was just using him, she told Jess again and again. But Jess didn't listen. He idolized Daugherty. Besides, he was having the time of his life. He didn't care who knew it.

13

ROCKEFELLER OF THE WEST

There was nothing especially prepossessing about Edward L. Doheny, certainly nothing that signified this was one of the wealthiest, most ambitious, and most powerful oilmen in the world. Unless it was his eyes. Blue gray, they seemed to look right through you. Otherwise, "the Rockefeller of the West" wasn't someone who stood out in a crowd. "At no point does Mr. Doheny seem commanding," a journalist noted on meeting him for the first time.

Short, portly, and slightly stooped at sixty-five, Doheny had a gleaming white mustache set off by a ruddy, weathered complexion, and reddish brown hair that by 1921 had gone mostly gray. The son of Irish immigrants, he could easily have been taken for the beloved neighborhood pub owner or a sympathetic parish priest known for doling out lenient penances at confession. The role he created for himself—one he played to the hilt—was that of the self-deprecating old codger with the heart of gold and the requisite twinkle in his eyes. Even though he'd amassed one of the great fortunes of the era, Edward Doheny hadn't lost the common touch or his humility.

Doheny was born in Fond du Lac, Wisconsin, on August 10, 1856. He graduated valedictorian from high school at age fifteen, excelling at arithmetic. After his father, Patrick, who had migrated from Tipperary during the Great Famine, died the following year, Doheny set off to Indian country to make his fortune. That much we know to be true. We also know that he spent much of the next twenty years prospecting for gold and silver in Mexico, the Southwest, and as far north as the Dakotas, always looking for a big score. Beyond those basics, it is difficult to sort fact from fiction.

In later years when he became a target of the Teapot investigations, Doheny hired a battery of high-priced publicists and commissioned authors to produce romanticized, invariably flattering accounts of his life on the frontier, all of which were calculated to make him come across as admirable, sympathetic, and certainly not the kind of individual who would bribe a cabinet officer simply to get his hands on more than a hundred million dollars' worth of government oil. At one point, the oilman even had Hollywood director Cecil B. DeMille halfway convinced to make an epic film about his life. Walter Huston would have been ideal as the lead.

According to his well-compensated and imaginative biographers, Doheny's early heroics included single-handedly cleaning up the mining town of Kingston, New Mexico, which had been overrun by desperadoes, cattle rustlers, and claim jumpers. After Doheny, who was five feet seven and then weighed 120 pounds soaking wet—not that he had many opportunities to soak in the desert—had dispatched the bad guys, nimbly dodging sixteen bullets during the fight (who was counting?), "Kingston breathed a little easier," reported *The New York Times*, drawing from an account of the incident provided by Doheny's publicists.

Doheny's war stories always featured the plucky little Gaelic gamecock going yet another round with destiny. He made and lost several small fortunes; fell one hundred feet down a mine shaft and broke both his legs; spent the recovery period teaching himself law, getting a degree, and opening up a practice; wrestled a mountain lion, getting his hand badly mangled in the fight; fought off attacks by Geronimo's Apaches on the mining camps in New Mexico Territory; fought off Sioux war parties in the Black Hills. There were certainly elements of truth in these yarns. He did read a little law, as an example, while his legs were mending after a mine shaft fall, but he never got a degree, never hung out his shingle. The reality of those prospecting years was far grimmer and more commonplace than his publicists indicated.

In fact, until 1892 Doheny's life had largely been a succession of failures and missed opportunities. In the spring of that year, we find him, now approaching his thirty-sixth birthday, sitting alone on the front porch of a cheap rooming house at 6th and Figueroa streets in Los Angeles. Upstairs in a seedy room are his sick seven-year-old daughter, Eileen, and his wife of ten years, Carrie, a failed singer. Chronically ill and likely manic-depressive, Carrie self-medicates with gin, whiskey, whatever she can get her hands on. Doheny doesn't drink, doesn't touch the stuff. Instead, he broods and worries about how he's going to feed his small family and pay the back rent. Doheny is tapped out, has no prospects, nothing to show for all those years of prospecting.

What follows is a Frank Capra moment. There's Doheny maybe wishing he hadn't been reared a strict Catholic (his mother wanted him to be a priest) so he wouldn't have to worry about eternal damnation if he put a revolver to his head. As an old horse-drawn wagon lumbered by the rooming house—the driver by one account, at least, an elderly black man—Doheny's prospector's instincts suddenly kicked in. The wagon was loaded with a tarry black goo that had a distinct smell to it.

"What is that?" Doheny asked, approaching the driver.

"*Brea,*" the driver responded, using the Spanish word for pitch, an oil exude that is combustible when mixed with soil.

"What do you do with it?"

"Oh, they burn it instead of coal," the driver explained.

"Who does?"

"Why, the factories."

"And where does it come from?"

"A hole out near Westlake Park."

Curious, Doheny took a trolley out to the nearby park, where he found "a great hole oozing with gobs of *brea,*" today's La Brea tar pits. At the time, the failed prospector had one friend in Los Angeles, Charles Canfield, whom he had known in New Mexico. Unlike Doheny, Canfield had walked away from the silver mines with a modest fortune, most of which he had subsequently blown in land speculation and at the racetrack. Still, Canfield was better off than Doheny. After visiting the tar pits, Doheny went to Canfield and proposed that the two of them go into business together selling *brea* as a cheap alternative to coal. Canfield came up with the $400 the new partners needed to lease a parcel of land near the park. There, using picks and shovels, they began trying to dig a well through the oil-soaked soil to get to the source of the *brea*—the oil that lay somewhere below.

Remember, this was 1892. Oil wasn't much in demand, and the process of extracting "black gold" from the earth was rudimentary at best. After several weeks of backbreaking work, it dawned on Doheny and Canfield that sweat equity had its limitations. They borrowed enough money to buy a drill and erect a derrick, striking oil at two hundred feet on April 20, 1893. It was the first free-flowing oil well in the city of Los Angeles. Their success triggered the great Southern California oil boom and provided Doheny with the capital he needed to build a petroleum empire. Within a year, he and Canfield had eighty-one wells pumping away in Los Angeles and had begun drilling in Fullerton and the San Joaquin Valley. Doheny was just getting started.

14

BACK IN THE DAY

Edward Doheny and Albert Fall had a shared history. Both had prospected in New Mexico Territory during the mid-1880s, encountering each other at the poker tables at Pretty Sam's Casino Saloon in Kingston and in the mining camps. At the time, Doheny was a popular, moderately successful figure in the area, having been a member of the original party that discovered a rich vein of silver in the nearby Black Range. Fall was simply passing through. He remained in Kingston only a few months, long enough to witness Doheny being chased and shot at by a drunk whose wrath he had somehow incurred. After Doheny finally retaliated by shooting his wild-eyed pursuer, carefully targeting a leg rather than the upper body, Fall was the first to congratulate him on his coolness under fire. Theirs had been a casual, passing acquaintance, although in later years Doheny tried to portray them as having been "lifelong friends" in order to justify a "loan" he made to Fall.

It was another thirty years before their paths again converged, by which time Woodrow Wilson was in the White House, Albert Fall was a U.S. senator, and Edward Doheny controlled a petroleum empire in Mexico that encompassed the states of San Luis Potosí, Tamaulipas, and Veracruz. Doheny had originally come to Mexico in 1900 as the guest of then president Porfirio Díaz and the Mexican Central Railway Company. Both were eager to develop Mexico's heretofore untapped petroleum resources and needed American help and capital to do so. Traveling by train in his own private, air-conditioned, walnut-paneled railcar—now worth millions from his California oil holdings, Doheny no longer roughed it—the Californian and his party explored the Gulf coastal plains area west of Tampico.

A blind man could have determined there was an abundance of oil in the region. You could smell it from miles away if the wind was right, great pools called *chapopotes* that had seeped up through the soil. Doheny began buying up vast ranchos from their Spanish owners, who had no idea they were sitting on almost unimaginable quantities of black gold. Ultimately, he acquired almost 1.5 million acres around Tampico and along the Huasteca coastal plain to the south and began drilling.

It was almost ten years before Doheny's efforts in Mexico began to pay off, but when the gushers finally came in, they exceeded all expectations. The first, Casiana No. 7, erupted on September 11, 1910, spewing out oil at a rate of 70,000 barrels a day. Oil blackened the surrounding jungle and quickly overflowed the storage reservoir. The drilling crew resembled creatures from middle earth.

Other gushers followed, one more spectacular than another. Drilling in a tranquil meadow in February 1916, Doheny's men brought in what at the time was the greatest oil well in history, Cerro Azul. Initially, it produced 250,000 barrels of oil every twenty-four hours. The earth seemed to be hemorrhaging. "The gusher was like a volcano," one veteran of the great Tampico oil boom reported. "The cap rock pierced, gas raged for nine hours before the first crude burst forth, hurling drilling tools 120 feet in the air, burying them 16 feet in the earth. The oil gushed 600 feet into the heavens. The roar was so terrible that men had to get half a mile off to hear each other's shouts."

After Díaz was ousted in 1911 as the result of the Mexican revolution and went into exile in France, Doheny and most of the other American oilmen in Mexico threw their support behind the counter-revolutionaries led by General Victoriano Huerta, whose nickname was El Chacal, "the Jackal." The oil and copper companies urged President

Wilson to take action to support Huerta, send in troops if need be. Wilson refused largely because, one, the general had a nasty habit of having anyone who stood in his way shot, and, two, Huerta banned free elections and was arguably the worst leader Mexico had ever produced. Instead, the president decided secretly to provide aid and arms to Huerta's chief rival, the constitutionalist Venustiano Carranza.

When Carranza took over as Mexico's constitutional president in 1917, his administration promptly drafted a new constitution, giving Mexico direct domain over all its subsoil resources—meaning minerals, oil, and gas. The old, bearded billy goat Carranza, Doheny feared, intended to expropriate Doheny's wells and storage facilities just when the Tampico fields were at the height of their productivity.

Knowing he wasn't going to get any help from Washington—Wilson had already granted de facto recognition of the Carranza regime—Doheny decided to create his very own petroleum state, a country within a country. This entailed hiring and arming a six-thousand-man private army to secure the Huasteca oil fields and keep Carranza's *federales* at bay. Doheny found just the man to command this force, a local warlord, General Manuel Peláez, whose price was $15,000 a month American. Once the general had signed on, Doheny had his public relations people and lobbyist announce to the world that Peláez, as the father of a new counterrevolutionary movement—"the Huasteca Home Defense Movement"—was determined to rid Mexico of Carranza and return the country to the good old days when Americans could exploit Mexico's resources without being harassed by revolutionaries.

In an attempt to legitimize Peláez, Doheny had his chief lobbyist in Washington, Harold Walker, orchestrate a campaign targeting the U.S. State Department. In letters to various State Department officials, Walker characterized the general as "the friend of America from the start. He sided . . . with us against Germany in the Great War. . . . Thanks to him and his protection, the oil and gas shortage has not been felt . . . and [there is] enough gas to run over 500,000 cars every day, all shipped to the United States."

Doheny was determined to undercut President Wilson's support of Carranza and oust him at all costs. In the Senate, he found an influential and powerful ally, the chair of the Foreign Relations Subcommittee on Mexican Affairs and the most vocal critic of Wilson's noninterventionist policy in Mexico—his old acquaintance Albert Fall.

By the time Albert Fall took over as interior secretary in 1921, Venus-tiano Carranza no longer posed a threat to American oilmen or Uncle Sam. While fleeing from the forces of his bitter political rival, General Álvaro Obregón, the stoic Carranza was assassinated as he lay sleeping in a hut near Puebla. His successor, Álvaro Obregón, a wealthy Sonoran farmer and sometime poet, had emerged as one of the dominant military leaders of the revolution. On taking power, the general determinedly sought American recognition for his new government.

To the collective relief of Doheny and other American industrialists with holdings south of the Rio Grande, Obregón stated that he had no intention of confiscating American property as long as he remained in power. Unfortunately, the one-armed general—he had lost his right arm in an artillery blast—was short of cash, Carranza having fled Mexico City with the entire, and as yet unrecovered, national treasury in bars of gold. Doheny's man in Mexico City, Frank R. Seaver, took care of the matter, short term, at least, personally delivering advance taxes in the form of gold so that Obregón's government could meet its large military payroll.

Working in tandem, Doheny and Albert Fall had played a critical role in ousting Carranza and putting Obregón in office. Doheny was a prominent Democrat who had dined at the Wilson White House. Fall ranked as one of the most powerful Republicans in the Senate. What they shared was a strong dissatisfaction with Wilson's noninterventionist policy on Mexico. Both the oilman and Fall, chair of the Foreign Relations Subcommittee on Mexican Affairs, had repeatedly pressed the president to send an armed force of as many as five hundred thousand men for a full-scale invasion in order to protect American interests in Mexico. On each occasion, the president refused. After Wilson suffered his stroke in late 1919, the White House went silent altogether on the Mexican question. Carranza chose that moment to dispatch troops to shut down American oil wells that had been drilled without permits, most of them Doheny's.

Doheny's rent-a-general Manuel Peláez and his mercenaries managed to keep Carranza's forces at bay. Meanwhile, "[Fall] and Doheny were doing all possible to foment difficulties between the two countries," Latin American journalist Carleton Beals wrote. As chair of subcommittee hearings dealing with the issue of protecting American lives and property in Mexico, Fall took the lead in inflaming anti-Mexican sentiments. "[Americans] have civilized Mexico," he railed. "They pay the taxes. They develop mines. They build factories. Every enterprise in the Republic of Mexico today of any consequence . . . was built and operated by foreigners, not by Mexicans."

Americans had invested billions of dollars in Mexico, he continued. And what had the United States of America gotten in return? Under Carranza, more than five hundred American citizens had been murdered (actually the number was twenty-one); American women had been raped by the score; while five thousand Americans had been driven from the soil of Mexico "at the muzzles of guns held by bandits," Fall maintained.

In his unrelenting efforts to discredit Carranza, Fall even managed to uncover a conspiracy, the so-called Plan of San Diego. The brainchild of an imprisoned Mexican radical, the plan called for Mexican forces to recapture all the territory lost to the United States. All Anglo males over the age of sixteen who inhabited what had once been Mexican land were to be put to death. Fall had received intelligence from mysterious, unidentified sources that Carranza had dispatched secret agents into the United States to foment anarchy. You can imagine what Doheny's good friend William Randolph Hearst and his newspapers made of this bogus threat. MEXICANS PREPARE FOR WAR WITH U.S., one Hearst headline declared. Of course, once the pro-American Obregón took office, Hearst's stance changed 180 degrees. At Doheny's urging, the newspaper overlord traveled to Mexico to meet with Obregón, later leading the chorus for U.S. recognition of the new Mexican leader.

During the Mexican hearings, Doheny's chief oil lobbyist, Harold Walker, fed Fall intelligence that helped the senator make his case. While most oilmen kept a low profile regarding their Mexican operations, Doheny gave Fall's committee $100,000 through the Doheny Foundation and happily appeared twice as Fall's star witness, on each occasion urging intervention and recounting horror stories about his difficulties in dealing with Carranza. "The hearings for the first time put the newly established Fall-Doheny alliance on public display," noted Fall's biographer, David H. Stratton.

Criticized for his unstinting support of his old prospecting pal, an unrepentant Fall responded, "I would do anything possible to assist him." At the same time, he assured a reporter that "I never owned a dollar of oil stock in my life. I never represented an oil company in Mexico." True, but Fall had represented a number of U.S.-owned mining companies in Mexico and secretly still co-owned several mines in Sonora with Cleveland industrialist Price McKinney. An impartial committee chair he wasn't.

On May 28, 1920, a week after Carranza's abrupt demise, Fall issued a 2,235,000-word report—a document roughly ten times the length of Joyce's *Ulysses*—of his subcommittee's findings. The overthrow of Carranza, he boasted, was due to his subcommittee's ongoing denunciation of the late *presidente* and the support of great Americans like Ed Doheny. Of course, Carranza's assassins—his own bodyguards—deserved a pat on the back as well. What mattered in the end, however, was that the pro-American Obregón was running Mexico. For now, Doheny's petroleum state and the holdings of other American industrialists were secure.

15

POWER GRAB

At Interior, Fall moved decisively to take control of the nation's resources, putting the naval oil reserves at the head of his list. His first act was to fire the conservationists in the department and replace them with his own people. He didn't want Pinchot's bright-eyed acolytes undercutting his policies or talking to the press. Already, Pinchot's former lieutenant, conservation watchdog Harry Slattery, was nosing around trying to get wind of what Fall was up to. Fall wanted to be sure no one on his staff gave Slattery the time of day.

Fall moved on the naval reserves within a few weeks after taking office. On April 1, 1921, he met with Navy Secretary Edwin Denby in the White House to discuss the transfer. According to Fall, Denby brought up the problems the navy was having with drainage of its oil reserves. Oil wells adjacent to the reserves were tapping into, or draining, navy oil, Denby asserted. Maybe the Department of the Interior, which included the Bureau of Mines and the U.S. Geological Survey, would be better able to manage the reserves and deal with the drainage issue than the navy, he suggested.

At least that was Fall's account of what transpired. More likely, Denby knew that Fall was hell-bent on gaining control of the reserves and decided to offer them up without a fight, especially since Fall seemingly had the president's blessing. The transfer, Denby confided to his staff, "was full of dynamite. I don't want anything to do with it." He subsequently designated Assistant Secretary of the Navy Theodore Roosevelt Jr. to serve as intermediary between the Navy Department and Interior. Let the late president's ambitious young son take the political heat that was sure to accompany the transfer.

In a brief meeting with Fall and Denby, Harding indicated he approved of putting the reserves under Interior. Fall then drafted an executive order for the president to sign authorizing the transfer and drew up a covering letter to be signed by Denby requesting the change. These he gave to thirty-four-year-old Ted Roosevelt with the understanding that Roosevelt was to get a final sign-off from Denby as well as Admiral Robert S. Griffin and Commander H. A. Stuart, both of whom administered the reserves.

Even though his father had been the nation's first conservation president, Ted Jr., a war hero and a product of Groton and Harvard, initially hadn't any qualms about turning over the reserves to Fall. Surely it must have occurred to him that the interior secretary might open the navy oil, which had been set aside to deal with a possible national emergency, to commercial development. Before joining the Harding administration, Roosevelt had been a director of one of Harry Sinclair's oil companies. He counted Sinclair as a personal friend and didn't hesitate to call upon him for favors. At Roosevelt's request, Sinclair had given Ted's younger brother Archibald a sinecure as vice president at one of his oil companies. In addition, Roosevelt presumably knew that many of the major oil companies, particularly Sinclair Oil, were eager to gain access to both the Teapot fields in Wyoming and the Elk Hills reserves in California.

However, he also viewed Albert Fall as a straight shooter. After all, the interior secretary had been a great supporter and admirer of Ted's father, their differences over conservation notwithstanding. Like the senior Roosevelt, Fall was a man of action. He had been one of Roosevelt's Rough Riders, although to his lasting regret, Fall hadn't accompanied Roosevelt to Cuba. In Washington, Fall took on young Ted as a protégé, included him in poker games at the McLean mansion, and enthralled him with tales of the wild frontier, firsthand accounts of the gunman John Wesley Hardin, Billy the Kid, and Pat Garrett, whom Fall counted as a friend and had defended successfully in a murder trial.

In Ted Jr.'s eyes, Fall could do no wrong. When Harry Slattery came to the Navy Department to see Roosevelt, bringing with him a letter of introduction from his father's friend Gifford Pinchot, he told the assistant secretary that Fall's proposed stewardship of the reserves was suspect, given his poor conservation record. Roosevelt "hit the ceiling," demanding that Slattery not speak a disparaging word "about his great, good friend." In anger, he showed Slattery the door.

Denby had no problems with either the draft of the executive order or the letter Roosevelt delivered. He was prepared to sign his name to both documents. Admiral Griffin and Commander Stuart, however, were anything but sanguine. Griffin, Stuart, and several other senior officers who had been involved in establishing and running the reserves strongly opposed the transfer and dismissed the drainage issue as bunkum. They had been closely monitoring the reserves for years and had seen no perceptible drainage. So vociferous were they that even Ted Roosevelt began to question the wisdom of the transfer and said as much to his superior. Griffin reminded Denby that the navy had been fighting for ten years to retain its oil reserves. If the secretary turned their administration over to the Interior Department, "we might as well say good-bye to our oil," he warned.

Denby was sympathetic, but there was nothing he could do, he claimed. The president, his commander in chief, wanted the transfer enacted. Harding had made that clear in his earlier meeting with the navy secretary and Fall. Frustrated, Griffin, Stuart, and several other senior officers revised Fall's draft, salvaging what they could and inserting a key paragraph giving the navy final say about leasing the reserves. Interior could do nothing "without the approval of the Secretary or Acting Secretary of the Navy."

By now, you know Fall well enough to imagine how he reacted to the navy's revisions. While the messenger, Ted Jr., stood by nervously, Fall struck out the paragraph that Stuart and Griffin had added and replaced it with one stipulating that he had to *consult* with the navy secretary or acting secretary if he chose to lease the reserves, an important distinction. He didn't need the secretary's approval. After the mere formality of a discussion with Denby, or in his absence Roosevelt, Fall had complete authority to lease the reserves. It was Roosevelt who brought the letter and revised executive order to the White House. Harding signed it on May 31. Did the president actually bother to read it? Likely not. Harding was not much for details.

Ed doheny was one of the few people besides Fall, Denby, and the president who knew anything about Fall's plans regarding the navy's petroleum. In fact, the Californian was prepared to begin limited drilling on Reserve No. 1, one of the Elk Hills fields, as soon as the president okayed the transfer.

Although he was a lifelong Democrat, Doheny began ardently courting Harding and his new interior secretary immediately after the election. Although he had given the Harding campaign a modest (for him) $25,000 contribution, out of an allegiance to his party Doheny had backed Cox, donating at least $75,000 in campaign funds. That had clearly been a mistake, one Doheny was most eager to rectify. "It is in sackcloth and ashes that I come to your feet to beg forgiveness and admission among the ranks of the sane people of the Country," he wrote Fall on November 4, 1920, only a day after he offered the use of *Casiana* to Harding. Now that the blinders had been stripped from his eyes by Harding's resounding victory, Doheny recognized that the Republicans had been responsible for "saving this Nation and Democracy from the fatal error of committing itself without reservations to the League [of Nations] as proposed."

Laying the blarney on even thicker, he concluded that Harding's victory provided "greater cause for rejoicing than the signing of the armistice on November 11, 1918, or any other event or day since the eventful day in 1776 which gave birth to this Republic."

No doubt touched by this sentiment, crusty old Interior Secretary Fall sent off his own valentine. "I have always had a very warm feeling for you, while we have met casually since the old days, and that feeling has grown as I have met you oftener in the last year or two," Fall wrote Doheny on November 15.

At Interior, Fall's regard for Doheny likely intensified when he learned the Californian had hired many of Wilson's cabinet members, including his predecessor at Interior, Franklin Lane, to highly paid executive positions. Eager to find work in the private sector that could offset all those years of getting by on a U.S. senator's modest salary, Fall had agreed to take the Interior post for only a year. "Making up for lost time financially had become an obsession with him," wrote Fall biographer David Stratton. "It warped his judgment and had a significant bearing on the most important decisions he ever made, as a cabinet officer or otherwise."

On a list of desirable employers, Doheny was at the top. At Interior, there was much Fall could do to win favor with his prospective boss. Doheny, Fall was aware, had approached the navy unsuccessfully in an attempt to drill twenty-two offset wells on Reserve No. 1 at Elk Hills. Six weeks after Harding signed the transfer order, Fall awarded Doheny the lease for the offset wells. It wasn't a big contract, but the conservationists and the navy officers who had opposed the transfer saw it as a confirmation of their worst fears and a harbinger of what was to come. In a speech in Washington, Harry Slattery warned, "I think Mr. Fall will be asked a few questions about . . . the leasing of oil lands in Naval Reserve Number One to a Doheny interest."

Commander Stuart and another officer also spoke out about the offset lease and tried to block it. Not good career moves. Fall expressed himself as "dissatisfied with both of them" and had Denby transfer Stuart to Charleston, South Carolina, and the other officer sent off to the Pacific, Stuart later testified, thus clearing the way for Doheny to get a foothold in the entire Elk Hills reserves.

On July 8, 1921, four days before he gave Doheny the lease, Fall wrote the Californian that he had matters firmly in hand. "There will be no possibility of any further conflict with Navy officials and this department, as I have notified Secretary Denby that I should conduct the matter of the naval leases under the direction of the president, without calling any of his force in consultation unless I conferred with him personally upon a matter of policy. He understands the situation and that I shall handle the matter exactly as I think best and will not consult with any officials of any bureau in his department, but only with himself, and such consultation will be confined strictly and entirely to matters of general policy."

In other words, nothing stood between Doheny and the California reserves except Albert Fall.

16

SURE THING

Usually, Harry Ford Sinclair's driver picked him up in front of his Fifth Avenue apartment and took him directly to his office downtown on 45 Nassau Street. Not today. Today, Sinclair had an important meeting at 10:00 a.m. at the Vanderbilt Hotel on Park Avenue.

A short, broad-chested, bull-necked man, balding with shoe-polish black hair—what was left of it—Sinclair, one reporter noted, resembled "a butcher shop foreman who enjoys his work." In reality, the forty-five-year-old Sinclair was, along with Ed Doheny and Standard Oil of Indiana's chairman, Robert Stewart, one of the three biggest oilmen in the country. *Time* magazine called him "the burly Destiny man."

Like Doheny and Stewart, Sinclair was a midwesterner, though he'd been born near Wheeling, West Virginia. His father, who owned a pharmacy in Lawrence, Kansas, sent him to the University of Kansas to study pharmacy. Soon after Sinclair graduated, the elder Sinclair died, leaving Harry the business. Pushing pills and making nice with arthritic old ladies, however, was not for Harry Sinclair. He let the business slide, played poker and hunted much of the time, accidentally blew off a toe with a shotgun, got a $5,000 check from his insurance company, and used the stake to get into the oil business, peripherally, at least. At the time—this was 1903, 1904—southern Kansas was experiencing an oil boom. Harry used his insurance check to buy "mud sills," the big logs the oil companies, most of them little independents, used to shore up their derricks.

With his booming laugh and enormous energy, Sinclair soon became a fixture in the still fledgling southwestern oil business. He had almost a second sense when it came to targeting a potential rich field. When Sinclair got started in the oil business, there was no science or technology to assist in finding gas and oil deposits. Sinclair developed his own criteria for pinpointing a likely drilling site. He would rely on "closeology," meaning the site should be in proximity of a producing well. The other telltale mark of a rich field, Sinclair believed, was the blackjack oak. Where there were blackjack oaks, there was likely oil, Sinclair believed. More often than not, he was right.

Sinclair would target a field, buy or lease it, develop it, maybe sell it off, always keeping the best fields for himself. Of course, he drilled his share of dry holes, but most of the time his wagers, particularly those in the oil business, paid off handsomely. Sinclair, as an example, had taken out leases on Oklahoma's Glenn Oil Field well before it proved to be one of the richest fields in the world, producing more wealth, it is said, than the California Gold Rush and the Colorado Silver Rush combined.

By 1920, Sinclair had already begun courting Soviet officials in hopes of securing Russian oil, had his sights trained on Persia (Iran), and was opening fields in Venezuela and Colombia. He had established sizable drilling operations in Mexico, Nicaragua, Costa Rica, Panama, Colombia, and Angola in Portuguese West Africa. "Sinclair's technique was to approach the government of the country with the flyleaf of his check book showing," one of his biographers noted. After paying off the proper officials, Sinclair typically received a franchise from the country's oil with the understanding that the government in question could have his entire output except for a million or so acres along the coast.

Married with one daughter, Sinclair had his own railroad car, *Sinco*, an estate in Great Neck, Long Island, a Fifth Avenue town house, a Thoroughbred racehorse farm in Rancocas, New Jersey, and a fleet of oil tankers. He controlled Sinclair Consolidated Oil, which in turn controlled some twenty companies. He had amassed one of the largest fortunes in the United States and seemed such an exemplar of the Midas touch that the bankrupt country of Albania offered to make Sinclair its king as long as he'd fatten the depleted royal treasury with some of his fortune and share his knack for making a buck.

Harry loved to gamble. He was a high roller, a player in every sense of the word. He played poker superbly, though sometimes he lost large sums of money to government officials who might have balked at taking an outright bribe. Harry loved baseball and owned a team in the short-lived Federal League, a rival to the American and National leagues, before it folded in 1916. Most of all, he loved racehorses and was determined to win the Kentucky Derby with one of the Thoroughbreds from his own stable.

Which was certainly not an unrealistic expectation. Harry was used to winning. Of late, however, he had been on a losing streak. And when he lost, Sinclair lost big. Sinclair had wagered $90,000 that the Chicago White Sox would defeat the Cincinnati Reds in the 1919 World Series. Unfortunately for Sinclair, his bookmaker was Arnold Rothstein, who would gain fame as the man who "fixed" the series. Harry Sinclair holds the dubious distinction of having been the patsy in America's most notorious sports scandal.

More recently in the 1921 Kentucky Derby, Sinclair had two horses that seemed like sure winners, Don't Know and Grey Lag. Don't Know got sick before the race, and Grey Lag pulled up lame in his last workout. Sinclair and the guests he'd brought down from Washington aboard *Sinco* had to watch another horse win.

He'd also suffered a setback when Jake Hamon had been shot by Clara. He and Jake knew each other from their days at the University of Kansas and the Oklahoma oil fields. For a time, they had both lived in neighboring mansions in Tulsa. In exchange for putting Harding in the White House, Jake was supposed to take over Interior and give the Teapot Dome lease to Sinclair and Robert Stewart in exchange for a cut. Then the damn fool got himself shot. That left Sinclair in a fix. He had shelled out $1 million to help get Harding elected, and the Republicans still had a postelection campaign debt of $1.5 million. Will Hays wanted Harry to bail out the RNC, but Sinclair wasn't giving another nickel until he got his oil.

SINCLAIR JOINED THE others in the suite at the Vanderbilt. Those present included Colonel Robert W. Stewart, chairman of Standard Oil of Indiana, the flagship of what remained of the Standard Oil empire. Stewart had come to New York from Chicago, where his company was headquartered. Two of the other oilmen in the suite essentially worked for Stewart and Sinclair. Harry M. Blackmer ran a Standard Oil subsidiary, Midwest Refining Company, while James O'Neil headed up Prairie Oil and Gas Company, a Sinclair subsidiary.

Also in attendance were A. E. Humphreys, who (like Sinclair) came from West Virginia but (like Blackmer) was based in Denver; and a Canadian lawyer, Harry Osler, who had come down for the meeting from Toronto. These gentlemen had gathered at the Vanderbilt at Harry Sinclair's behest to complete a major transaction: The previous year, Humphreys had made a major oil strike in Mexia, Texas. In March, Sinclair, Stewart, O'Neil, Osler, and Blackmer traveled by train to Mexia to check out Humphreys's fields. Now, in New York they were buying fifty million barrels of the Mexia oil from Humphreys in what seemingly was a straightforward business transaction.

There was a second deal under way here as well, however, one that would generate the payoffs needed to obtain the Teapot lease, clear the remaining Republican debt, and add substantially to the participants' finances. It centered on a fraudulent Canadian-based corporation—Continental Trading—and was so cleverly devised, complex, and outlandishly ambitious that it would take investigators another three or four years to begin to put the pieces together. By that time, Blackmer and O'Neil had fled to France; Humphreys had blown off much of his forehead with a shotgun; Osler disappeared into darkest Africa on an extended big-game hunting trip; and Sinclair and Stewart were in court fighting to stay out of prison.

All because Harry Sinclair made one boneheaded mistake.

17

BLACK BAG

While Harry Sinclair and his associates were buying up A. E. Humphreys's oil, Albert Fall was in the process of acquiring another ranch in New Mexico in order to obtain valuable water rights. The three-thousand-acre ranch in question, the Harris ranch, was situated at the head of the valley in which Fall's ranching kingdom was based. It came with prized water rights for one of the forks of the Three Rivers, which flowed through Fall's property. With southern New Mexico experiencing a prolonged drought, Fall needed the Harris water desperately. With it, he could perhaps finally make his Three Rivers ranch profitable and complete ambitious plans to build a hydroelectric plant. "[It was] worth more to me than anyone else and [would render] my holdings much more valuable," Fall said of the Harris property.

Fall had been hoping to buy the Harris place for several years and had even arranged for Cleveland industrialist Price McKinney to provide the necessary funding. Fall and McKinney owned some gold mines in Sonora. These were in McKinney's name since Fall wanted his participation in the venture kept confidential, for good reason. As the Senate's chief advocate for protecting American rights in Mexico, Fall could not be seen as having a personal agenda.

After meeting with then president-elect Harding at Brownsville, Texas, in November 1920, Fall had visited McKinney in Chandler, Arizona. He later claimed that McKinney at the time provided him with a credit line of up to $250,000 based on Fall's equity in their joint Mexican ventures. Fall intended, he said, to use the money to buy the Harris place as soon as it came up for sale.

Which it did the following year. Fall got word from New Mexico that in order to settle the estate of its previous owner, the Harris place was going to be sold quickly—within seven days. The price was $91,500, and a rival buyer had already expressed interest. Fall had been given first opportunity to purchase the property, but he had to come up with the cash fast.

Fall later claimed he tried to reach McKinney but had been unsuccessful, the Cleveland multimillionaire having chosen late November to visit his mines on Michigan's Upper Peninsula. Fortunately, Fall had also discussed the Harris purchase and a possible loan with Doheny's lobbyist, Harold Walker, and Doheny. Doheny had earlier volunteered, "Let me lend it to you." All Fall had to do was ask, and the loan was his.

THROUGHOUT THE SUMMER and autumn of 1921, Fall had showered Doheny with political favors. These ranged from small gifts such as an autographed photograph of the president to important concessions. One of the latter involved a naval officer who would play a significant role in helping Doheny gain the Elk Hills oil.

After a summer tour through the national parks, Fall visited Doheny in California. During the visit, Doheny told Fall about Captain John Keeler Robinson, an Annapolis graduate who during the war had been in command of the USS *Huntington,* the ship on which Doheny's only son, Ned, served briefly as a lieutenant. Visiting Ned's ship at Pensacola, Florida, in 1917, Doheny had spent an hour or so meeting with Robinson in his private quarters and discussing the naval oil reserves. Robinson asked Doheny's opinion about how the oil reserves were being handled. "Well, it's being handled very well [as an unintended benefit] for the people you have as neighbors," Doheny's biographer Margaret Leslie Davis quotes him as telling Robinson. He went on to

explain that the oil drillers on adjacent fields could tap into the navy reserves using slant wells, wells that drilled at an angle instead of verti-
cally. Robinson was taken aback by Doheny's assertion. Such culpability
had apparently never occurred to him. "It opened my eyes to a situation
I never dreamed existed," he later said.

After four years, Doheny remembered Robinson fondly and was indebted to him. During their initial meeting, he had secured assurance
from Robinson that Ned would be kept out of danger. Much to the an-
noyance of some of the other officers aboard the *Huntington*, Doheny's
son received preferential treatment after his father's visit. Soon after, he
was transferred to a cushy shore job in Washington, D.C., where he was
entirely out of harm's way.

Robinson, Doheny believed, would be an excellent candidate to replace the uncooperative and recently exiled Commander Stuart as the
officer in charge of the oil reserves. Clearly, he sold Fall on the idea,
likely during the interior secretary's California visit. Soon after Fall's return, Secretary of the Navy Denby announced that he was putting
Robinson, a large, florid-faced man who barked orders in a booming
voice, in charge of the naval petroleum reserves and appointing him his
liaison with Fall. The move had Fall's fingerprints all over it. In gratitude, Robinson, now a newly appointed admiral, wrote Doheny on October 6 telling him of his good fortune in securing command of the
reserves.

The following month when Doheny and his second wife, Estelle,
visited Washington, Fall rolled out the red, white, and blue carpet, getting the Dohenys invitations to the dedication of Arlington Cemetery's
Tomb of the Unknown Soldier on November 11. Fall also wrote Secretary of War Weeks to obtain tickets for the Dohenys to the Army/Navy
football game and brought them to the White House to meet President
Harding.

Writing to Fall after the meeting, Doheny thanked him profusely for "the interview which we had with the President. It was most
satisfactory, and demonstrated to my friends that we have a real President, one who meets the people and recognizes that their interest in
public affairs is worthy of consideration." In closing, he extolled Harding as "a great president" and described Fall as "Lincolnesque in
stature."

In Washington, Fall and Doheny also discussed the oil leases. In response to Doheny's complaints that the royalties he had to pay on the oil taken from the offset wells at Elk Hills were too high, the accommodating interior secretary offered to give him additional leases on the Elk Hills reserves and preferential leases on any additional California naval reserves. In other words, the entire California naval oil reserves, an estimated three hundred million barrels of oil, was Doheny's for the asking. What Doheny had to do in return, under a tentative agreement worked out by Admiral Robinson and Fall, was to build a large fuel-oil storage station at Pearl Harbor. As early as 1920, some in the U.S. military believed that the next great war would be between the United States and Japan in the Pacific and recognized that Pearl Harbor would be strategically critical to the United States if war came about.

The Pearl Harbor project would cost tens of millions, Doheny estimated, but the potential payback was enormous. The Elk Hills and Buena Vista naval reserves held as much as three hundred million barrels of oil, and Doheny typically cleared $1 profit per barrel drilled. On November 28, Doheny gave Fall and Admiral Robinson a formal proposal to construct the Pearl Harbor facility in exchange for all the crude oil from the two California reserves. No oil company other than Pan American Petroleum and Transport, Doheny's company, was asked to bid on the project.

That night, Doheny went on to New York, where he and Estelle were staying at the Plaza. Early on the morning of November 30, a Wednesday, Fall called him. The topic was the Harris ranch. Fall said "that he was prepared now to receive that loan," meaning the $100,000 he needed to buy the additional property. And he needed the money in cash.

Doheny said he would have the money by the end of the day. There was one stipulation, however, at least according to Fall's version of the incident. This was to be a business transaction, not just a loan from one exceedingly rich old buddy to a needy pal, as Doheny and his lawyers would later characterize the deal. Doheny wanted assurances that on leaving the Harding administration, Fall would go to work for him. He was to oversee his Latin American affairs, focusing principally on Mexico and Doheny's need to shore up the Obregón government. Like Fall's predecessor at Interior, Franklin Lane, Fall would receive a generous salary of $50,000 a year (a small fortune in 1921), a liberal expense account, and likely valuable stock options, as Pan American Petroleum, Doheny's company, was publicly traded.

From Fall's salary, Doheny suggested—again, this was Fall's account—Fall could repay him the $100,000 incrementally. Fall was delighted with the terms. After all, he had been looking for a lucrative post in the private sector, and this seemed an ideal match. "I was egotistical enough to believe at the time . . . that Doheny was desirous of securing my services . . . because of my supposed knowledge on Latin American laws and customs and . . . familiarity with the Spanish language," Fall later said. Apparently, it hadn't occurred to him at the time that in agreeing to this arrangement, he had been bought and paid for.

TWENTY-SEVEN-YEAR-OLD Edward "Ned" Doheny Jr. happened to be in New York at the same time. With him was his constant companion, secretary, and bodyguard, a former garage mechanic named Hugh Plunkett. Doheny was in town staying with his parents at the Plaza and shopping for an apartment on Manhattan's East Side. He came to New York often, loved the city and especially the theater—so much so that he was contemplating buying several theaters on Broadway.

Edward Doheny adored his only son, but Ned, whom he was grooming to take over the Doheny oil empire, hadn't measured up to his father's exacting expectations. Not even close. Tall, athletic, and just short of handsome, Ned lacked the elder Doheny's drive, ambition, and discipline. No student, he had flunked out of Stanford, finally graduating from the University of Southern California. In 1914, young Doheny married his high school sweetheart and quickly fathered two daughters. After joining the navy in 1917 as a full lieutenant, Doheny lobbied consistently to be stationed in Los Angeles on recruitment duty rather than be sent to sea far from his family. One of his superior officers, Commander Alfonso Henry Woodbine, characterized him as a pampered malcontent.

By 1921, Ned had been made an executive vice president of his father's oil companies, but he was easily distracted and spent much time out of the office, collecting expensive cars, working on behalf of the USC alumni association, or socializing at the Los Angeles Country Club or the Los Angeles Athletic Club. At first, the elder Doheny let his son do pretty much as he pleased. After all, Ned had had a hellacious childhood. Doheny Sr. was almost always away from home. Embittered by her failed singing career and deteriorating marriage, Ned's mother and Doheny's first wife, Carrie, frequently retreated to her bedroom for days on end. A chubby, musically inclined boy, Ned was left to fend largely for himself. In 1899, just as Doheny was experiencing his first success in the California oil business, Carrie walked out on him, taking Ned and his sister with her to San Francisco. The following year, a few months after Doheny and his second wife, Estelle, were married, Carrie committed suicide by downing a bottle of battery acid. Ned's sister died soon after. Estelle Doheny, a former long-distance telephone operator whose dulcet speaking voice captivated Ed Doheny before he even met her, drew stepmother duty, rearing Ned as best she could while her husband drilled for black gold in Old Mexico.

Doheny had spoiled Ned, given him anything he wanted, but by late 1921, it was time for the young prince to assume his rightful place as the heir apparent. "I was endeavoring at that time to work [him] into every phase of the business of handling the fortune that I expected sometime or other he would handle all of," Doheny would later explain. The old man wanted Ned to learn something, "gain something in experience," get his well-manicured fingers a little dirty. And what better way to get one's hands soiled than by delivering a $100,000 "loan" to a U.S. cabinet officer?

As soon as he got off the phone with Fall, Ed Doheny called Ned and told him to go down to Blair & Company, an investment banking firm where both Dohenys had substantial accounts, and withdraw in cash from Ned's own account the sum Fall had requested. This Ned did, accompanied by his sidekick, Hugh Plunkett. At the bank, an obliging assistant teller organized the money into five $20,000 stacks, wrapped each with a rubber band, and placed them in a black parcel bag Ned had brought with him. Ned and Hugh took a train to Washington and a cab to the Wardman Park Hotel, where Fall had an apartment and the Dohenys frequently stayed. Recognizing young Doheny, the doorman greeted Ned warmly, as did Albert Fall when he glimpsed the black bag;

he immediately began counting out his money, a million dollars or so in today's currency.

After presumably offering the boys a drink, Fall wrote out an IOU, thanked Ned and Hugh, who went right back to Manhattan, and began packing himself. In the morning, Fall was leaving for New Mexico to make a deposit on the Harris ranch.

18

ALL ROADS LEAD TO THREE RIVERS

Santa came early to the Three Rivers ranch, bringing with him a shiny tin box filled with $100 bills. Upon arriving in El Paso, the nearest large town, on December 5, Fall went straight to the office of his son-in-law, customs collector Clarence C. Chase, to meet with the Harris ranch heirs and make a down payment of $10,000. With Chase, the Harris heirs, and their lawyer looking on, Fall made a show of counting out the money on the desk. When Chase's wife, Alexina—one of Fall's two surviving daughters—walked into the room, she said she'd never seen so much money. Playfully, she picked up one of the rubber-band-wrapped $20,000 stacks and started for the door. "Here's where I go to Mexico," she said, according to M. R. Werner and John Starr in their book *Teapot Dome*. Her father called her back, she later testified, and told her she was absconding with the mortgage on their ranch, money Ed Doheny had loaned him.

To Alexina and later to various investigators, Fall failed to mention that on the train trip from D.C., he had met up with the no longer elusive Price McKinney in Chicago and traveled with him all the way to El Paso in McKinney's private car. Had Fall so desired, he could have easily gotten the funding he needed from McKinney, repaid Doheny for the "bridge" loan, and used his own money to buy the Harris ranch, thereby avoiding any impropriety.

Settling in for Christmas on the ranch, Fall got a telegraph on December 22 from the Interior Department informing him that Harry Sinclair and his lawyer, J. W. (Bill) Zevely, were eager to see Fall at the end of the month "on a very urgent and important matter." If the interior secretary could make time for them, they would travel to New Mexico with their wives aboard Harry Sinclair's private railcar, *Sinco*.

Fall didn't know Sinclair well, though the oilman of late had become a conspicuous figure in Washington. Fall ran into him at K Street house poker games, at the McLeans', where both were frequent guests, or in the White House when Sinclair was staying overnight as a guest of the Hardings. The Kentucky-born Fall had also talked horse racing over mint juleps with Sinclair at the Kentucky Derby. Every year, both religiously attended the Derby, the interior secretary as the guest of Price McKinney. Since becoming interior secretary, Fall, who had fought to protect American petroleum interests in Colombia much as he had in Mexico, had arranged a meeting between the Colombian ambassador and Sinclair. Otherwise, their relationship had been social and entirely amicable, stoked by a shared passion for Thoroughbred racehorses and poker.

Sinclair's party arrived on December 30, leaving Sinclair's railcar on a siding at the Three Rivers station. Ostensibly, the "urgent matter" that had brought Sinclair and Zevely all the way to the southern reaches of New Mexico was a problem Sinclair was having with an oil lease on the Osage Indian Reservation. Fall, who wanted to open all Indian lands to oil and gas exploration without compensation to Native Americans, addressed the matter promptly with a telegram to the Interior Department, while the visitors and their wives toured the ranch by horseback. Several of Fall's hired men took Sinclair and Zevely hunting for quail, deer, and wild turkey. On New Year's Eve, the Falls and their guests attended a party at the Three Rivers schoolhouse that ultimately developed into a drunken brawl. The combatants smashed chairs, fired pistols into the air, and cold-cocked one another. This was still the Wild West. Sinclair and Zevely had the time of their lives, though they were quick to hustle their spouses back to the safety of Sinclair's private railcar.

Sinclair hadn't come all the way from New York, however, for a taste of the frontier or for Fall's assistance with Osage oil, a matter that could have easily been addressed with an exchange of telegrams or letters. What brought him to Three Rivers was the Teapot lease, the plum he had been seeking since before the 1920 Republican convention. According to what Fall later told Harding, he and Sinclair discussed Teapot only briefly during the visit, and then almost as an afterthought. "The day that Mr. Sinclair left Three Rivers, he, for the first time, asked me if I were contemplating the opening up of the Teapot Dome," Fall explained to the president. "I answered immediately that I was considering the matter, but was yet awaiting final reports from the Bureau of Mines experts in that field upon the danger of immediate drainage."

We'll give Fall the benefit of the doubt here and assume that Sinclair actually restrained himself until the last day of his visit to press his host on the Teapot leases. In all probability, though, Fall and Sinclair and their subordinates had discussed Teapot well before Sinclair's visit and were already in the process of arranging for Sinclair and his business associates to take over the Wyoming fields. The previous November, Sinclair and his partner in seeking the leases, Standard Oil of Indiana CEO Robert Stewart, had secured funding from the fraudulent Continental Trading transaction that would be used to pay off Fall. That same month, Edward Doheny, likely at Fall's urging, had dropped a pending claim he had on the Teapot leases, thus clearing the way for Sinclair to move on the Wyoming fields. With Solomon-like judgment, Albert Fall had managed to divvy up the until now government-owned petroleum resources into two more or less equal parcels, each containing millions of barrels of oil. Doheny would be allocated the California reserves, Sinclair and friends Teapot. In broad strokes, the matter had been largely decided well before Sinclair started off to Three Rivers.

THERE WAS MORE at stake here, however, than Teapot and the California fields. One of the lingering misconceptions regarding the Teapot scandal is that it involved only the naval oil reserves. There was another oil reserve at stake, however: the Salt Creek fields, which were adjacent to Teapot and contained substantially more oil. Taken together, Teapot and Salt Creek in outline resembled a bowling pin, Teapot the neck,

Salt Creek the pin. Salt Creek wasn't a naval reserve, but it was owned by the federal government, which meant that Albert Fall had the final say as to who got the Salt Creek oil. At the time, Salt Creek was the richest oil field in the world.

Now follow closely here, because this was a three-card monte game involving some extremely deft sleight of hand. When investigators began later to unravel the fraudulent machinations of Messrs. Sinclair, Stewart, Blackmer, and Fall, they determined that Sinclair and Stewart had hatched a master plan by which Sinclair would gain Teapot and Stewart would take over Salt Creek. They would then share the bounty and jointly build a pipeline linking both fields to a Standard Oil of Indiana refinery. This is how the rich get richer—that is, if the rich happen to be oil barons.

One minor hurdle had to be cleared before Stewart could take control of Salt Creek, however. In 1911, Standard Oil had been broken up by the U.S. Supreme Court because old John D. Rockefeller's company at the time totally monopolized the U.S. oil industry. As a result, the oil megagiant Standard Oil had been divided into a number of separate corporate entities, among them Standard Oil of New Jersey, Standard Oil of California, and Stewart's company, Standard Oil of Indiana. Each were huge companies in their own right but individually smaller than their mutual corporate parent.

In 1921, Harry Blackmer, who had made a lot of money in silver mining and oil, controlled 95 percent of the Salt Creek field leases along with several partners from Colorado through Midwest Refinery. Stewart wanted to buy out Blackmer's share of Midwest so that Standard Oil of Indiana would have full control of Salt Creek. Because of the old antitrust ruling, however, Standard was precluded from taking a majority stake in government-owned fields. As it was, Standard Oil of Indiana was already the dominant petroleum producer in Wyoming.

Stewart and Blackmer needed a friend in the Harding administration who had the clout to have the law changed so that Standard could take over Midwest's Salt Creek operations. Which was why Stewart and Blackmer also paid a visit to Albert Fall at Three Rivers. According to testimony later given by Fall's son-in-law Clarence Chase, Sinclair had scarcely pulled out of the Three Rivers station when Stewart and Blackmer arrived. We have to surmise what was discussed during their visit, since none of the three participants, bound perhaps by an oilman's omertà, ever discussed the meeting or acknowledged that it took place. We do know, though, that as soon as Albert Fall got back to Washington, he convinced Harry Daugherty's Justice Department to clear any legal obstacles that prevented Standard Oil of Indiana from buying out Harry Blackmer. Likely, Fall and Daugherty were well compensated for their efforts on Stewart and Blackmer's behalf.

19

UNFINISHED BUSINESS

Albert Fall arrived back in Washington on January 27 to find that the conservationists had been raising all kinds of hell in his absence. In December, Gifford Pinchot had sent out letters to six thousand newspapers railing against the interior secretary's efforts to pry the Forest Service from the Department of Agriculture The ensuing press coverage, in Pinchot's view, had stalled Fall's plans. "I think we have won our fight in the transfer," he wrote his brother Amos over Christmas.

Pinchot and Harry Slattery had gotten the little redheaded Henry Wallace, Harding's secretary of agriculture, all worked up as well. Wallace "had his fighting clothes on," Fall was told when he got back. Wallace, the populist former Iowa newspaper editor, was a golfer who played frequently with the president at the Chevy Chase Country Club. Between holes, he'd apparently been trying to persuade Harding that the Forest Service should stay put—that is, remain part of Agriculture. Fall didn't play golf. He'd always had better things to do than whale away endlessly at a little white ball. The idea that Wallace used these outings with Harding to undercut Fall's agenda angered the interior secretary no end. At the first opportunity, he complained to the president about the "vicious and unwarranted attack" being mounted against him by Wallace, Pinchot, Harry Slattery, and the rest of the conservationists.

Fall would have been better off—certainly far happier—staying on at Three Rivers and retiring, but he'd be damned if he was going to let Pinchot's crowd drive him out of town. He also had some important unfinished business in Washington, notably the Doheny and Sinclair leases. On his return to the Interior Department, his first order of business was to meet with Admiral Robinson. Based on Fall's discussions with Sinclair and Zevely at Three Rivers and whatever research Robinson had conducted in Fall's absence, Fall and Robinson decided to develop all of Reserve No. 3—the entire Teapot field. A few days later on February 3, Fall summoned Sinclair and Zevely to his office to give them the news and express his gratitude for the generous gifts Sinclair had sent along after his visit: six heifers, a yearling bull, two young boars, and four sows. As a bonus, Sinclair threw in an English Thoroughbred racehorse from his Rancocas breeding farm for Tom Johnson, Fall's foreman. Zevely had sent the lot down to Three Rivers in a special railroad car.

Sinclair said he was willing to take out all the oil in the reserve on a royalty basis, at which point Fall and Sinclair asked an Interior Department geologist, Arthur Ambrose, to come up with an estimate of the amount of oil in Teapot and the extent of drainage. The numbers were eye-opening, higher than either Fall or Sinclair had anticipated. Teapot, Ambrose estimated, held 135,050,000 barrels of oil; the Salt Creek field, which would be included as part of the overall package but leased separately, contained 360,270,000 barrels. Typically with the price of oil at all-time highs in 1921, producers such as Sinclair and Doheny estimated they could make a profit of $1 a barrel less royalties, which in the instance of the Teapot lease averaged between 16 and 17 percent. To Sinclair and his associates, then, the Wyoming fields could be worth almost $495 million less 17 percent. If Sinclair was willing to give Fall a small piece of this—not the 33 percent that Hamon supposedly demanded, but say 10 percent—the interior secretary could likely buy up every ranch in New Mexico.

One problem with the lease, however. Ambrose had apparently been under the impression that his boss, the interior secretary, actually wanted him to calibrate the risk of drainage instead of coming up with numbers supporting Fall's contention that drainage was a significant problem. Meeting on February 18, 1922, with Fall, Zevely, and Sinclair, poor Ambrose announced there was no immediate danger of drainage. A possibility of some loss, maybe, over the next six or seven years . . . always that possibility. But . . . no "immediate danger." We are left to imagine the scene that followed. Dead silence. Ambrose becoming aware that he has just kissed his future with the Interior Department good-bye; Fall glowering at the geologist from the other side of his desk; Sinclair's bug eyes all but popping out of his head; Zevely discreetly admiring the two stuffed eagles perched on one of the office tables, ready to take flight.

Fall composed himself. No need to worry. Ambrose's drainage estimates would not be a problem if no one outside Fall's office knew about them. Fall ordered Ambrose to work with Zevely in the lawyer's Washington office in drawing up the contract. Meanwhile, Sinclair headed back to New York, where on February 28 he announced the organization of a corporation called Mammoth Oil Company, a new subsidiary of Sinclair Consolidated Oil Company, the parent company for all Sinclair's holdings. There was no mention that Mammoth had been created solely to extract the Teapot oil.

In the midst of all this harried preparation—with the conservationists up in arms, secrecy and expediency were paramount in wrapping up both the Sinclair and the Doheny leases—several of Fall's subordinates, including H. Foster Bain, director of the Bureau of Mines, had the temerity to suggest that it might be prudent to have Attorney General Daugherty review the leases to determine their legality. Fall wouldn't hear of it. Absolutely not. Fall had forgotten more about oil law than Daugherty and his entire crew at Justice knew. Besides, Daugherty would only pass the matter on to "some law clerk, someone who was not at all interested in getting anything done, but who was simply interested in never writing an opinion that anybody could ever possibly find fault with and that under those circumstance the chances were at least even . . . and that if the Attorney General signed such an opinion . . . then we would be stopped from doing anything."

More likely, Fall didn't want the attorney general or his dandied-up department-store floorwalker Jess Smith nosing around trying to get a piece of the action. Let Daugherty work his side of the street. Oil was exclusively Fall's province.

A month after Mammoth was incorporated, Robinson okayed the

final draft and gave it to Fall for his signature, Fall signing on April 7 as "Secretary of the Interior" and "for the Secretary of the Navy." Hold on. One of Fall's subordinates suggested that it might be a good idea if Denby actually signed the lease himself. Lest we forget, Denby *was* secretary of the navy. This Denby did on April 12.

Harry Sinclair and his new best friend, Admiral John Keeler Robinson, celebrated the event playing poker and drinking champagne in Sinclair's suite in Washington's Carlton Hotel. Robinson actually claimed to have lost $2 to Sinclair, making him perhaps the only public official ever to lose money to Sinclair in a poker game. Fall was already on his way west for a visit to the ranch and a tour of some reclamation projects.

SOME OF ALBERT FALL'S fellow cabinet officers had been trying to keep abreast of what was going on at Interior. There were rumors, all kinds of speculation. Washington in the 1920s really was a small town. Harry Sinclair and the smooth-talking, monogrammed-shirt-wearing Zevely were seen coming and going. Some cabinet officers had a vested interest in these developments. Postmaster General and former RNC chairman Will Hays had substantial holdings in Sinclair Oil. Through a blind account at the Washington brokerage house of Hibbs & Company, Daugherty and Jess Smith also owned fourteen thousand shares of Sinclair stock. In January 1922, the stock had been selling on the New York Stock Exchange for $18. By the second week in April, it had doubled. That was a pittance, however, compared with what others were making from Sinclair investments. During one of his runs to deliver the Ohio Gang's monthly take to Mal Daugherty, Jess Smith complained to Roxy Stinson, "Some fellows—five fellows—made thirty-three million the other day in two or three days."

"Were you and Harry in on it?" Roxy asked.

"No," Jess said. "That's what we're sore about. They were friends of ours, too."

BEFORE FALL LEFT Washington on April 12, he locked the twenty-year Teapot contract in his desk and gave strict instructions to his number two, Assistant Secretary of the Interior Edward C. Finney: No one in the department was to breathe a word about the leases until after his return. He didn't want to announce the Teapot transaction until after the Doheny contract was complete. Then, when he got back, Fall would announce the two contracts concurrently. That way, the naval reserve transactions would be a fait accompli. The conservationists couldn't do a damn thing about them.

That, at least, had been the plan, but on April 14, *The Wall Street Journal* broke the news in a front-page story that the Department of the Interior had leased U.S. Naval Reserve No. 3 in Wyoming to Harry Sinclair's Mammoth Oil Company. Unnamed Interior officials were quoted as saying, "The arrangement . . . marks one of the greatest petroleum undertakings of the age . . . and signalizes a notable departure on the part of the government in seeking partnership with private capital for the working of government-owned natural resources." Conservation watchdog Harry Slattery was responsible for the story. He had learned about the lease from a source at Interior—he refused to divulge the name—and then leaked the information to the *Journal*.

At Three Rivers, Fall did his best to exert damage control. There was "nothing sensational" about the lease, he told reporters. No one was trying to "put over anything whatsoever." On April 18, on Fall's orders, Finney issued a press release officially announcing the Sinclair contract. He also instructed Finney to go ahead with the Doheny transaction—what Fall now called the "Pearl Harbor" contract. Later, though, he tried to distance himself from the Elk Hills deal by claiming that he'd been out of town when the bids were opened. When he learned that the Doheny bid was the best, "I authorized Finney to go ahead with it, *provided* [Fall's emphasis] it met the approval of the Secretary of the Navy." He had, he later said, been just one of "25 men directly or indirectly connected with drawing these contracts or shaping the policies and terms of the contracts."

Of course, none of the other twenty-four men connected to the lease had received a six-figure loan from Edward Doheny.

FALL HAD EXPECTED that Pinchot's conservationists would take the lead in protesting the leases, but instead the most immediate and vigorous concerns were voiced in Congress. Learning that Sinclair had locked up Teapot, a number of politically well-connected Wyoming oilmen immediately complained to Senator John B. Kendrick, a Wyoming Democrat. Why, they demanded, hadn't there been competitive bidding for the navy oil? And why was the entire Teapot field being developed when Wyoming was already producing an excess of petroleum? When Kendrick and Representative F. W. Mondell of Wyoming pressed Act-ing Interior Secretary Finney on the matter, Finney replied that no con-tract for a lease had been made. To similar requests, Secretary of the Navy Denby responded with a brief note saying that his counterpart at Interior, Albert Fall, had been in charge of the negotiations. Any infor-mation about the Sinclair deal would have to come from him.

Tired of getting the runaround, Kendrick on April 15 introduced a resolution in the Senate demanding that the secretary of the navy and secretary of the interior provide full disclosure regarding Teapot. Finney's April 18 announcement of the Teapot Dome lease, which also mentioned the pending Doheny contract, raised more questions than it answered. Urged on and fully briefed by the ubiquitous Harry Slattery and Pinchot, Wisconsin senator Robert "Fighting Bob" M. La Follette on April 28 introduced a resolution in the Senate calling for a full-scale investigation of the leases. "Who were the real organizers of the Mam-moth Oil Company who were to be favored by the government with a special privilege in the value beyond the dreams of Croesus?" he de-manded. With Vice President Calvin Coolidge presiding, the Senate unanimously passed the La Follette resolution the following day.

Fall learned about the proposed investigation on April 23. FRIDAY SENATOR LA FOLLETTE INTRODUCED RESOLUTION OF INQUIRY CON-CERNING LEASING RESERVE[s] . . . [and] CALLING FOR VOLUMINOUS DATA. NO ACTION TAKEN ON RESOLUTION UP TO PRESENT TIME, Assis-tant Secretary of the Interior Finney informed him in a cable to Three Rivers. Perhaps Fall believed the resolution would go nowhere in the Republican-controlled Senate. Like many Republicans, including the president, Fall viewed the Progressive La Follette as a gadfly— irritating, but essentially harmless. Or perhaps he was so preoccupied with ranch business and his dangerously overextended finances that he wasn't paying attention. He was also expecting important visitors. I HAVE AN APPOINTMENT WITH MR. DOHENY UPON SOME IMPORTANT MATTERS IMMEDIATELY AFTER THE FIRST [May 1, 1922], AND I HAVE BEEN INFORMED THAT MR. SINCLAIR WILL STOP OFF HERE ON HIS RE-TURN FROM MEXICO CITY ABOUT THE SAME TIME TO DISCUSS TEAPOT

DOME AND SOME OTHER MATTERS, Fall wired one of his subordinates on April 26, the day after Finney signed the Doheny contract on Fall's behalf. MR. DOHENY HAS BEEN AWARDED THE CONTRACT ON THE CALI-FORNIA OIL FIELDS AND DESIRES TO DISCUSS THE DETAILS WITH ME.

Fall never bothered responding to Finney's telegram regarding La Follette and hadn't seemed especially concerned when on April 29 the Senate, despite initial opposition from the Republican side of the chamber, passed La Follette's resolution. Fall welcomed "any investiga-tion senatorial or otherwise," he told reporters. He was entirely confi-dent the American public would applaud "the businesslike way" in which the navy's oil reserves were being managed.

EARLY IN MAY, Albert Fall headed back to Washington to deal with the brouhaha over the oil leases and meet up with another son-in-law, Mahlon T. Everhart. Everhart had been married to Caroline "Carrie" Fall, one of the two Fall offspring who died in the influenza epidemic of 1918. Tall and lean, Everhart managed Three Rivers as Fall's partner in the venture. He had come east to attend his mother's funeral. Fall wanted to see him on an important matter. He needed Everhart to col-lect a substantial payment from Harry Sinclair and bring it back with him to New Mexico, where it would immediately be put to use to pay off back taxes and refurbish the ranch. Fall and Sinclair had made arrangements for the payoff in advance. Fall later claimed that Sinclair had become so enraptured with the Three Rivers ranch that only a few weeks after receiving a contract worth millions of dollars from the Inte-rior Department, he had decided to purchase a one-third interest in the spread for $233,000.

This was the first of several payments Fall was to receive from the oilman as reciprocity for the Teapot contract. Instead of cash, however, Sinclair gave the money to the interior secretary in so-called Liberty bonds, government bonds that had been issued to support the U.S. ef-fort in World War I. Fall voiced no objections. After all, these bonds yielded at least 3.5 percent annually tax-free. They also had serial num-bers, a detail that both Sinclair and Fall apparently overlooked at the time.

Sinclair arrived in Washington with the money on May 8, 1922, only a week after the Senate had authorized the investigation into the naval leases. With Fall now under intense scrutiny, he sent Everhart to meet Sinclair in the Washington railroad yards, where his private car was parked at a siding. Later, Everhart would recall waiting in the car while the bulky oilman retrieved the bonds in $1,000 and $500 denominations from a safe, then carefully counted out $198,000 in bonds and handed them over to the rancher. Neither Sinclair nor Everhart documented the transaction with a bill of sale, a receipt, or even an IOU, which gave the lie to the story that Sinclair was buying a share of Three Rivers.

Everhart took the bonds back to Fall's Wardman Park apartment, where only five months earlier Ned Doheny had made a similar delivery. There Fall peeled off $2,500 in bonds for his personal use and gave the balance to Everhart. Fall, however, was dissatisfied. He apparently had expected a larger payment, substantially more than $198,000. Peeved, he instructed Everhart to visit Sinclair in his New York office before heading back to New Mexico and collect another $71,000. Sinclair obliged, giving the thirty-eight-year-old rancher $35,000 in Liberty bonds and $36,000 in cash. Again, neither party produced any written record of the deal.

20

A DOG'S BREAKFAST

On the evening of April 10, Albert Lasker dropped by the White House to see the president. Lasker, you'll remember, was the hotshot Chicago advertising and public relations executive who was instrumental in getting Harding elected. In gratitude, the president had appointed him chairman of the prestigious United States Shipping Board. Although he was not part of Harding's inner circle, Lasker was always welcome at the White House.

Under a long-standing agreement, the U.S. Shipping Board purchased much of the oil used by the U.S. Merchant Marine from the Salt Creek fields adjacent to Teapot. In his role as Shipping Board head, Lasker had ties with many of the nation's top oil operators. Earlier that day, he told Harding, Walter Teagle, president of Standard Oil of New Jersey, barged unannounced into his office and launched into a tirade. "I understand the Interior Department is just about to close a contract to lease Teapot Dome, and all through the industry it smells," he told Lasker. "I'm not interested in Teapot Dome. It has no interest whatsoever for Standard Oil of New Jersey, but I do feel that you should tell the president that it smells—that he must not let it go through."

Lasker had concerns of his own about the lease and the damage it might do to the presidency. At the time, Washington was rife with rumors about the navy oil transactions. Like it or not, the president was being dragged into the fray. A few days earlier, Senator La Follette had asked for a copy of the president's May 31, 1921, order transferring the reserves to the Department of the Interior. It had never been published. Lasker feared, correctly, that the Wisconsin senator intended to challenge the document's legality.

Harding didn't seem especially concerned by Lasker's news. "This wasn't the first time that this rumor has come to me," he told Lasker, "but if Albert Fall isn't an honest man, I'm not fit to be president of the United States."

And surely, the president believed, Edward Doheny and Harry Sinclair were above reproach as well. Harding had met Doheny only once, when Fall brought him to the White House, but Fall had the highest regard for the Californian. That was good enough for Harding. Sinclair had become a Harding favorite. Florence, in fact, had developed a personal relationship with him, given that Sinclair always took the time to chat with her when he came to the White House poker soirees and unfailingly sent gracious, flattering thank-you notes after one of his overnight visits. Of course, Sinclair had also funded a substantial portion of Harding's presidential campaign, which no doubt endeared him to the president and First Lady as well.

The president was further reassured when on June 7, 1922, the interior secretary presented him with a seventy-five-page report dealing with the oil leases, complete with attached exhibits. "I think you will find [it] fully and thoroughly comprehensive, if tediously long," Fall wrote in a cover letter. "I am handing you these documents in the sincere belief that the contracts entered into and the policy as formulated . . . will redound to the credit of your administration, both in the immediate present and in the distant future."

A forceful, direct, and lucid speaker, Fall produced a report that was an exercise in obfuscation, replete with half-truths, misstatements, arcane geological data, legalese, inaccuracies, and a self-justifying, revisionist history of the U.S. petroleum reserve policies and the drainage issue. As far as the president was concerned, it might as well have been written in Mandarin. In the report, Fall justified the Teapot lease as necessary to eliminate drainage, a threat that was at worst negligible. He claimed that in giving Sinclair the contract, he was breaking up "the absolute monopoly" Robert Stewart's Standard Oil of Indiana enjoyed in

Wyoming—this after Fall had cleared the way for Stewart to take over the Salt Creek fields. At the time, Fall knew full well from his discussions with Zevely and Sinclair that Stewart was Sinclair's silent partner in the Teapot deal, had half ownership of the Sinclair Crude Oil Purchasing Company, and with Sinclair shared control of the Sinclair Pipeline Company, which would build the pipeline that was to carry Teapot's oil to the Midwest. Stewart would benefit as much from the navy oil as Sinclair.

Fall also claimed that he had talked to other oil operators about leasing Teapot, but there had been no competitive bidding. Operating under Fall's mandate for absolute secrecy, Interior had never said a word publicly about the possibility of leasing Teapot until after the contracts had been awarded. Of course, nothing was mentioned about a loan from Doheny or Harry Sinclair's supposed purchase of one-third of Three Rivers. Moreover, Fall noted in the report that he had repeatedly apprised the president and the cabinet of his activities leading up to the lease transactions. The White House had supported and encouraged his efforts to privatize the reserves all along. By inference, any criticism of Fall's handling of the leases was a criticism of the entire administration.

Fall accompanied the report with the paperwork La Follette had demanded pertaining to the leases—thousands of documents, surveys, maps, memos, letters, and charts—drawn at great effort, Fall explained, from the General Land Office, the Geological Survey, the Bureau of Mines, and the personal files of the secretary of the interior. La Follette wanted facts. Let him choke on them.

Did the president even read the full report? Not that it would have mattered. Realistically, the chances that Harding would contest a report favoring a major campaign contributor were nil. He promptly sent along Fall's opus to the Senate, noting in a cover letter that the new naval reserve plan "was submitted to me prior to the adoption thereof, and the policy decided upon and the subsequent acts have at all times had my entire approval." It was in writing this brief endorsement of his interior secretary's actions that Warren Harding inexorably linked his name to the Teapot scandal.

As soon as Thomas James Walsh saw Albert Fall's papers being wheeled into room 210 of the Senate Office Building, where the Committee on Public Lands and Surveys held its hearings, he knew he didn't want any part of the Teapot investigation. The whole thing was a dog's breakfast, an unsavory mess. There were boxes and boxes of documents from the interior secretary, "a wagonload," Walsh later said. It would take him months just to wade through all this material.

An amendment to La Follette's resolution called for the Senate's Public Lands and Surveys Committee to investigate the naval leases. Walsh, the senior Democratic senator from Montana, was a member of the committee, but not its chair. Still, La Follette and Senator Kendrick from Wyoming, Walsh's neighboring state, pressed him "to take the leadership in investigating" the leases and serve as "the laboring oar of the inquiry." Unless the Montana senator assumed the role of the committee's prosecutor, La Follette and Kendrick feared that the Republican-dominated committee would either soft-pedal the investigation or simply let it atrophy.

Walsh was an anomaly in Washington, the antithesis of the hail-fellow-well-met political character. He had little time for small talk and suffered fools not at all. Those who didn't know him well, or didn't "get" his wry wit, claimed he was the only Irishman in town who lacked a sense of humor. As a "dry" who favored Prohibition, Walsh also contradicted the stereotype of the Irish infatuation with the bottle. Not that he was a prig. In private, Walsh took a drink himself now and again, and in later life he developed a palate for good French wine.

La Follette and Kendrick both had great respect for Walsh. No one in Congress was more qualified, they believed, to head the investigation. Of medium height, with an impressive handlebar mustache and steel blue eyes that one reporter noted "seem to bore through a witness," the intense, politically progressive Walsh was viewed as the ablest constitutional lawyer in the Senate, a man who lived by the strictest personal probity. Born June 12, 1859, he was the third of eight children. His parents, Felix and Brigid Walsh, were Irish immigrants who had settled in Two Rivers, Wisconsin. Walsh had learned to read by the age of five, encouraged by his mother, who was entirely illiterate. A brilliant student, he attended public schools, and studied law at the Law Department of the University of Wisconsin at Madison, paying his tuition by teaching in one-room rural schools. After graduating and being admitted to the bar in 1884 at the age of twenty-five, he began practicing law in what was then Dakota Territory with his younger brother John, also a lawyer. At one point, the two young Democrats thought about establishing an office and possibly entering politics in Fargo, only to discover that the region was predominantly Republican. Democrats need not apply. One afternoon while the brothers were having lunch outside of town, both gazed down at the Red River. "Tom, isn't that river flowing north?" John asked. Somewhat surprised at the revelation, Tom agreed. "Tom," John continued, "let's go on. I don't feel right about a place where rivers run north and Irishmen vote the Republican ticket."

With its big Irish population, its prosperity, and then its strong Democratic leanings—a Democrat, Joseph K. Toole, had recently been elected the first governor of the new state—Helena, Montana, the copper mining capital of the West, was more to their liking. Both moved there in 1890. Walsh had married a Chicago woman, Elinor McClements, a few months earlier. With his new wife, a baby on the way, and $350 in savings, Walsh bought a modest home on the west side of town and established his own law office. With assistance from Elinor, a suffragist who became involved in Montana politics and ran Walsh's office when he was traveling, Walsh emerged as one of the state's leading attorneys, often representing miners in suits against the powerful Anaconda Mining Company. "He had a marvelous energy and an unremitting mental activity," one admirer noted at the time. He also became a power in Montana's Democratic Party, winning election to the Senate in 1912 despite strong opposition from copper interests.

La Follette and Kendrick were certain Walsh had the tenacity, drive, and intellect to get to the bottom of this Teapot business, but Walsh declined. He was already overextended with more committee assignments than anyone else in the Senate. He had always been extraordinarily industrious. His wife, Elinor, had died of cancer three years earlier. After recovering from a nervous breakdown, he had thrown himself into his work, often putting in sixteen-hour days. He simply didn't have time to take on this business of the naval oil reserves, even though it was a topic he knew well.

Besides, Walsh hadn't been entirely sympathetic to La Follette's resolution, even though he had voted to adopt it. Both Fall, who had entered the Senate a year ahead of Walsh, and Ed Doheny, a fellow Irish Catholic who (like Walsh) came from Wisconsin, were acquaintances. Both, especially Doheny, had been especially kind to Walsh after Elinor's death.

He was also suspicious of Pinchot's crowd. Although not as vehement in his dislike of the conservationists as Fall, Walsh as a westerner shared the interior secretary's distrust of the Pinchotites, especially the "true believers" who were seemingly indifferent and oblivious to the concerns of ranchers, miners, and oilmen whose livelihoods depended on their use of public lands. Walsh suspected that the Teapot matter had as much to do with furthering the conservationists' agenda as it did with uncovering a deal that La Follette characterized as being "befouled with corruption." La Follette and Kendrick would have to find someone else to champion their cause.

At least that had been his view until he learned something that caused him to alter his thinking entirely.

21

THE BEST-LAID PLANS

Harding's endorsement of the Teapot deal had taken some of the heat off the Department of the Interior—for the time being, at least. Emboldened, Fall resumed pushing for the rest of his agenda—opening up Alaska, Indian land, the forests, and coal reserves to commercial development.

At about the same time Fall took office, substantial oil deposits were discovered in the Four Corners area, where the boundaries of New Mexico, Arizona, Colorado, and Utah converge. Soon Farmington, New Mexico, the only town of any size in the region, was overrun with oil company representatives looking to acquire drilling rights. Four Corners, however, was situated on the Navajo Reservation, which meant that outsiders who wanted to drill there had to first get approval from the tribal council, share in royalties, and cut through reams of red tape. In the oil industry, time and patience were in short supply in 1922, when oil prices were at record highs.

In June, Fall interceded on behalf of the oil companies, designating millions of acres of the Navajo Reservation as public lands, which meant that the petroleum interests suddenly had carte blanche to drill there. It also meant that royalties from any drilling in areas designated by the interior secretary would accrue to the states where the drilling took place—mainly New Mexico and Arizona—as well as to the federal government. This was good for cash-strapped western states, good for Uncle Sam, bad for the Navajo. The Navajo, in fact, wouldn't receive a penny for oil drawn from land that had been set aside for them by presidential order.

Even though the Indian policy reform movement was gaining momentum at the time, Fall's shenanigans with Navajo land probably wouldn't have drawn much attention had he not appointed a greedy reservation agent who overthrew the tribal council and established himself as the resident dictator. In this exalted role, he sold off as much land as possible, including one especially promising drilling site, Rattlesnake Dome. This went for $1,000 to a friend, who promptly resold it to one of the oil companies for $3 million. Fall apparently didn't benefit from the transaction and likely didn't know about it until after the Indian agent's entrepreneurial exploits were uncovered. Moreover, his views about matters such as putting Native Americans under the jurisdiction of state and local courts and forcing them to assimilate into the white world were widely shared by many government officials at the time. Even so, Indian rights champions such as John Collier and Eleanor Roosevelt later characterized Fall as epitomizing all that was unjust and exploitative in the government's dealings with its native peoples.

THE CRITICISM THE interior secretary encountered over Teapot didn't slow him down an iota in regard to Alaska. With its seemingly boundless tracks of forest, its coal, oil, phosphate, and potash, Alaska Territory was the crown jewel in Fall's master plan to privatize the nation's resources. In preparing his Alaskan initiative, Fall did his homework, sifting through all kinds of reports, studies, and maps detailing Alaska's natural treasures. With his enthusiasm and newly acquired expertise on the topic, Fall had no trouble selling Harding on his vision for developing vast tracts of Alaskan wilderness. In fact, the Hardings had been looking forward to taking an extended trip to Alaska Territory for several years. In the summers of 1921 and 1922, they'd had to cancel at the last minute because of unexpected crises—in the summer of 1922, a national railroad and mining strike. "I'll believe in that Alaskan trip when I've taken it," said a disappointed Florence Harding after the second postponement. The president had been equally dejected. As Florence

Harding's biographer noted, Harding revealed to a friend that Florence's health might prevent them from ever taking the much anticipated journey and spoke lyrically about his wish to "plunge boldly out into the open ocean and approach the Arctic Circle . . . up into that far northland greeted by a midnight sun."

Just as he had with the naval reserves, Harding gave Fall his blessing on Alaska, telling the interior secretary "to go ahead and carry out the program which [we] both are convinced will mean a greater Alaska." Working with Navy Secretary Denby and Scott Bone, a Harding crony whom the president had named governor of Alaska Territory, Fall in May 1922 transferred the Matanuska coal fields, which had been part of a naval coal reserve in Alaska, to the Interior Department with an eye to leasing them to private interests. As he had with the oil reserves, the by now thoroughly housebroken Denby signed the transfer documents, at which point Fall shut down operations at Matanuska altogether, presumably until he could find a suitable outside company to lease the mines.

Concurrently, Fall sent a team of government geologists to Alaska to study its oil potential. He subsequently sent along their findings to his future boss, Ed Doheny, before making them public, so that the Californian could have first crack at the Alaskan fields. In early August, after receiving letters of introduction from Fall to Governor Scott Bone and Alaska Engineering Commission head Frederick Mears, Doheny sailed north aboard the *Casiana* to scope out the western Alaska oil fields for himself. On the way, he entered into a verbal deal with two Seattle-based oil "boomers" to develop a syndicate of oil claims they had located earlier at Kachemak Bay in Alaska. Fall had hoped to join Doheny on the trip, but with the nation's railroad industry at a standstill because of the strike, he had to remain in Washington. Neither the interior secretary nor the Hardings would be visiting Alaska that summer.

Fall's plans for Alaska called for the president to assume responsibility for administration of all the territory's disparate resources, which Harding would subsequently turn over to Fall. Drawing on a revolving fund of $5 million, Interior would build paper factories, sawmills, factories, and even railroads and operate them until they could be sold or leased to private investors. Fall's stated goal: to create an economic boom in Alaska so great that the nation as a whole would share in the economic windfall.

This hugely ambitious undertaking might have been successful had it not been for the Teapot revelations. As a result of Fall's shady dealings with Sinclair and Doheny, the conservationists were quick to charge that the interior secretary was in bed with the paper manufacturers who coveted the dense pulpwood forests of Alaska. There is no evidence this was the case. Nonetheless, the Pinchotites again went on the attack. John Ballaine, builder of the original Alaskan railroad and the leading champion of Alaskan conservation, charged that the negotiations and terms Denby and Fall used to co-opt the navy coal reserves "ran along lines exactly parallel with the negotiations and terms of the lease of the Teapot Dome oil reserve." Meanwhile, American Forests, the nation's oldest nonprofit citizens' conservation organization, was waging an all-out public relations vendetta against the interior secretary.

Sensing he finally had the strength he needed to halt the Fall juggernaut, Secretary of Agriculture Wallace played his trump card. In a July cabinet meeting, Wallace announced that if the president gave Fall the U.S. Forest Service, he would "expose the case against Fall, his colleagues, forests, oil, and everything to the nation." We have no record of Harding's response, but soon after Wallace made his threat, Harding backed down on surrendering the Forest Service to Fall and began to distance himself from the interior secretary's Alaskan plan. It was one thing to have La Follette sounding off about Fall's misdeeds. La Follette was always moaning about some perceived injustice. But Harding could not afford to have one of his own cabinet officers—the popular and well-respected Wallace—telling the world that Albert Fall was a crook.

Tired of being beaten up by the conservationists and embittered by Harding's vacillation, Fall by late summer walked away from a fight he couldn't win, not without the president's full support. Fall hadn't the time, temperament, or patience to fight on alone. "The reorganization plan [for Alaska] seems to have gotten nowhere," he wrote his former law partner, W. A. Hawkins. "Whether it will ever be carried out or not I don't know, and insofar as I am personally concerned don't care."

22

NAPOLEON AND THE DUTCHMAN

Frederick Bonfils and H. H. Tammen, owners of the *Denver Post*, listened intently as J. Leo Stack told his story. Denver being a small town and the *Post* its eyes and ears, Bonfils and Tammen already knew why Stack had come to see them. Still, they registered appropriate expressions of shock, disbelief, and sympathy as Stack's tale unfolded.

A lobbyist for oil interests, young Stack was abrim with righteous indignation. He had come to Bonfils and Tammen after being, he believed, shortchanged in an oil deal involving the Teapot fields. Now he wanted his due. He needed allies who had what it took to stand up to some powerful, unscrupulous people. Of course, he would give his prospective partners a piece of what was owed him, once the sum was collected.

Stack had come to the right place, certainly the right people. Let's take a moment for introductions here. The tall, dark-haired, swarthy, mustached man at the table was Frederick Bonfils. He was sixty-two, handsome in a stern, straight-backed military way, rigorously fit, an outdoorsman, and a gambler. Of Corsican descent, Bonfils claimed to be a direct descendant of Napoleon Bonaparte. He was a native of Troy, Missouri, the son of a probate judge, Eugene Napoleon Bonfils. The judge had military aspirations for his son, which were realized when Frederick was accepted into the class of 1878 at West Point. The young, athletic Bonfils cut a dashing figure in uniform but wasn't cut out to be an army officer, his family ties to Napoleon notwithstanding. Two years into his stay at West Point, Bonfils was either kicked out or left to marry a young woman from nearby Peekskill.

Thereafter, Bonfils held a number of jobs, none for very long. He was fired abruptly for some long-forgotten impropriety while working as a salesman at the Knox Hat Store in New York. He later worked in the Chemical National Bank in New York, where he learned the rudiments of high finance. It wasn't until the early 1880s, however, that he discovered his true avocation. Bonfils was a natural-born con man, swindler, and extortionist. World-class. Using aliases including M. Dauphin and Silas Carr, he was involved in various real estate swindles. During and after the Oklahoma land rush, he operated a crooked lottery and a newspaper blackmail scheme in Kansas City before coming to Denver.

Which brings us to Bonfils's partner, H. H. Tammen. Of Dutch descent, Tammen was born in Baltimore in 1856. He worked in beer gardens as a kid, went on to become the top bartender at Chicago's Palmer House before he was twenty-one, and soon moved to Denver, where he gained a reputation as the best bartender in the West. "Tammen took to the West and the West to Tammen," his biographer wrote. Short, blond, and built like a beer keg on sticks, Tammen quickly accumulated a little capital the old-fashioned way—filching from the till—and decided to go into business for himself, drawing on his inherent talents as a huckster, promoter, and showman, a high plains P. T. Barnum. His first enterprise, a mail-order western curio business, proved a smashing success. To unsuspecting easterners and tourists seeking genuine relics of the frontier, he sold "authenticated" headdresses that had once belonged to great chiefs such as War Cloud. For $5, customers could acquire genuine scalps of foes slain by Geronimo (Tammen also managed to sell Geronimo's authenticated personal scalp on numerous occasions at a significantly higher price), Sioux arrows, arrowheads, and beaded moccasins.

Of course, his entire inventory was bogus, manufactured by workers in Denver, many of them high school kids and elderly women seeking a little pin money. Tammen also holds the dubious distinction of being one of the first dealers in the country to sell Navajo blankets that were manufactured in eastern textile mills. He and Bonfils complemented each other perfectly, Tammen the joker to Bonfils's king of spades.

Together, in 1895—with some of the estimated $800,000 Bonfils had accumulated from his various scams—these two acquired the *Denver Post,* then an afternoon rag that had a dwindling circulation and a dubious future. They resuscitated it as a razzle-dazzle mix of populist politics, sensational features, and yellow journalism. The paper, the new owners announced, would serve as a champion of the people. True to their word, Bonfils and the irreverent Tammen took on the big money and political interests in the Rocky Mountain region, especially if the aforementioned didn't advertise in the paper. A businessman who spent his advertising dollars at the rival *Rocky Mountain Daily News* instead of the *Post* soon discovered that the *Post*'s society column writer would refuse to mention the important luncheon his socially ambitious wife was hosting at the Denver Country Club. Often when a business failed to advertise, Bonfils and Tammen sent out their top reporters to dig for dirt—the use of child labor, say, in a department store's stockroom. As investigators would later learn, Bonfils retained a number of operatives specifically to seek out information that might be used for blackmail. "Bonfils was a frequent employer of secret agents [through which] he collected a large mass of information which he used for blackmailing purposes whenever opportunity offered," a Secret Service investigator later reported. "He did not employ regular detective agencies, using instead persons of the 'underworld' of Denver, Kansas City, and other places." These strong-arm tactics earned Bonfils and Tammen the enmity of the Denver establishment and a soaring readership. By 1922, the paper, Bonfils bragged, had the largest per capita circulation of any major newspaper between New York and California.

LEO STACK NEEDED "Bon" and "Tam," as the *Post*'s owners were known locally, to take on none other than Harry Sinclair. Prior to Teapot being leased to Sinclair interests, Stack had been one of numerous independent oil operators who had staked out preliminary claims on parts of the Teapot field. In March 1922, a month before he took over the entire Teapot field, Harry Sinclair had bought up most of these claims, including those owned by the Pioneer Oil Company. At the time, Stack had a contract with Pioneer calling for him to participate in any profits realized from Teapot. Sinclair paid Pioneer $1 million to acquire its holdings. When Stack finally found out about the deal after being given the runaround, he went to Pioneer for his cut. Pioneer offered him a certified check for $50,000. "Do you have any more funny stories to tell?" Stack responded, reminding the Pioneer representatives that they had no right to sell off his share, which in Stack's mind was worth far more than $50,000. Even though he had only $187 to his name at the time, Stack told the Pioneer people what they could do with their check. He then headed over to 16th and Curtis streets, headquarters of the *Post*.

When Stack got through with his story, Tammen and Bonfils looked at each other with likely the same thought: There was indeed a God in heaven. Hallelujah and amen! What Leo Stack didn't know was that Tammen and Bonfils were already on to the Teapot Dome story. The *Post* was the first newspaper in the country to get wind that something wasn't entirely kosher in the oil fields of Wyoming. A month or so earlier, one of Albert Fall's secretaries had been hospitalized after working day and night to further her boss's oversize ambitious. Fall hadn't bothered to send flowers or even a get-well card. Her nose out of joint, the secretary complained about her boss's negligence to a woman friend in Denver, noting as an aside that the secretary of the interior was giving away oil leases to his friends like "kisses at a wedding." As it happened, the woman friend in Denver was married to a subeditor of the *Post*. "He saw in the letter a lead to a startlingly important story— the country was being stolen," recalled Gene Fowler, a *Post* reporter in the 1920s. "He left the breakfast table on the run and soon was closeted . . . with Bonfils."

After reading the letter, Bonfils told the editor he wanted to sit on the story for a while and in the meantime send one of the *Post*'s star reporters, D. F. Stackelbeck, to New Mexico. It didn't take the *Post*'s man long to discover that Albert Fall's finances had taken a significant turn for the better. From the railroad agent at Three Rivers, Stackelbeck learned about the racehorse, cattle, and other livestock Sinclair had sent Fall from his Rancocas farm. From Fall's old enemy, Carl Magee, editor of the *Albuquerque Morning Journal,* he also heard that the formerly broke interior secretary was suddenly flush and spending large sums adding to and improving Three Rivers. Magee and his lone reporter,

Clinton P. Anderson, had launched their own investigation of the Teapot leases.

Stackelbeck left New Mexico hurriedly after some of Fall's friends discovered his identity and threatened to break one or more of his limbs. Still, he came away with enough information to convince Bonfils and Tammen that a number of important people would pay significant money to ensure that the *Post didn't* publish what it had learned about the leases. Bonfils had scarcely locked up Stackelbeck's report in his big office safe when in marched young Leo Stack. The oil operator's claim against Sinclair was just the leverage Bonfils and Tammen needed.

AFTER THEIR MEETING with Stack, Tammen and Bonfils summoned their lawyer, H. H. Schwartz, to look over the contract Stack had with Pioneer. Satisfied that Stack had a legitimate claim, the *Post*'s owners then drew up an agreement with Stack offering to help him collect— not from Pioneer, but from Sinclair, who had acquired Pioneer's interests and therefore, Bonfils and Tammen reasoned, was liable for its debt. They wanted $1 million, the same amount Sinclair had paid Pioneer. Of that, Stack was to get slightly less than half, while Bonfils and Tammen collected the rest minus 7.5 percent to the lawyer Schwartz. Stack was also to receive the first $50,000 up front before Bonfils and the others got a thing.

The agreement was signed on April 14. The next day, the *Post*, self-proclaimed champion of the little people, ran the first of a series of front-page editorials under the banner "So the People May Know." The subject, of course, was the Teapot deal. "If carried out, it will consummate one of the baldest public-land grabs in history," asserted the editorial written by Bonfils, with an assist from Schwartz. Bonfils and Tammen, who knew Harding and corresponded with him, sent the president, every member of the cabinet including Fall, the entire U.S. Senate, and select members of the House of Representatives copies of the editorial.

THE INTERIOR DEPARTMENT had a man in Denver, M. D. McEniry. As soon as the *Post* launched its Teapot campaign, McEniry began reporting regularly to Fall as to what was going on behind the scenes. He told

Fall about Stack's unhappiness with the Pioneer offer and about meeting with Stack shortly after the agreement with Bonfils and Tammen had been signed. "Alone I could not do very much, so I have assigned one-half my interest in this contract to Fred Bonfils," Stack told McEniry. McEniry added that "Bon" could shake down the oil crowd much more effectively than Stack, or so Stack believed.

McEniry had also learned that "Bonfils and Tammen had been trying for several years to edge on the oil game in Wyoming with a minimum expenditure of their already huge fortunes—but without success thus far." When Sinclair acquired the Pioneer rights, Bonfils and Tammen learned that John Shaffer, publisher of the *Rocky Mountain News*, the rival newspaper, was part of the Pioneer syndicate and had received a substantial payout. The mere mention of the *News* or its publisher would trigger what Tammen described as Bonfils's "Peer Gynt temper."

"Bonfils has the idea that John C. Shaffer, the publisher of the *Rocky Mountain News* . . . got in on the Teapot Deal with Sinclair and the Standard Oil crowd for practically nothing. . . . I think this is the main reason . . . why Bonfils is trying to make all this publicity against the Sinclair interests," McEniry wrote Fall. "You know everything with which his competitor is connected is poison to Bonfils."

It had been the *Post*'s editorials, McEniry added, that had stirred up the oil independents in Wyoming, who had subsequently complained to Senator Kendrick. The *Post* boasted the largest circulation, forty thousand, of any paper in Wyoming. It "is largely, if not wholly anti-administration, and sees an opportunity to raise what they call a lot of political stink, despite the fact that Mr. Harry Tammen exchanges personal letters with the president," Stack concluded.

Believing they had enough leverage on Sinclair to make him amenable to their demands, the *Post*'s owners asked Sinclair and his lawyer, J. W. Zevely, who had known Bonfils in Missouri, to come to Denver and resolve the situation. Sinclair quickly made it clear that he had no intention of traveling to Denver. If Bonfils, Tammen, and Stack wanted to discuss their claim, they'd have to come to New York. If they "desired to talk with me about the matter, it was for them to set an appointment and that when convenient, I might grant same," Sinclair said.

At a July 5 meeting in Sinclair's New York office, with Zevely present, Sinclair took a hard line, insisting he'd bought out the Pioneer claim knowing nothing of Stack's deal with Pioneer. If anyone owed Stack money, it was Pioneer, not Sinclair. He had no intention of paying Bonfils and the others anything at all. As far as Sinclair was concerned, there was nothing more to discuss.

Sinclair not only refused to negotiate with the Denver contingent, but had humiliated Bonfils and the others by having them come all the way to New York to give them his answer. Though Zevely met with an enraged Bonfils the next day and said he'd try to get Sinclair to reconsider, Bonfils and the others weren't assuaged. "I was invited when just recovering from my illness to go to New York City to meet Mr. Sinclair," Tammen said. "I did not seek the invitation but was asked to go on this contract in which we are associated with Leo Stack. After traveling two thousand miles to New York City, I was told by Mr. Sinclair that he had nothing to settle and that he was not interested in the contract one way or the other. Is that any way to treat a man?"

Before departing, Bonfils reminded his old acquaintance that the *Post* could prove a good ally to Sinclair in the West, where the oilman planned to do business for many years to come. It could also prove a formidable enemy, Bonfils warned, unless Zevely went to Denver immediately "to arrange to secure the friendly cooperation of the *Post*."

23

SUMMER OF THEIR DISCONTENT

The president was already having a terrible summer. Everything seemed to be going awry, beginning with his love life. On the first Sunday in June, he had Jim Sloan smuggle Nan Britton into the White House for a pre-church tryst. Nan brought along a photograph of her daughter by Harding that had appeared recently in one of the Chicago papers. Little Elizabeth had locked herself in the bathroom of Nan's apartment on Lafayette Parkway. Nan had to call the fire department to rescue her. Harding took one look at the photograph, which coincidentally appeared next to a headline that read INTIMATE CHAT AT THE WHITE HOUSE, and momentarily forgot all about *amore*. "I can remember we were sitting at his desk, and I can just see his face twist and the impatient gestures of his hands as he lay the picture down upon his desk," Nan later recalled.

Nan was full of surprises. Later, as she and Harding were spooning together on the big leather couch in the Oval Office, Nan confided to the president that she had begun to keep a diary, which included accounts of her visits to see Harding in the White House. "Oh, dearie, you *mustn't* keep such a book around," Harding said when he'd composed himself. "You must destroy it as soon as you return to Chicago. Promise, Nan, that you'll destroy it immediately."

Shortly after Nan's visit, Harding learned from Daugherty that William Eastbrook Chancellor—the former professor who was obsessed with proving that Harding had African American blood—was back in the country. After Harding had been elected, Chancellor had been threatened by several of Billy Burns's agents and had fled to Canada. Now he'd returned and was planning to come out with *The Illustrated Life of President Warren G. Harding,* a book that promised to reveal everything from Harding's affair with Carrie Phillips to what the author claimed was the president's Negro ancestry.

Chancellor, Daugherty learned, was having the book printed in Ohio. On Daugherty's orders, Billy Burns dispatched a number of his agents to stop publication, but they arrived too late. Several hundred copies were already in circulation. For the next few weeks, several dozen of Burns's agents, accompanied by Jess Smith and Gaston Means, traveled through Ohio, seizing every copy of the book they could find, along with Chancellor's printing plates.

Fearing the attorney general intended to silence him by committing him to a mental institution, Chancellor fled to a former college roommate's house in Maine. Meanwhile, Jess Smith, Means, and their merry band of bibliophiles returned to Washington in an armored car carrying the entire print run of the book. Since it was a distinct legal "no-no" to suppress books during peacetime, Smith and Means decided it would be imprudent to destroy their haul on federal grounds. Instead, they chose the rear grounds of Friendship, the McLeans' estate in Virginia's hunt country that included a private golf course where Harding often played, a duck pond, and a ménage of animals that included goats, donkeys, waddling geese, and a band of mischievous monkeys. With Evalyn and Ned looking on from the house at the surreal scene and a montage of assorted critters watching from the shadows, Smith and Means burned the evidence. "I myself had helped to light a bonfire that burnt up the entire edition of the book—copyright and all," Means later boasted.

This would not be the last time documents relating to the president's personal and political doings would be burned at Friendship.

At least during their visits to Friendship the president and Florence could escape the worst of the unrelenting summer heat. But back at the

White House, Harding had to contend with the railroad and mining strike, which threatened to paralyze the nation. Then there was the uproar about the naval leases. No sooner had Harding managed to still some of the criticism with his cover letter to the Senate in support of the Fall report than his interior secretary marched into the White House demanding to send the U.S. Marines to Teapot Dome.

Marines to Teapot? Was this some early manifestation of senile dementia, Fall reliving, as his biographer suggested, the days when he used to dispatch his quick-triggered hired hands to deal with some adversary in a range war? In this instance, he wanted the marines to deal with an old friend and political backer of Harding's, Colonel James G. Darden, who held claims on part of the Teapot field that predated the Sinclair lease. Darden had gone into the deal with the attorney general and Jess Smith, and in June he started drilling on land Fall had already leased to Sinclair. When Fall, who despised Darden, discovered what the colonel was up to, he threw a tantrum that was off the Richter scale.

Fall's demand to send marines immediately to Teapot to eject Colonel Darden's "squatters" put Harding in one of those quandaries from which he was continually trying to extricate himself. Deploy the marines and alienate a friend and backer, not to mention the attorney general. Reject Fall's demands and . . . God only knows what the interior secretary's reaction would be. The president managed to buy a little time by telling Fall he'd talk the matter over with Darden.

The discussion went as follows: Darden arrived at the White House, where he was greeted by Harding's secretary, George B. Christian. "George, the president wants to see me," Darden said.

"He's busy or playing golf or something," Christian said.

Darden: "I will come back."

Christian: "No, wait."

Finally, Harding appeared. "Jim, how about the property you think you own in Teapot Dome?" he inquired.

Darden: "I don't know; I couldn't tell you. We feel naturally we own it, because we spent some money to get it."

Harding: "Fall doesn't think you own it. He is TNT. What are you going to do?"

Darden: "I guess we have to go to court, Mr. President."

Fall, meanwhile, kept after Harding to take action. He wouldn't let the matter rest. On Saturday morning, July 29, he took up the subject with the president again. Again Harding said he didn't want to send in the marines because an officer of the company (Darden) that was trespassing was a close personal friend and had contributed to his campaign fund. "Darden is a low-down son of a bitch," Fall countered, reminding the president that he had earlier expressed similar sentiments about the colonel despite Darden's having sent him a campaign check. So he had, Harding conceded, finally consenting to Fall's request.

Before Harding could change his mind, Fall sent a note to Ted Roosevelt Jr. This being a Saturday, Denby was out of the office. Roosevelt was in charge. Fall asked the acting secretary of the navy to come to his office at Interior at once. There, Fall informed Roosevelt of the situation and told him he needed Darden's crew put off the Teapot property by a marine detachment. When Roosevelt appeared skeptical, Fall assured him there was a legal precedent for such an undertaking. This was Fall improvising. There was no such precedent, but Roosevelt was nonetheless reassured. Surely Albert Fall wouldn't lie about something so important.

Roosevelt's next move was to send for the commanding officer of the marines, Major General John A. Lejeune (yes, it's the same general after whom Camp Lejeune was named), and ask him to select an experienced officer to lead a detachment of marines on a delicate mission into the wilds of north-central Wyoming. Lejeune selected a World War I veteran, Captain George K. Shuler. Roosevelt approved, but of course Fall had to have final say in the matter. In a meeting at Interior, he asked Captain Shuler what he'd do if a federal judge served him with an injunction telling him he couldn't carry out this mission. When Shuler responded that (a) he'd never laid eyes on an injunction, and (b) he'd ignore it entirely, Fall knew he'd found his man.

When Shuler went back to report to Lejeune, the general asked him how many men he'd need. Shuler responded, "If we are going out there and fight the whole state of Wyoming, we would probably have to take quite a few." Lejeune responded that Shuler simply had to "eighty-six" a few roughnecks, not, fortunately, take on the entire state. Four marines would probably do the trick, Lejeune calculated.

The following morning, Captain Shuler, four young marines, and Arthur Ambrose (the geologist who almost ruined his career by claiming there wasn't drainage at Teapot) left Washington for Wyoming. From the Halls of Montezuma to the wells of Teapot Dome. In Casper, they were met by Interior Department officials and a couple of newsmen, including a reporter for the *Denver Post*. The party then proceeded forty-five miles north to the portion of the Teapot field in dispute, section 30. "This is your battlefield," one of the Interior officers told Shuler, pointing out an oil rig surrounded by a high barbed-wire fence.

At the gate, Captain Shuler faced off with the rig foreman. Shuler had orders to shut down drilling, he explained. The foreman countered that he had orders to keep out all trespassers. The marines had carbines, pistols, and enough ammunition to take on a small army of oilmen. There was much macho posturing on both sides of the fence. Shuler threatened force. The foreman conceded that the marines looked as though they meant business. Captain Shuler assured him that such was the case. The reporters were frantically taking notes. The foreman had to send for his supervisor. Of course, the supervisor was "rather peeved" (Shuler's description), but he gave in, asking the marines to lunch after Shuler and his men slapped NO TRESPASSING signs all over the rig and barbed-wire fence. Mission accomplished. Back in Washington, Roosevelt told Captain Shuler, "You did excellently and confirmed our pride in the ability of the Marine Corps to measure up to whatever it was put up against."

24

SHAKEDOWN

The *Post* couldn't have asked for a better story if Bonfils and Tammen had dreamed it up themselves. On August 7, McEniry wrote Fall that the *Post* had run a two-column editorial attacking both the motives for leasing Teapot Dome and the Harding administration for sending in the marines to protect Sinclair's interests. McEniry had just run into Leo Stack, who told him that "the action of the government in bringing in the Marines to the Teapot Dome to eject the Mutual Oil Company [Darden's outfit] has given the *Denver Post* a hammer with which to pound the government and [Harry Sinclair's] Mammoth Oil Company."

Stack added that the *Post* proposed to use the hammer during the next few weeks inasmuch as Sinclair was dragging his heels in settling Stack's claim. Meanwhile, Tammen wrote the president a letter protesting the use of the marines and describing the Teapot affair as a "good deal of a mess."

Since returning from their meeting with Sinclair in New York, Bon and Tam, Tammen said, had "been looking everywhere for ammunition" to use in the blackmailing scheme. If Harry Sinclair thought he could give them the bum's rush, he had made a costly mistake. On August 18,

McEniry wrote Fall alerting him that Bonfils had sent two men to New Mexico, "endeavoring to find something in your long residence in that State to your disparagement." McEniry had learned this from Stack, who also told him that Bonfils had his investigators snooping around in El Paso, where the Falls had their winter home. They had discovered that Sinclair, Stewart, and Blackmer had visited Fall at Three Rivers; that Fall not only had cleared the obstacles preventing Standard Oil of Indiana from buying out Blackmer's Midwest Refining Company, but had granted Sinclair and Stewart a pipeline franchise connecting the Teapot and Salt Creek fields to a Standard refinery in Missouri; and—most damaging—they claimed to have a witness who'd seen Fall collecting a payoff from Sinclair in the latter's railcar during the Three Rivers visit. Stack told McEniry the sum would more than fill a suitcase with $1,000 bills. "Mr. Fall will know what that means and he will know that the *Post* has something, too," he warned.

Bonfils intended to reveal the whole story unless he got what he wanted.

After the New York trip, he had expanded his target to encompass all Sinclair's allies in the oil business as well as Fall and the Harding administration. Bonfils and Tammen announced that their lawyer intended to appear before the La Follette committee to question the whole Teapot gang: Harry Sinclair, Robert Stewart, Harry Blackmer, and James O'Neil, "relative to the understanding these men may have had among themselves and with the Interior Secretary prior to Sinclair's contracting with Fall for the Teapot Oil."

They planned to start by taking Fall's deposition and revealing the whole "secret inside history" of Teapot and Salt Creek. Their fellow Denverite, Harry Blackmer, was to be a prime target of the questioning. "We expect to lay out every intestine of Blackmer's on the table in the committee room and look them over very carefully," Bonfils warned.

Of course, if Sinclair agreed to a settlement, Bonfils offered, the *Post* would lay off and try to kill "any proposed legislation by Congress of any matters pertaining to Teapot Dome, and while the La Follette investigation is likely to continue, the Teapot Dome affair would not figure in any way."

The following day, the *Post* ripped into Fall and Sinclair and the naval leases again in a "So the People May Know" editorial written by Bonfils. Drawing on information from his investigators, Bonfils claimed that negotiations between Fall and Sinclair began in the latter's private car the previous January on a siding near Fall's ranch at Three Rivers, New Mexico, and continued throughout the subsequent trip to Kentucky and Washington. This was incorrect in part. Fall hadn't traveled on with Sinclair but had stayed behind to meet with Stewart and Blackmer.

Meanwhile, the *Post* continued to get mileage out of the marines story. Wyoming governor Robert D. Carey wired Harding complaining about the invasion of his state. Of course, the *Post* promptly echoed Carey's criticism in an editorial that was picked up by the Hearst papers and run nationally. Briefly, Bonfils became so caught up in the role of crusading newspaperman that he momentarily thought of dropping the blackmail scheme altogether. "If we were patriotic, we would blow this thing to hell instead of trying to make a settlement," he announced to Stack.

"If I had as much money as you, I could afford to be patriotic, but that is not my idea. I want a settlement for just claims," Stack responded.

THE PRESIDENT HAD been preoccupied much of the summer of 1922 with the mining and railroad strike. He was drinking heavily. In an Oval Office meeting with the rail workers' union president, B. M. Jewell, he'd been downing shots of whiskey from a bottle on his desk. Brother Jewell claimed Harding had been so drunk, he couldn't talk.

By August, however, Harding had grown concerned about all the negative publicity surrounding the Teapot leases. He'd received numerous letters and cablegrams questioning the administration's handling of the Teapot matter, including those from the governor of Wyoming and Tammen. On August 10, he asked Assistant Navy Secretary Ted Roosevelt for detailed information about dispatching the marines to Wyoming in order to respond to the correspondence he'd received.

For a time, the White House could ignore the *Post*'s attacks on the leases or dismiss them as scurrilous exercises in partisan politics. After all, the *Post* was known as a largely anti-administration paper. But in August, the Hearst newspapers began reprinting the *Post*'s editorials in all of Hearst's twenty-eight newspapers around the country. Bonfils had threatened to create a "political stink." He was suddenly succeeding on a national level. On top of his other worries, Harding didn't need to contend with a scandal.

On August 25, the *Washington Times*, one of Hearst's newspapers, ran a front-page story with the headline FALL CALLED ON CARPET IN OIL LAND DEAL. According to the piece, publication of the incidents leading up to the secret agreement between Fall and Sinclair "was causing grave concern to the Administration." A highly agitated Harding had detained Fall the previous day for an hour after a cabinet meeting, demanding that the interior secretary explain what was causing all the controversy regarding the Wyoming oil leases. We don't know Fall's response—he refused to comment on the story—though it's likely he gave Harding pretty much the same story he'd given to others: Stack had a legitimate claim, but Bonfils and Tammen were "scoundrels" who were exploiting the situation in an effort to get the same amount from Sinclair, $1 million, that the oilman had paid out to Pioneer. In his earlier report, he'd already told the president that the subject of Teapot had come up during Sinclair's visit to Three Rivers. The assertion that he continued the negotiations riding back to Washington in Sinclair's private car was entirely false. For certain, he didn't mention Bonfils's claim that Fall had taken a suitcase filled with thousands of dollars in bonds from their mutual friend "Sinco" in exchange for the Teapot lease.

Fall reassured Harding that he had already written Hearst asking the newspaper owner not to reprint any more of the *Post*'s editorials. In the past, the Hearst papers had consistently backed Fall's tough stance on Mexico, where the newspaper titan had substantial holdings. When Hearst responded on August 28, "I have told our people not to print any more such articles," Fall was grateful beyond measure. The *Post*, he claimed, had spawned "the most malignant, vicious and untruthful criticism" of him. He was most eager to prove himself above reproach. In fact, he was more than willing to document his innocence "to any responsible man you might send to me," he told Hearst. He had nothing to hide.

ULTIMATELY, BONFILS, TAMMEN, and Stack got their money, the entire $1 million. According to the story that was circulated at the time, the payoff came about as the result of a meeting in Kansas City between Sinclair and Zevely and Bonfils and a prominent Republican lawyer and oilman from Denver named Karl C. Schuyler. Schuyler was representing Harry Blackmer's interests in these talks, Blackmer having decided to bring in his own legal talent after Bonfils had threatened to eviscerate him—figuratively, of course. Tammen, Stack, and Schwartz had remained in Denver.

At the outset of the meeting, Sinclair had offered $100,000. "One hundred thousand dollars is a lot of money, and Stack ought to be happy with it," he said.

Schuyler responded that it wasn't nearly enough. "Mr. Sinclair," he said, "if any man came to you today and created a situation for you . . . to secure an oil property as valuable as the Teapot structure, would you think of valuing his services for less than one million dollars?"

After some thought, Sinclair finally responded, "Well, it's big, and perhaps you are not asking too much." By the end of the talks, Sinclair added $900,000 to his offer, which was promptly accepted.

That, at least, was Schuyler's account of what transpired. There's another, more sinister version of what actually happened, however, one that has never become public even after more than eighty years. According to several men who were privy to the negotiations, including Bonfils's son-in-law C. V. Berryman, it was President Harding who pressured Sinclair to make the payoff. Berryman claimed that in late August, when Bonfils was still threatening to depose Fall, Sinclair, and the others in conjunction with the La Follette investigation, Harding asked for Bonfils and Tammen to come to the White House. There, Harding demanded that the *Post* must "let up on that oil business in Wyoming."

At this, Bonfils struck the desk with his fist, saying, "Not unless I get two quarter sections of land on Cat Creek [a stream that runs through the Teapot field] and $1 million in cash." Harding assured him that this would be done and went so far as to invite Bonfils along on his Alaskan trip the following summer.

Berryman was not the most reliable of sources. One of the Secret Service men investigating Teapot suspected he might be a "hophead." Moreover, his tale of Harding's direct involvement didn't reach Teapot's chief investigator, Thomas Walsh, until after Harding's death, at which time no one was eager to "look beneath the shroud," as one newspaperman noted. Still, there are a number of factors that lend credibility to Berryman's account: For starters, Bonfils, whose newspaper had savaged the Harding administration, in fact did go to Alaska as the Hardings' invited guest. On boarding the ship, he presented the Duchess with a sealskin coat as a gift—a little something to keep her warm on those cold Alaskan nights. Additionally, after Sinclair made the payoff, Bonfils became persona grata in Washington. Although Fall would have nothing to do with him, Secretary of the Navy Denby invited Bonfils on a navy warship cruise in tropical waters.

Albert Fall resigned from the cabinet in January 1923. Before he left Washington, however, he ever so quietly gave Sinclair a five-year renewable contract to buy all the so-called royalty oil from the Teapot fields that had originally been given the U.S. Shipping Board. This amounted to close to two million barrels of oil a year that Sinclair bought and then sold at a profit that more than made up for what he paid Bonfils. Remarkably, the contract went largely unnoticed at a time when Teapot was much in the news. It had the full approval of Harding, who wrote Fall on October 30, 1922, two weeks after Fall gave out the contract: "I have no concern about Wyoming oil matters. I am confident you have adopted the correct policy and will carry it through in a way altogether to be approved."

Likely, as Berryman claimed, Harding did summon Bonfils and Tammen to Washington and agreed to the payoff in order to suppress any more damaging information about the leases. Likely, too, Harding—through Daugherty, who did most of the president's dirty work—asked "Sinco" to pay up, assuring him that he'd be taken care of later. The negotiations in fact took place in Kansas City, a neutral site. As for Schuyler's account, perhaps he really believed that in the course of what he described as an hour-and-a-half conversation, he convinced a hard case like Harry Sinclair to up his $100,000 final offer tenfold. More realistically, he was aware that Sinclair had already committed to the million-dollar payoff before he ever got to Kansas City.

Schuyler and Bonfils got back to Denver on September 22, 1922. "Schuyler and Bonfils returned from Kansas City, and no one is talking, not even Stack," McEniry wrote Fall several days later. "Bonfils has told everyone—Tammen, Stack and Schwartz—not to speak with anyone. . . . I feel that those fellows . . . are now working overtime on soft-pedaling everything about Teapot Dome." In fact, the *Post*'s attacks on Sinclair, Fall, and the Teapot deal ceased entirely. Any mention of Harry Sinclair in the paper thereafter was effusively laudatory.

25

THE UNRAVELING

The last time Roxy Stinson had seen Jess Smith, her ex-husband seemed highly agitated. "He was in constant fear of being closed down upon," Roxy later testified. He had asked her "to bolster him up, to cheer him up."

Over lunch at the Deshler Hotel in Columbus, Smith kept glancing apprehensively at a man seated at the nearby table. Smith thought he might be one of Billy Burns's agents. Roxy assured him the man looked like a traveling salesman, not one of Burns's operatives. Similarly, on the train back to Washington Court House, Smith cautioned Roxy to speak quietly. The man sleeping across from them looked suspicious. "Don't talk so loud," Smith told Roxy. "He'll hear you."

Although Smith didn't discuss the details with his ex-wife, the corruption that was rampant in Washington had begun to attract unwelcome scrutiny. Teapot, of course, had cast the administration in an unfavorable light, but more recently, a series of letters from the wife of former Washington State senator Miles Poindexter to a Seattle paper had caused an uproar in Washington. Marion Denby, Martha Weeks—the wives, respectively, of the secretary of the navy and the secretary of war—and other cabinet member wives had been portrayed by the ex-senator's wife (Poindexter had been appointed ambassador to Peru) as throwing wild parties and commandeering government cars, War Department aides, and even navy ships for their personal travel use. The letter was published at a time when Washington, D.C., was rampant with gossip dealing with everything from the doings of the Ohio Gang and Colonel Forbes's crooked deals at the Veterans' Bureau to Harding's philandering. "Many threatening rumbles . . . had come to light and were being hinted at and discussed in the newspaper," said Gaston Means.

Jess, who was as well plugged into the Washington rumor mill as anyone in town, feared a Sodom-like reckoning was at hand. As the weak link in the chain, he also feared that he was going to end up being the fall guy. "I'm not going to be anybody's scapegoat," he told Means.

In Ohio, Jess gave Roxy stocks to sell and opened a blind account for her at the brokerage firm Ungerleider & Co., which was used by members of the Harding administration, or at least Harding, Daugherty, and Smith. The owner, Sam Ungerleider, had owned breweries before Prohibition. He had subsequently gone into the brokerage business and counted Daugherty, an old friend from Columbus, as one of his best clients.

Before heading back to Washington, Jess instructed Roxy to burn all their correspondence as well as any papers regarding his financial dealings she had in her possession. Jess, who despised firearms, also bought a pistol to bring back east with him. Roxy was so alarmed that she expressed her concerns to Evalyn McLean, whom she had met earlier in Washington and liked. Jess was a basket case.

Back in Washington, the usually ebullient Smith had attended a dinner party at which he'd seemed despondent. When a fellow guest asked what was wrong, Smith responded, "It's all up with me. They're going to get me." Two days later on May 29, Jess called the McLeans at Friendship, their place in Leesburg, Virginia, and asked if he could come visit for three or four days. Evalyn had just quit drinking. She'd had a goiter operation and wasn't feeling well. It wasn't a good time. Still, she liked Jess and agreed. She'd have her meals in her room while Jess was visiting.

At about 10:00 p.m., Jess called back. Evalyn answered and inquired how he was. "I'm fine but a little nervous," Jess responded.

"Now, now," Evalyn said, trying to comfort him. "What's wrong with you?"

"Oh, I'm just a little upset," Jess said. Harding had summoned Daugherty to come to the White House and spend the night. "Sinco," who was in Washington on business, was staying over as well. Daugherty had asked his secretary, Warren F. "Barney" Martin, to spend the night in the Wardman Park apartment he shared with Jess.

"Well, get some sleep and you'll feel better," Evalyn said. Jess thanked her and said he'd be out at the farm the following evening at 7:00. When Evalyn, a late sleeper, woke around noon the following day, her twelve-year-old son, Jock, was standing wide-eyed beside the bed. "Jess Smith is dead," he said. "He shot himself, the paper says."

Barney Martin had discovered the body at 6:40 a.m. Jess was lying on the floor next to his bed, a .32-caliber revolver in his right hand. Martin immediately called Billy Burns, who lived on the floor below. Burns took charge. By the time the Washington police arrived, a Sergeant J. D. Marks and two policemen from the Tennallytown sub-precinct station, Burns had somehow misplaced the pistol. The bullet had entered Jess's left temple and exited the right side of the skull. Odd that a right-handed man would shoot himself in the left temple. There was no residue of gunpowder found on either hand, never a postmortem examination of the body.

Roxy thought her ex-husband had been murdered. Evalyn McLean believed so as well. Alice Longworth quipped that Jess had died of "Harding of the arteries." Daugherty said he was certain it was suicide. Jess had been drinking heavily, in poor health, depressed.

Either way, the weak link had been eliminated.

26

DEPARTURE

On June 20, 1923, the president and the First Lady were in high spirits as they embarked on the long-anticipated trip to the Far West and Alaska. Harding looked forward to being the first U.S. leader ever to visit Alaska Territory, while Florence had been talking of almost nothing but the journey for months. Though she had been in ill health during much of the last half of 1922 and was still fragile, the Duchess had been hoping to make the trip since Harding was in the Senate. "I have been wanting to go to Alaska for six years," she said, "and they're not going to talk me out of it."

They'd also just experienced a sizable and much welcomed windfall. In 1923, Harding's salary was $73,000 annually, a substantial sum in those days but hardly enough to ensure a comfortable retirement. At the time, the president of the United States didn't receive a pension. Once Harding left office, he would either have to go back to running the *Marion Star* or find some other livelihood. He had already been offered $25,000 a year to write for a newspaper syndicate and could earn $750 per speech if he chose to bloviate professionally.

Just two days before he was to leave for Alaska, Harding got a visit from Louis H. Brush and Roy Moore, who ran a chain of small-town newspapers in Ohio. Harding already knew Brush. He was the top Republican fund-raiser in Ohio, a friend of Daugherty's, and a Harding supporter. As such, he had access to the White House and was well known in Washington.

The president's visitors had a proposition. They wanted to buy the *Marion Star* for $500,000, paying most of the amount in Liberty bonds. Harding accepted on the spot. The *Star* had a circulation of nine thousand. It was profitable. Still, $500,000 was a lot for what some rival publishers characterized as a "one-horse newspaper." Consider that Carl Magee had acquired the comparable *Albuquerque Morning Journal* for $115,000. That Brush, a shrewd moneyman, seemingly paid two or three times what the *Star* was worth and paid in Liberty bonds—Harry Sinclair's preferred means of payment—would later lead to speculation that Harding was being rewarded indirectly by "Sinco" for turning a blind eye to the naval leases.

With the deal signed and payment forthcoming, Harding summoned Sam Ungerleider, the brokerage firm owner, to the White House. Ungerleider had an office nearby, which was convenient because he did so much business with the Ohio Gang. Harding was already a client with a modest account that he'd been gradually increasing. After telling him about the newspaper sale, Harding asked Ungerleider to buy $500,000 worth of stocks on margin, assuring the broker he'd give him the money on his return from Alaska. By then he'd have received the proceeds from the *Star* deal.

There's a certain malodor emanating from this transaction. The president didn't use his own name on the account but instead listed it in the name of Walter Ferguson, one of his Secret Service men. Why? Was Harding trying to hide something? But let's not spoil the upcoming journey with untoward speculation. On one of those ungodly humid and hot Washington summer days, June 20, the president's ten-car train started west. The Hardings rode in the last car, the *Superb*. The president and the Duchess, who was shading herself with a parasol, waved farewell from the rear platform as the train pulled out of Union Station.

This was to be one of the longest trips ever undertaken by an American president, fifteen thousand miles across the continent by way of St. Louis, Denver, Seattle, and Tacoma, then on up to Alaska by ship and back, stopping again along the West Coast before heading on down through the Panama Canal. From there, the Hardings would go on to

New York. The journey was expected to take two months. Only President Taft had traveled farther on behalf of his country.

Accompanying the Hardings was an entourage of seventy-five, including the new secretary of the interior, Hubert Work, and his wife; Herbert Hoover, the secretary of commerce, and his spouse; Secretary of Agriculture Henry Wallace; the president's secretary, George Christian, and his wife; various congressmen with spouses; U.S. Army and Navy brass; ten Secret Service men; newspaper correspondents and photographers; and newsreel cameramen and telephone company technicians who were charged with setting up the means of relaying the president's speeches nationally. Aside from the Hardings' shared desire to visit the country's northernmost possession, this was a barnstorming trip designed to offset reports (this was before the days of polling) that Republican popularity was at a low ebb and to shore up support for the 1924 elections. With his hail-fellow heartiness, Harding was good at connecting with people. "He gains friends wherever he goes," *The Washington Post* noted just before the Hardings' departure. "There is no reason to suppose that the people of the middle and far West will prove different from those in the East in their liking of the President's personal side."

"I want people to see their president," Florence said.

THERE ARE HARDING biographers who continue to maintain that the president knew nothing of the Teapot malfeasance until after the fact, wasn't complicit in any way, and sought to distance himself from the scandal and those who perpetuated it. Which supposedly was in part what the Alaska trip was all about.

According to this still prevalent scenario, when Harding finally found out what Fall and Sinclair had been up to, he felt betrayed and was so dismayed that his stress and disappointment contributed to his untimely death. This theory hinges on two wobbly pegs. Riding across Kansas from Kansas City to Hutchinson, Harding gave a now famous interview to newspaper editor William Allen White, saying, "I have no trouble with my enemies. . . . It's my friends that are giving me trouble." In light of subsequent revelations about the naval leases, the inference has been that Harding was speaking about Fall. Not so.

Second, according to the wife of Congressman Arthur Capper, who was aboard the train with her husband, a veiled and distraught Emma Fall visited the president's train briefly in Kansas. Mrs. Capper claimed to have seen Harding emerge from the meeting "perturbed and obviously shaken." Emma must have "told him something that was a wallop on the jaw," she concluded. The suspicion that arose pursuant to this tale was that Emma told the president about the extensive home improvements being conducted at Three Rivers as a way of 'fessing up to her husband's culpability.

This story begs the question: Why would Emma come all the way to Kansas to bare her soul to Harding? Send a letter. Call. Actually, the Hardings had learned that Emma was going to be in Kansas and asked her to dine with them aboard the train. "The evening was delightful," Emma later wrote. "I went with them to hear him speak, and they left me at my hotel."

Harding didn't feel betrayed by Fall. Nor was he trying to distance himself from his former interior secretary. Prior to Fall's leaving the administration, Harding had offered him a seat on the Supreme Court. When Fall declined and took an interim assignment with Sinclair to travel to Russia, he stopped by the White House to give his former boss the news. Sinclair wanted Russian oil, and the Soviet government sought U.S. recognition. Obviously, as a former cabinet officer, Fall gave Sinclair's mission at least a semiofficial status. Upon hearing the news, Harding offered Fall his blessing and advised him "to make as much money as he could."

Hardly the sentiments of a man betrayed.

Nor did Harding try to distance himself from the other culprits in the leasing fraud. In Denver, Frederick Bonfils joined the presidential entourage, presenting Florence with the aforementioned sealskin coat. He went along officially as the *Denver Post*'s press representative, though he didn't file a single word regarding the trip. After the payoff from Sinclair, the newspaper owner had become one of Harding's most ardent admirers. After the president's death, he headed up a committee in Denver to build a monument to Harding. Presumably, he contributed a portion of the ill-gotten gains Harding had helped him secure.

IN DENVER, before an audience of twelve thousand, Harding spoke out about the need to enforce the Prohibition laws. This predictably raised a few eyebrows in the crowd. It was no secret that Harding liked to take a drink or two. Florence had been after him to go "on the dry," as the Irish say. He had vowed to do so, but this trip to Alaska would have been enough to test Prohibitionist Carry Nation's willpower. Everywhere the president went—Cheyenne, Salt Lake, Butte, or Meacham, Oregon—he was feted, asked to speak, and, of course, had to ooh and ahh at the local sights. In Utah, Senator Reed Smoot prevailed on Florence to have the president visit Zion National Park near Cedar City, where the daytime temperatures averaged three figures in summer. Despite a raging case of hemorrhoids, the president was persuaded to go on a horseback ride through the park. Bad mistake. When he returned sweating and sunburned to Zion Lodge around noon, the Duchess clapped her hands, calling out, "Warren"—she pronounced the name "Wurren"—"you look just like a great big Indian." It was probably fortunate for Florence that her spouse wasn't armed with a war hatchet at the time.

Florence seemed to be enduring the grueling journey far better than her husband, who looked exhausted. Despite all the sun he'd gotten, Harding's face had a grayish pallor; his lips were purple. Aboard the refurbished army transport ship *Henderson* during the four-day cruise from Tacoma, Washington, to Alaska, Herbert Hoover, with whom the president played bridge for much of the trip, noted that the president seemed edgy and distracted. At one point, he summoned Hoover into his cabin and asked, "If you knew of a great scandal in our administration, would you for the good of the country and the party expose it publicly or would you bury it?"

"Publish it, and at least get credit for integrity on your side," Hoover responded.

Harding noted that this approach might prove politically damaging. He said he had received disturbing rumors involving some of Jess Smith's activities in connection with cases in the Justice Department. "Harding gave no information about what Smith had been up to," Hoover recalled. "I asked what Daugherty's relations to the affair were. He abruptly dried up and never mentioned the question again."

HARDING HAD ALREADY tried to bury one potentially disastrous scandal when he sanctioned Sinclair's payoff to Bonfils and Stack. Now on this western trip, he seemed to be trying to make amends by taking an even-handed approach to conservation, balancing the interests of the public sector with those of the private. In Utah, both the Duchess and Warren had expressed enthusiasm for the newly created Zion National Park. Earlier in Wyoming, when Harding first took in the towering, snow-capped Tetons and the Snake River Valley, he advocated adding a big part of the Jackson Hole basin and part of the Tetons to the public domain.

In Alaska, likely influenced by the pro-conservationist secretary of agriculture, Henry Wallace, Fall's old nemesis, Harding set aside twenty-three million acres of the north slope of the Brooks Range, designating it "Naval Petroleum Reserve No. 4." This, of course, was a return to the policy that Fall had earlier dismantled. But Harding wanted the oil boys to get their taste as well. On his return to Seattle, in a speech before sixty thousand people in the University of Washington stadium, he noted enthusiastically that some of the larger oil interests were already developing what he described as Alaska's "measureless oil resources."

What alarmed Hoover and any others who were actually paying attention to the speech was that the president kept saying "Nebraska" when he meant to say "Alaska."

WARREN HARDING APPARENTLY did not intend to run again. In making the western trip, he was seeking to undo the damage that had resulted from his sanctioning the naval leases and to refurbish his legacy as president. As for his own complicity, Harding hadn't actively sought payback from those who benefited from his oil policies—and in the end they were *his* oil policies—but he wasn't averse to pocketing whatever came his way as a result of the leases, no questions asked.

Before leaving for Alaska, the president met Oregon governor Walter Pierce. The brief discussion affords us a window into the president's frame of mind at the time. Pierce later recounted the meeting, noting that after some discussion regarding the Alaskan trip, Harding had asked: "Going to be a candidate for reelection, I presume, Governor?"

Pierce said he didn't have much of a chance. "Much of the publicity in Oregon is against me . . . so I am enjoying the term I'm now serving."

At this point, Harding looked at the Duchess. "What do you say, Mrs. Harding?"

"I think you ought to invite him," she responded. "We need a few Democrats, and I think he is just what we want."

The president explained, "I am going to serve only one term as president, and when my term is out, we are going around the world. The arrangements have been made for an oceangoing yacht to leave New York on a world trip, carrying from fifty to seventy people whom I have the privilege of inviting. It will take nearly a year. We are going to see the sights of the world; read; study; and lecture; stenographers aplenty to take down our thoughts; all expenses paid. You are invited to be one of the guests."

Harding didn't say whose yacht they would be using or who was footing the expenses, but it was likely "Sinco"—an offer he'd made during one of those convivial nights spent at the White House. Sinclair's best friend and most valued employee was an international mystery man and adventurer named Henry Mason Day. One of Day's responsibilities was to take VIPs—heads of state and important business associates—on extended cruises. In this case, the VIPs likely were the Hardings and sixty or so of their closest friends.

Pierce said he'd love to go, but he didn't think financially he could afford to take the time off.

"Well, well, I am sorry to hear that," the president said. "You know, Mrs. Harding and I are much better off than we thought we were." He went on to say that he'd recently sold his newspaper. "We knew the *Marion Star* was a fine property . . . but we never imagined it was worth the money it proved to be. . . . A couple of boys came by and offered us $500,000 in bonds for it. We took them."

"They pay four and a quarter percent interest," Florence added.

A half million in Liberty bonds that produced $17,500 annually in income and a year on the high seas all expenses paid—that's what Harding would come away with. Plus the fees for writing a column and the speaking engagements. That made for a comfortable nest egg, even for an ex-president with expensive tastes. Of course, he never got to enjoy either the money or the cruise. On August 2, only a week after his return from Alaska, Warren Harding died of a stroke in San Francisco's Palace Hotel. He was three months short of his fifty-eighth birthday.

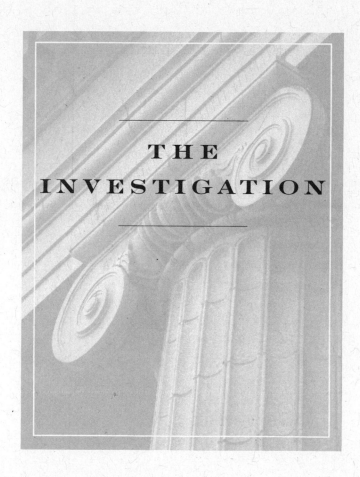

THE
INVESTIGATION

27

COOLIDGE

Vice President Calvin Coolidge had just gone to bed when his seventy-eight-year-old father came upstairs with a telegram. Coolidge and his wife, Grace, were vacationing in Plymouth Notch, Vermont, the little town in the foothills of the Green Mountains where Coolidge had grown up. He and Grace had retired at 10:30. They were staying at the old Coolidge family homestead, a two-story frame house without electricity, indoor plumbing, or a telephone.

A few minutes after they'd gone up to bed, a driver arrived from nearby Bridgewater with a telegram. Old Colonel Coolidge brought it upstairs. "I was awakened by my father coming up the stairs and calling my name," Coolidge recalled. "I noticed that his voice trembled. As the only times I had ever observed that before were when death had visited our family, I knew something of the gravest nature had occurred."

Coolidge's father told him the telegram was from San Francisco, the Palace Hotel. President Harding was dead. Coolidge came downstairs a few minutes later, dressed in a black suit and black necktie. He was fifty-one, of English stock, a slender, taciturn son of the Green Mountain State. His wife, Grace, followed him down the narrow, rickety staircase, wiping tears from her eyes. Before coming down, she and

Calvin had knelt and prayed together upstairs, Coolidge asking God to bless the American people and give him the power to serve them.

By now, a number of people who'd learned of the president's death had begun to arrive, among them Porter Dale, who represented Vermont's Second District in Congress and lived not far away. On greeting Coolidge, Dale expressed concern that the country was now without a president—and would remain so until the vice president took the oath of office.

Coolidge asked his father if he'd retained his notary public license. Fortunately, he had. Was it legal for the senior Coolidge to administer the oath? After a brief discussion, the vice president and the others present decided that, yes, the elder Coolidge could swear in his son. First, though, the colonel insisted on going upstairs to shave and freshen up for the impromptu ceremony.

At 2:47 a.m., the colonel, the vice president, his wife, and their guests gathered in the parlor sitting room. There, by the canted lights of two oil lamps placed on the center table, John Coolidge swore in his son as the thirtieth president of the United States. "It seemed a simple and natural thing to do at the time, but I can now realize something of the dramatic force of the event," Coolidge later wrote.

CALVIN COOLIDGE SEEMED even less suited to the presidency than his predecessor. At least the robustly handsome Harding had looked the part. Coolidge was a slight, red-haired man with sharp Yankee features, a prominent nose, and a sourpuss expression. The latter belied a dry wit and a shyness that had stayed with him since childhood. He was born in Plymouth Notch on July 4, 1872, the son of the village storekeeper and local constable and a mother, Victoria, who died of a burst appendix when Calvin was twelve. After graduating from Amherst with honors, Coolidge entered law and politics in Northampton, Massachusetts; in 1905, he married Grace Anna Goodhue, who had the gregarious, animated temperament that was so conspicuously lacking in her husband. "Mrs. Coolidge . . . has vivacity and savoir-faire, and was . . . beloved by Republicans and Democrats alike," noted Daisy Harriman, a prominent figure in Washington. When she first met her husband-to-be, Grace was teaching at a school for the deaf. Aware of Coolidge's reputation as a man of few words, one of her fellow teachers noted: "Well, Grace has taught the deaf to hear. Maybe she can teach the mute to speak."

Coolidge's political career progressed steadily and largely without incident. The circumspect and increasingly conservative Coolidge was a rock-no-boats politician. He was elected mayor of Northampton in 1910 and then elected to the state senate in 1912, serving as president of that body in 1914 and 1915. In 1916, he became lieutenant governor, then governor in 1919.

It was as governor that Coolidge gained sudden national prominence. In 1919, in the wake of World War I, the country was experiencing sharply rising costs and a shortage of jobs with the return of hundreds of thousands of servicemen. The situation was so dire that one-fifth of the nation's labor force would strike during the year—harbor workers in New York, a general strike in Seattle that shut down all business for a week, a steelworkers strike in Chicago in which 350,000 workers went out as part of a drive by the American Federation of Labor (AFL) to unionize the industry and reduce the workday from twelve to eight hours. Murderous race riots erupted in almost two dozen cities, fueled by inflation, unemployment, and racism against last-hired, first-fired African Americans. Conservatives, management, and the nation's "yellow press" blamed the unrest on Reds, the Industrial Workers of the World (the Wobblies), radicals, and undesirable immigrants, especially those from southern and eastern Europe who were seen as carriers of the potentially deadly and highly infectious Bolshevism virus.

Boston was especially hard hit. In April, a strike by Boston telephone operators shut down much of the phone service in New England. Elevated train operators walked off the job. The largely Irish police department had been threatening to strike for several years. The city hadn't given new recruits a pay increase since 1857. Officers worked as much as ninety-eight hours a week with one day off every two weeks. Their grievances ignored by Boston's Protestant establishment, almost three-quarters of the force went on strike in September. Rioting and modest property damage ensued. On September 11, in a rare movement of public assertiveness, Governor Coolidge called out the state guard and effectively fired all 1,500 of the police who'd gone on strike. When AFL president Samuel Gompers asked Coolidge to reinstate them, he responded: "There is no right to strike against the public safety by anybody, anywhere, any time." It was a stance that Ronald Reagan, who counted Coolidge among his heroes, would assume years later in dealing with striking airline traffic controllers.

Immediately after, Coolidge regretted having taken such a strong position, fearing it would cost him the next election in pro-labor Massachusetts. "I have just committed political suicide," he told a friend. Instead, he became a national figure, "a hero to the mass of private citizens who, alienated by postwar strikes, felt that labor was becoming contemptuous of the public interests," noted one of his biographers. On the strength of his handling of the police strike, Coolidge was not only reelected Massachusetts governor, but won the vice presidential nomination as well.

In his two and a half years under Harding, however, Coolidge had been so inconspicuous that a booking agency for public speakers with whom he signed couldn't get a gig for the vice president even at discount rates. He often went unrecognized at public events, and when he identified himself as the vice president, the response was often, "Of what?" As the first vice president ever to attend cabinet meetings, he typically remained silent at these weekly gatherings and rarely asserted himself in his role as presiding president of the U.S. Senate. Still, in assuming the presidency, Coolidge announced, "I think I can handle this."

His first days in the White House were disrupted by Florence Harding, who had returned to Washington immediately after Harding's August 10 funeral in Marion to pack her possessions and burn any of her husband's personal and business papers and letters that might portray the late president in an unfavorable light. The Coolidges graciously gave her the run of the White House, staying at the nearby Willard Hotel, until finally, after almost a week, Florence retreated to Friendship, the McLean estate, where she continued burning records in one of the McLeans' fireplaces. At the same time, according to Thomas Walsh, Daugherty burned Harding's papers to which he had access.

On finally settling in, Coolidge vowed to continue Harding's programs—that is, to further reduce the $22.3 billion national debt, continue to tighten restrictions on immigration, and press for U.S. membership in the World Court. One of his more pressing challenges was the upcoming Teapot investigation, which was scheduled to commence in October 1923. As the new Republican president, he hoped to minimize its impact on his party and his own chances of winning the presidency in 1924. He asked his close friend and former president William Howard Taft how to best accomplish this. "Do nothing" was Taft's advice. "In the returning prosperity people are glad to have a rest from watching Washington, and . . . your wisest course is to be quiet for a while."

The Democrats, however, believed it wouldn't be easy for Coolidge to distance himself from the scandal. "Teapot Dome is going to be a heavy load for Mr. Coolidge to carry," Washington lawyer Harold L. Ickes said soon after Coolidge took office. "His position is not improved by the circumstances that he sat in . . . the cabinet when the deal was considered and approved."

28

GETTING READY

In mid-September, Thomas J. Walsh returned to Washington to complete his final preparations for the Teapot hearings, which were scheduled to commence on October 15. Walsh had agreed to investigate the leases only after the junior senator from Montana, Burton Wheeler, told him of a meeting with Tom Arthur, a leading Montana Democrat. Arthur told Wheeler Teapot "was a crooked deal" that deserved a complete public airing.

In June 1922, Walsh agreed to take command of the Senate inquiry, but he proceeded slowly and without much evident enthusiasm. According to journalist Mark Sullivan, a friend of Walsh's, this was due at least partially "to a lack of strong conviction [on Walsh's part] that corruption could be shown."

At this juncture, Walsh had no reason to believe that Albert Fall, who was at the center of the investigation, was anything less than honest. Nor did he bear a grudge against Fall despite their political differences. As a staunch Democrat, Walsh had been one of Wilson's closest advisers. He had managed Wilson's 1916 western campaign from headquarters in Chicago and led the fight for confirmation of the nomination of Louis Brandeis to the Supreme Court.

Walsh and the intensely partisan Fall were often at loggerheads.

Walsh had taken a leading role in Senate support of American entry into the League of Nations and the Treaty of Versailles. Fall, who reviled Wilson, had emerged as one of the more vocal opponents of the League. Walsh strongly opposed American intervention in Mexico to protect U.S. interests. Fall, of course, had long been intervention's most vocal champion in the Senate. Even so, the two remained on cordial terms and as western senators shared a number of similar views. Both favored leasing public land to private interests, for instance; both favored opening up Indian land—Fall the Navajo Reservation, Walsh the Blackfoot Reservation and Flathead Reservations—to white settlement. Walsh, according to Fall's biographer, had even written Fall congratulating him on his appointment as interior secretary, a position that was "scarcely second in importance to that of the presidency, far as the material interests of the people of [my] state are concerned," Walsh said. Certainly, there were those in the Senate whom Walsh disliked—for one, Henry Cabot Lodge, whom he characterized as a pompous twit—but Albert Fall wasn't among them.

So much obfuscation, confusion, and controversy surrounded the leasing issue that it was difficult for Walsh to know where to begin. "Sherlock Holmes could not have been presented with a more tantalizing case than that facing Senator Thomas J. Walsh in September 1923," noted Walsh biographer J. Leonard Bates. Walsh knew nothing about the payoffs to Fall at this point, nothing about Continental Trading and the Liberty bonds. In fact, neither Walsh nor anyone other than Fall and his associates was entirely sure what had been leased—and to whom. Fall had parceled out the leases with such secrecy that Walsh didn't learn that Ed Doheny had been granted Naval Petroleum Reserve No. 1 (Elk Hills) and Reserve No. 2 (Buena Vista) until October 23, 1923, the day before the first witnesses began appearing before Walsh's committee and eighteen months after the lease had been signed.

Walsh approached the investigation with his usual slow deliberateness. "With characteristic thoroughness, he began by refamiliarizing himself with the laws affecting public lands—he had known them fairly well in his private practices—and with the history of them," Mark Sullivan said. Intermittently over the past sixteen months, he'd reviewed and analyzed the leases and thousands of documents—much of them Interior Department detritus—Fall had provided and even sent letters to all journals that had run articles dealing with the leases, requesting they share their sources with him. In all, it was "a laborious study" of the evidence, he said. And a solitary one.

On his return to Washington, however, he had been counting on getting assistance from others in gearing up for the hearings, especially from Wyoming senator John Kendrick. It was Kendrick along with La Follette who had urged Walsh to investigate. Like Walsh, Kendrick was a member of the Committee on Public Lands and Surveys, one of the few Democrats. On September 21, Walsh wrote Kendrick, telling of his "most delightful summer" visiting his only child, Genevieve Walsh Gudger, who was married to a navy officer stationed in Manila. Upon his return to the United States, Walsh spent the remainder of his vacation, he told Kendrick, "going about Montana renewing old acquaintances and making many new ones."

Now that he was back in D.C., Walsh wrote Kendrick that he was "counting definitely on your being here and hope very sincerely that you can come soon, as your counsel will be invaluable in the preparation which I am undertaking. Meanwhile, I shall be pleased to have a letter from you with such suggestions as you may think helpful."

Kendrick, who had a ranch outside Sheridan, Wyoming, responded that the cattle business and other matters would keep him from returning to Washington until Congress reconvened in mid-October. Similarly, Josephus Daniels, the former navy secretary under President Wilson, wrote Walsh that he couldn't come up from Raleigh, North Carolina, where he owned the *Raleigh News & Observer*, to meet with the Montana senator as had been planned earlier. As navy secretary, Daniels had fended off numerous attempts by oil operators to take control of the reserves and had established a supervisory board to manage and protect the navy petroleum. Fall, Walsh had learned from a geologist involved with La Follette's earlier probe of Teapot, had dismantled the board by having the officers who served on it transferred to other, often remote posts. Walsh had hoped to confer with Daniels on the matter as well as Fall's allegations that under Daniels the California fields had been drained of almost seven million barrels of oil as the result of drilling on adjacent lands. "I regret very much that you find it impossible to give me the assistance I had hoped would come from a conference with you," Walsh wrote Daniels on October 8, only a week before the hearings were scheduled to begin. Others who had initially offered help, including ex–interior secretary John Barton Payne, also proved otherwise occupied, while the press seemed entirely indifferent. When approached by Walsh to write about Teapot Dome, journalist Christopher Connolly responded that with the economy on the rebound and so many publications depending on big business for ads, "muckraking" had become "extremely unpopular." President Taft's assessment, it seemed, had been right.

With the hearings coming up, it was left then almost entirely to Walsh and his able young clerk, John G. Holland, a Georgetown law student, to frame questions and gather evidence regarding the legality of the leases, the lack of competitive bidding, the drainage issue, and the surreptitiousness under which the transactions were carried out. "The duty of assembling the evidence has, in a way, devolved upon me," Walsh wrote Daniels. "At least, I am assuming it chiefly because no one else seems to be giving himself any concern about it."

29

TWO MASTERS

On leaving the cabinet, Albert Fall had planned to retreat to Three Rivers for an extended stay with Emma and his family. The beneficiaries of his petroleum-leasing policies, Messrs. Doheny and Sinclair, however, couldn't wait six months. Both were in the midst of sensitive, high-level negotiations—Doheny in Mexico, Sinclair in the Soviet Union—and both believed that having the former interior secretary and close friend of the president on their payroll could tip the balance in their favor. At stake were hundreds of millions of dollars and a significant share of the world's oil.

In March, two months after Fall's resignation, Doheny wrote urging that Fall come with him and other oilmen to Mexico to assist in settling some differences between the Obregón government and American oil interests operating there. "I answered this letter, and again in various personal conversations, explained my position to Mr. Doheny and my desire not to tie myself up after at least six months given to my own personal affairs and recreation," Fall later said.

Fall passed on the Mexican trip, only to be visited by J. W. Zevely in May 1923. At the time, Zevely's boss, Harry Sinclair, was on the verge of eclipsing wizened old John D. Rockefeller, who still controlled the Standard Oil empire, and Sir Henri Deterding, founder of Royal

Dutch/Shell and "the Napoleon of Petroleum," as the world's dominant oilman. To expand his empire into the Soviet Union, Sinclair planned to develop the oil resources of Sakhalin Island, where he'd already been granted a concession. At the time, the island was claimed by both the Soviet Union and Japan. Sinclair was targeting other concessions in the USSR as well. He wanted Fall to come to Russia to advise on the negotiations.

Sinclair's success in Russia, Zevely explained, hinged on a number of factors. Royal Dutch/Shell was also in the hunt for Soviet oil. Sinclair and his associates would have to top Sir Henri in the bidding. In addition to a share of whatever concessions it granted, the Lenin-led Soviet government wanted a "sweetener" to revive its economy—a substantial loan. And there was one more matter. Sinclair would be given the concession if the United States recognized the Soviet government, a tall order given that the United States was at the time in the thrall of a "Red scare."

Which was one of the reasons Sinclair was eager for Fall to accompany him. With his expertise in international law and in oil, his understanding of how to get things done in Washington, and his well-known and still enduring friendship with Harding, Fall might just possibly persuade Harding to recognize the Soviets, or at least give the matter serious consideration. It was well known that Fall was an ardent anti-Bolshevik. If he returned from the USSR saying the Commies weren't so bad after all, Harding just might be inclined to listen. At least, that was the impression Sinclair likely hoped to convey at the bargaining table. And certainly Sinclair was in an excellent position to ask for a big favor from the White House. He too was close to Harding and, as one journalist noted, "had paid off the Republican campaign debt—or he was about to."

Anxious to make some money, Fall cut short his R & R, agreeing to the trip on the condition that Sinclair pay him a $25,000 fee and $10,000 in expenses. If he was going, he was going first cabin all the way. Not a problem, Zevely assured him. The payment for Fall's fee would be made on his return, in Liberty bonds from the Continental Trading transaction. The expenses would be paid up front in cash.

Fall was to sail from New York under a passport that listed his occupation simply as "rancher." First, though, he stopped off in Washington to brief Harding, who was getting ready for his Alaskan trip. In what would be their last meeting, the president not only gave Fall his blessing, but, as Fall later recalled, "he said he was very glad for me to go to Russia, because he was satisfied he would get the truth of Russian conditions [from me and] he had not been able to get the true facts from any other source." Fall, his biographer noted, pledged not to support any contract that required diplomatic recognition, because, if it was granted, Harding would face accusations of being in "partnership with Sinclair."

Sinclair and his entourage—Archie Roosevelt, Teddy Jr's. brother and a Sinclair vice president; Zevely and some executives from Barnsdall Corporation, who were partnering with Sinclair on the Russian deal; various bankers from Chase Manhattan; and other Sinclair executives—had sailed on an earlier ocean liner. Fall caught up with them in London. There, the mysterious Henry Mason Day joined the party. Described by a journalist who knew him casually as "a soldier of fortune . . . tall, straight and swarthy, perfectly poised and seemingly impenetrable, almost sinister [but] always pleasant," Day was perhaps Sinclair's most trusted business associate and closest friend. He was intensely loyal to his boss. "Harry Sinclair is the salt of the earth," Day said.

No one seemed to know where Day came from or much about his early life except that he had two spinster sisters living somewhere in the States. Day himself lived in Paris and was married to a well-known mezzo-soprano who had served as a member of Field Marshal Kitchener's British recruiting staff during the war. Day acted as Sinclair's "fixer," dealing with problems, entertaining important officials, providing intelligence on the opposition, and doling out bribes. When he and Sinclair traveled together, as they did frequently, Day made the arrangements, took care of security, and paid the bills. On the road, they always shared a hotel suite—separate bedrooms with an adjoining sitting room. Day was so circumspect and protective of his boss that when he and Sinclair and whoever might be part of their entourage checked out of a hotel, Day went through every closet and drawer to make sure nothing had been left behind. He even burned all the desk blotters so that no one could decipher what Sinclair or Zevely, say, might have written during their stay.

Though Day sometimes came to Washington, he worked largely in Europe and Asia, scoping out new oil concessions for Sinclair in competition with Royal Dutch/Shell; another American giant, Standard

Oil; and the British-owned Anglo-Persian Oil Company. It had been Day who several years earlier had secured the rights to oil fields on remote Sakhalin off the Siberian coast after visiting there. Now Sinclair wanted to add to his Sakhalin operations.

More recently, in August 1922 Day had gone to Tehran in an effort to secure the country's northern oil concessions from the Iranian government, a move that was not well received by the British, who thoroughly dominated the country's oil resources through the Anglo-Persian Oil Company. By one account, Day won over the country's prime minister with a $275,000 bribe, then sealed the deal with an offer of a $10 million loan on behalf of Sinclair Oil to the Iranian government.

In London, Sinclair, Day, and the others had cause for celebration. A few weeks earlier, the Iranian Majlis, its Parliament, had passed a bill officially granting the northern fields to Sinclair, contingent on receiving the $10 million loan. The Brits, of course, would do everything they could to ensure the bill wasn't enacted. Even so, Day, who had just returned from Tehran, assured his boss that the company's interests in Persia were well looked after by Sinclair's agent there, a man named Soppier, and Major Robert Imbrie, the American vice consul at Tehran and a strong Sinclair ally. Within the year, Imbrie would literally be torn to pieces by a mob that the U.S. State Department believed was acting on behalf of the British government and the Anglo-Persian Oil Company.

In a jovial mood, Sinclair's party—by now numbering almost eighty—traveled in high style aboard a chartered luxury train to Moscow, where the Lenin government put them up in a former czarist palace. In meetings with Lenin and lesser Soviet officials, Sinclair expressed his interest in further developing Sakhalin, in drilling in the vast Caucasian oil fields, and—say this for Sinclair: His vision was boundless—in having his company take over control of virtually all Russia's oil production, distribution, refining, and international marketing. To this end, he was prepared to invest $115 million in developing the Russian fields and said he could raise another $250 million in New York—a Chase Manhattan Bank–backed bond offering—as a loan for the financially beleaguered Soviet government. It was an offer the Russians couldn't refuse, especially with the prospect of the diplomatic recognition pervading the discussions. His promise to Harding notwithstanding, Fall wasn't about to throw a wet blanket on the subject of U.S. recognition, especially since he wasn't to receive his $25,000 until he got back to the United States.

By any measure, the Russian trip was a great success. The Soviets gave Sinclair additional Sakhalin concessions and a green light on Caucasian development, and they were eager to follow up on the larger proposal. Of course, Sinclair downplayed the potential scope of the undertaking to the press in order not to tip his hand to competitors. "I came to Russia at the invitation of the Russian Government primarily to discuss operations of the Sinclair Consolidated Oil Company under its concession granted some time ago for the development of the rich petroleum resources in northern Sakhalin," Sinclair told an Associated Press reporter on July 24 just as he and the others were about to start back to London. "The general oil situation presents a number of problems, all of which, however, can satisfactorily be solved providing the proper business methods are used and sufficient cooperation is obtained." The one variable Sinclair hadn't foreseen occurred as he, Fall, and the others were sailing back to New York and the ship's captain announced that the president of the United States had died during the night.

The party didn't arrive until August 10, the same day Harding was buried in Marion. Fall, who was met by Emma in New York, missed the president's funeral, but he and Emma traveled to Washington to express their condolences to Florence Harding. While there, Fall also met for three and a half hours with the new president regarding affairs in Mexico and Russia—"Roosia," as Coolidge called it. With Emma, he dined with Commerce Secretary Herbert Hoover and his wife and also discussed his trip. Exhausted from his travels, Fall was looking forward to getting back to Three Rivers, but in Washington he got a cable from Ed Doheny summoning him to Los Angeles immediately.

30

OPENING ROUNDS

On Monday, October 23, 1923, at 10:00 a.m., the Teapot Dome investigation by the Senate Committee on Public Lands and Surveys finally got under way in room 210 of the Senate Office Building. It had been scheduled to begin October 15, but with many committee members not yet back in Washington, the hearings were delayed. Reed Smoot, a Mormon apostle and conservative Republican senator from Utah, called the committee to order. Present were Thomas Walsh of Montana (D); George William Norris of Nebraska (R); Irvine Lenroot of Wisconsin (R); John Kendrick of Wyoming (D); Edwin Ladd of North Dakota (R); Peter Norbeck of South Dakota (R); and the committee chairman, Reed Smoot.

It had been eighteen months since "Fighting Bob" La Follette had called for a full-scale investigation into the oil leases in a scathing speech before the Senate and then vice president Coolidge. La Follette had charged that under Fall, the Department of the Interior was the "sluiceway for 90 percent of the corruption in government." The resolution had passed unanimously on April 29, 1922.

In the interim, President Harding had died, Albert Fall had resigned, and the initial controversy surrounding the naval reserves had largely petered out. The ranking Republicans on the committee—

Smoot, its chair, and Irvine Lenroot of Wisconsin—were eager to lay Teapot to rest as expeditiously as possible—and not simply because the investigation could give the party a black eye or damage its chances in the upcoming election year. At the time the hearings got under way, the RNC, notably its former chairman, Will Hays, was counting on Harry Sinclair to pay off more than $1 million in debts that remained from the 1920 campaign. Meanwhile, the hearings commenced at a time when potentially billions of dollars' worth of Russian, Persian, Mexican, and Wyoming oil was in Sinclair's grasp. If Sinclair was found to have broken any laws during the course of the investigation, his hopes of establishing a global petroleum empire could well be dashed. Which would mean the RNC would lose its most generous sugar daddy.

Well before the hearings got under way, Sinclair and some of his associates had taken measures to protect themselves, pressuring Senator Smoot to derail the inquiry almost as soon as La Follette's resolution cleared the Senate. In May 1922, M. D. McEniry, the Interior Department's man in Denver, had written Fall regarding a conversation he'd had with Leo Stack, who at the time had just enlisted the *Denver Post*'s owners in an effort to collect $1 million from Harry Sinclair. Stack had told him that John C. Howard, president of the Utah Oil Refining Company and a leading member of the Mormon Church, was now in Washington and had been there for a week or more.

Utah Oil Refining was a subsidiary of Midwest Refining, which Harry Blackmer had recently sold to Robert Stewart of Standard Oil of Indiana, Harry Sinclair's partner in the Wyoming oil ventures. It was Midwest that sent Howard to Washington, "to help them out with Senator Smoot," Stack said. "Naturally, Blackmer and Sinclair, as well as their companies, wish to block as far as possible any action on Senator La Follette's resolution for the investigation of this Teapot Dome affair . . . and they hope through Howard's efforts to use Senator Smoot in blocking La Follette's resolution."

Smoot, whose party loyalty and prodigious energy were legendary, nearly succeeded. Prior to the hearings, he'd commissioned two geologists to investigate the degree of leakage at Teapot. "Smoot's geologists," as they were called, directly contradicted every previous study of the Teapot fields, including one by the Bureau of Mines. The bureau, which was part of Interior, had concluded the Teapot field held as much as two hundred million barrels of oil. Smoot's geologists claimed that adjacent private operators had drained so much oil from the naval reserve that no more than between twenty-one and twenty-five million barrels remained.

The Republicans made the most of this revelation, leaking the conclusions of the report to the newswire services four days before the hearings began. Then, on the first day of the investigation, Smoot had the geologists' report read into the record, after which the Utah senator announced: "If the reports of the experts are accepted, the theory that the government made a mistake in leasing this reserve has been exploded." Fall's action, he concluded, had been entirely justified.

For the most part, the press agreed. On October 23, *The New York Times* reported: "The hearings will be continued tomorrow, but all interest in its outcome has evaporated with the reports of the experts."

End of story. Almost.

ALBERT FALL WAS the committee's first witness. Since his return from Russia, the former interior secretary had been running several high-level errands for Ed Doheny having to do with Mexico. In August, the Obregón government agreed to honor foreign ownership rights of oil fields that were in place prior to 1917 as long as the operators could show that "positive acts" had been undertaken to improve the holdings. In return, the United States extended formal diplomatic recognition to Mexico. This, of course, was a boon to Doheny's Mexican Petroleum Company, but the Mexican government, like the Soviets, was strapped for cash. To ensure Obregón was able to retain power—and pay his army—Doheny agreed to lend him $10 million and invest another $9.5 million in Mexico. As a precondition, however, Doheny wanted assurances from President Coolidge that if Obregón defaulted, the United States would exert full-court diplomatic pressure on Mexico. In Los Angeles, Doheny briefed Fall on his dealings with Obregón, then sent him back to Washington to present the matter to Coolidge. First, though, Fall deigned to appear before the Committee on Public Lands and Surveys, making it clear at the outset that he hadn't been subpoenaed. He'd agreed to testify only as a favor to his old friend Reed Smoot. Nor was he sworn in, a highly irregular courtesy extended to Fall by Irvine Lenroot.

Walsh led the questioning. "Walsh was austere and carefully groomed, impeccable, soft-voiced, polite; he carried a formidable amount of information in his head," recalled Bruce Bliven, who covered the hearings for *The New Republic.* Meanwhile, the rest of the committee, which had only just returned from an extended summer vacation—in those days, Congress didn't reconvene until mid-October—seemed in equal measure uninformed and uninterested. For two days, the star attraction, Fall, "bore himself with somewhat more than his usual touch of quiet arrogance," said Mark Sullivan. Alternately, he was patronizing, prickly, fulsome, and forthcoming and seemed to have more important matters on his mind—perhaps his imminent meeting with Coolidge.

When Walsh asked him why he hadn't asked for bids, Fall responded: "Business purely, I knew I could get a better price without calling for bids." As for Walsh's questions as to why the transaction was carried out in secrecy, Fall raised the issue of national security, as would other witnesses to follow. "I have undertaken to explain that I regarded myself as a business agent of the Secretary of the Navy, acting in what I regarded as a military matter under the President of the United States, I did not purpose . . . to call attention to the fact that the contracts providing for enormous storages of oil for future use in a crisis were being made off the coast of certain parts of the country."

Walsh pointed out that it had originally been Congress that had given control of the navy reserves to the Department of the Navy, yet the executive branch had approved the transfer to Interior without so much as consulting Congress. "Does it not occur to you," Walsh asked, "that such a great question of national policy ought to be determined by Congress?"

"No, not necessarily," Fall answered. "The Congress of the United States has very little to do with this whole proposition. We took the responsibility, and I am very proud of the contract."

Who had been the authorized legal adviser to Interior in regard to the transfer? Walsh asked. "The Secretary of the Interior, largely himself," Fall responded in the third person. And what other oil companies had bid for the reserves? Regrettably, this was a matter of national security, Fall responded. "Unless this is considered absolutely necessary for the purposes of the hearing, I prefer not to name the oil companies."

Walsh pressed Fall about the Russian trip with Sinclair, to whom a year earlier he'd leased Teapot. Fall conceded he'd indeed made the trip but had been paid nothing more than his expenses. He failed to mention these had come to $10,000, nor did he acknowledge his $25,000 fee. As for his employment by Doheny, the other lessee, Fall alluded cryptically to his Mexican dealings: "I have been advising Mr. Doheny with reference to some important matters, of which I think our government is informed, but without any compensation at all."

So, according to his testimony, Fall had received nary a dime—other than travel expenses—from the recipients of hundreds of millions of dollars in naval oil. His actions had doubled the strengths of the Pacific fleet, he claimed. His only regret: Because of his actions, President Harding had been criticized. "He is dead now and cannot speak for himself," he concluded.

Before Fall left the committee room, Walsh said he might want to recall him for further questioning. Clearly, though, Fall had won the opening round. "On the whole, the impression made . . . was distinctly favorable. There was nothing in what he said, or in his manner, to excite suspicion. . . . The dispatches that went out to the country intimated that Walsh was on a preposterously false trail," Sullivan said.

DENBY, WHO WAS still navy secretary, Sinclair, and Doheny followed. Denby gave the impression that he was hearing about the naval leases for the first time. To almost all of Walsh's questions, he responded that he didn't know or couldn't remember the answer. Either Denby was a nitwit whose major accomplishment in the cabinet was leading the navy cheers in the annual Army/Navy game, as Mark Sullivan claimed, or he was simply playing the fool as a means of eluding all responsibility for the leases.

Doheny's appearance was brief. He and Walsh had known each other for a number of years. Both were Irish Catholics from Wisconsin; both were prominent in the Democratic Party. After Walsh's wife had died, Walsh had spent some time recovering at Doheny's place in Los Angeles. Doheny was someone for whom Walsh had had nothing but respect and affection up till now.

Like Fall, Doheny waved the flag, telling Walsh that he had accepted the leases only out of "patriotic concern." The leases were made strictly "in the interests of the United States Government, of which you are a senator and I am a citizen. . . . You cannot get me to admit it was a bad lease, because I certainly don't think it is."

"I only want the facts," Walsh responded.

Doheny did concede, however, that his actions weren't entirely altruistic. The two reserves he received could yield as much as two hundred million barrels of oil, he noted, producing a profit of roughly half that amount. Even by Doheny's vaulted standards, that was an impressive piece of change.

Taking the stand on October 29, Harry Sinclair was more forthcoming than the earlier witnesses. Yes, he'd visited Fall at Three Rivers: He conceded he'd sent Fall some cattle. He estimated that there was potentially $100 million to be made in the Teapot field. Fall had received no compensation from him other than the expenses for the Russian trip. At this point, Lenroot posited a rare question: "Mr. Sinclair . . . is there any profit to be received in this transaction, that Mr. Fall received, any benefit or profits, directly or indirectly, in any manner whatsoever in connection with you?"

"No, sir, none, unless he had received some benefit from the cows," Sinclair responded.

ON OCTOBER 30, the committee agreed to take a month's recess. Walsh was so discouraged that he was ready to close down the hearings. Lenroot and Smoot were openly hostile to the investigation, Walsh asserted, and had been doing everything they could to put a lid on the scandal. Other committee members on whom Walsh had been counting for support, such as Kendrick, seemed reluctant to revisit the scandal. Or utterly indifferent. As a result, Walsh was doing almost all the questioning. "Walsh *was* the committee," said Mark Sullivan.

A reporter for *The New York Herald* wrote on October 30 that "one Senator slept through most of the proceedings today. Another found it difficult to keep his eyes open." The press generally ignored the hearings or took the line that they represented an exercise in party politics designed to build political capital for the upcoming elections. DEMOCRATS TRAIN GUNS ON REPUBLICANS, a *Washington Post* headline read. The hearings were given such a low priority that at one point the committee had to vacate the spacious Senate chamber room and move to smaller premises so that the Senate wives could host a tea party there. No wonder Walsh said he was thinking of shutting down the hearings.

As for Albert Fall, he'd assumed that Walsh was only out to "pin something on the Republicans," his biographer wrote. If given enough rope, he'd hang himself. Perhaps Fall's greatest mistake in his first appearance before the Teapot Dome committee was to underestimate Walsh. By the time he realized his error, it was too late.

EVEN BEFORE THE hearings had started, Walsh had begun to hear rumors about Fall receiving funds from Sinclair; Sinclair funding much of Harding's campaign with a $1 million slush fund; Hamon buying Harding the nomination. Some of these vague reports were sent directly to Walsh from sources who claimed some inside knowledge of the scandal. Additional rumors reached Cordell Hull, chairman of the Democratic National Committee (DNC); Harry Slattery, the Washington lawyer and conservationist who'd been looking into the leases on his own; and others who had an interest in the hearings. Subsequently, they passed them along to Walsh, who had to decide which leads to ignore and which to follow up on—a task that became more difficult as the investigation progressed and the volume of incoming telegraphs, letters, and calls increased. He hadn't the resources or the time to chase down every lead, no matter how promising it might seem.

One lead he did pursue came from Cordell Hull. Before the hearings got under way, Hull forwarded Walsh a letter from Byron G. Beall in Santa Fe, New Mexico, claiming that Harry Sinclair had both purchased the Harris ranch and repurchased the *Albuquerque Morning Journal* from Carl Magee on behalf of Fall. As New Mexico's chief tax commissioner, Beall seemingly knew of what he spoke. Walsh wrote Beall directly on September 25, asking Beall for more information and copies of the records of the transfer of the Harris ranch.

During the actual hearings, Walsh received dozens of similar reports, chasing down as many of them as possible. He didn't hit real pay dirt, however, until October 30, the day the hearings went into a month-long recess. A Scripps-Howard newspaperman in Denver, Sidney B. Whipple, wired him regarding D. F. Stackelbeck, the *Denver Post* reporter whom Bonfils had sent to New Mexico to dig into Fall's various business dealings. Of Stackelbeck, Whipple said:

> His report was made to owners of *Post* and then forwarded to Washington where it is in the hands of officials unknown to me. Confidentially Stackelbeck told me two months ago that his report had much

to do with Fall's resignation. . . . Sinclair is said to have met owners of *Post* and after that the *Post*'s attacks on the deals ceased and there appeared a eulogistic article about Sinclair. I saw Stackelbeck last night and believe he would like to talk, but wouldn't dare unless forced.

Walsh authorized Whipple to subpoena Stackelbeck and then summoned him to Washington. In meeting with Walsh in November, Stackelbeck proved eager to reveal what he knew. After all, he'd uncovered the greatest scoop of his career, only to have it spiked by his blackmailing bosses. Yet he still needed his job, which meant that he couldn't be seen to be talking voluntarily. Thus the need for the subpoena.

Stackelbeck wouldn't be called to testify before the committee, but he proved invaluable to Walsh's case. In Washington, he briefed Walsh on what he'd learned about Fall during his visit to New Mexico. He also brought along his notes, a copy of the report Bonfils had suppressed, and notarized documentation of Fall's purchase of the Harris ranch. At the time, the ranching business in New Mexico was in dire shape because of a prolonged drought and the decline in cattle prices. Yet Fall, who Stackelbeck had learned had been broke, mysteriously came up with $91,500 in cash to acquire the Harris place.

Before leaving Washington, Stackelbeck promised Walsh "to keep you informed regarding any information I might obtain regarding Teapot Dome scandal." He also gave Walsh a list of potential witnesses to call, all from New Mexico and all familiar with some aspect of Fall's dealings and his financial affairs. One name stood out—the newspaper editor Carl Magee, with whom Stackelbeck had conferred several times during his two visits to New Mexico. If anyone in the state had the goods on Fall, it was Magee, Stackelbeck said.

31

THE CRUSADER

Carl Magee appeared before the committee on November 29, having taken the train up from New Mexico. After his fractious encounter with Albert Fall in the offices of the *Albuquerque Morning Journal*, the newspaper owner had learned firsthand what Fall had meant in threatening to "put him on the rack." Short of tar and feathering him, or dispatching him with a .44, Fall's cronies had done just about everything in their power to get Magee to exit the state. "I have withstood personal assaults, advertising boycotts, civil libel suits, criminal libel convictions, social ostracism, and personal vilification in carrying the banner of decency against Fall and his New Mexico gang," he later said.

Beginning in late 1921, the banks from which he'd borrowed money to buy the *Journal* began putting the financial squeeze on him. After a bank in Kansas City called in a $60,000 loan, Magee finally sold the *Journal* in April 1922. "I sold the journal to local special interests, but only after the bitterest fight in the annals of newspaper making and only when I had bankruptcy staring me in the face," he said. The First National Bank of Albuquerque purchased the paper for $200,000, but Magee suspected that one of Fall's friends—possibly Sinclair—was behind the purchase. Indeed, the new owner proved to be Joshua Reynolds, the bank's retired president. He is the "father-in-law of James J.

McNary, president of First National, El Paso, whom Fall tried to put over for Comptroller of the Currency and failed," Magee informed Walsh. Under its new ownership, Albert Fall was untouchable.

Still, Magee was not to be intimidated. He promptly started a new weekly paper, *Magee's Independent*, later to become *The New Mexico State Tribune*. This he funded by going to his readers and supporters with what proved a successful bond offering. As a slogan for the new periodical, he borrowed a phrase from Dante: "Give Light and the People Will Find Their Own Way." In his weekly column, Magee relentlessly lambasted Fall and a number of his cronies, especially the old guard Republican establishment in San Miguel County. One of his frequent targets, District Judge David J. Leahy, said he would rather deal with horse thieves than Magee. Leahy tried to send Magee to prison for a year on trumped-up charges. A pardon from the New Mexico governor, Democrat James F. Hinkle, kept him out of jail.

Before coming to Washington, Magee had gone up to Denver to see D. F. Stackelbeck at the *Denver Post*. The two had met earlier when Stackelbeck had been in New Mexico investigating the interior secretary. In fact, Magee had been one of Stackelbeck's prime sources. In Denver, Stackelbeck told Magee that he had learned about Sinclair's visit from the Three Rivers stationmaster. From the same source, he'd heard about the racehorses and cattle that Sinclair had subsequently sent to Fall's ranch. Most important, Stackelbeck told him about his bosses' successful efforts to blackmail Sinclair. On November 23, Magee wired Walsh from New Mexico after being served with a subpoena to appear before the committee:

> YOUR WIRE RECEIVED. SUBPOENA SERVED. ASSUME IT CARRIES MILEAGE. EXPECT TO ARRIVE WEDNESDAY NIGHT, SAW STACK-ELBECK IN DENVER MONDAY. SATISFIED LESSEE (SINCLAIR) MADE DEAL WITH DENVER SUPERIORS (BONFILS AND TAMMEN) TO REPRESS TESTIMONY. SUGGEST SUBPOENA FOR PROPRIETORS DENVER NEWSPAPER. LIKELY TO UNCOVER SCANDAL IN EFFORT TO BLOCK YOU.
>
> —CARL C. MAGEE

Magee spent much of his first day in Washington in conference with Walsh, explaining what he'd learned about the Teapot deal and

Fall's seeming sudden prosperity. The following morning, he told the committee under questioning from Walsh how he'd purchased the *Journal* from Fall and how Fall had told him he was flat broke, owed back taxes on the ranch, and needed money for improvements. At the time of his visit to Three Rivers, Magee stressed, Fall's ranch had been in a severely run-down condition.

At this point in the hearings, Walsh interrupted Magee to present tax records showing that Fall had paid no taxes on the Three Rivers ranch from 1912 to 1922. In June 1922, however, he'd paid all back taxes for the preceding ten years. Walsh then continued questioning Magee. The editor testified that in August 1922, he'd driven by Three Rivers while on a speaking tour. He didn't recognize the formerly dilapidated ranch because it had undergone so many improvements. The road leading from the Three Rivers railroad station to the ranch house was unimproved and in bad condition when he was first there. In August, it was being paved. Impressive new pillars flanked the ranch entrance. New cement cattle guards had been installed. In town, he talked to a number of locals who had recently been hired to work on the property by Fall, including an electrician who said he was doing a $40,000 electrical job on the ranch. Some of the other committee members, who had remained silent for much of the hearings, now began shifting uncomfortably in their seats, especially Smoot and Lenroot. Wasn't there bad blood between you and Fall? Smoot asked of the witness. "[Isn't] a great deal of this testimony of yours politics anyway?"

Magee responded, "Well, I didn't ask to come here, Senator, and I said what I said here under oath with reference to it." Politics or no, it was clear even to those members of the committee and the press that Albert Fall had some explaining to do. Smoot wired him that night, saying he needed to come up from New Mexico. The following morning, many of the nation's newspaper's carried banner headlines: FALL UNDER A SHADOW: "Suspicion of Graft Seen in Testimony," read the *Ogden Standard Examiner's* front page. *The Fresno Bee* ran a similar piece: SENATE BOARD PROBES FALL'S TAX PAYMENTS: EDITOR MAGEE TELLS OF TEAPOT DOME OIL LEASE. Now it was Fall's turn on the rack.

32

THE CRACK-UP

In November, Albert Fall was back at Three Rivers, enjoying a respite with his family before officially beginning his new job with Doheny on January 1, 1924. His posthearings meeting in Washington with the president had gone better than expected. Once Fall had assured Coolidge that the $10 million to Obregón was a legitimate loan to be repaid out of oil royalties accruing to Mexico—a transaction that wouldn't embarrass the administration—the president agreed to Doheny's request: Should Obregón default, the United States would exert diplomatic pressure. "Upon my report [to Doheny] of the interview with the President the loan was made," Fall's biographer quotes him as saying.

As for the committee hearings, Fall, like much of the Republican establishment, assumed that Walsh's investigation had run its course. Not even when Smoot informed him that Walsh had summoned the *Denver Post*'s star reporter D. F. Stackelbeck to Washington was Fall especially worried. Stackelbeck had been on the journalistic equivalent of a witch hunt. But Magee's testimony and Walsh's revelations about the tax payments on Three Rivers amounted to a far more serious matter. Still, despite Smoot's request that Fall come to Washington as soon as possible to counter Magee's testimony, Fall decided to stay put. For the past five months, he had been traveling extensively on behalf of Sinclair and Doheny. He was exhausted, in failing health, and getting along in years. On November 26, he'd celebrated his sixty-second birthday.

Rather than go to Washington himself, he decided to send his son-in-law Clarence C. Chase. En route, he wanted Chase to stop off in Cleveland to meet with Price McKinney, Fall's old friend and former business partner. In the past, the steel magnate had offered to loan Fall the money for the Harris purchase. Now Fall wrote McKinney asking him if he "would state that I had made the loan for the purchase . . . of the property bought in New Mexico." Meanwhile, he summoned Chase up to Three Rivers from El Paso, where his son-in-law worked as a customs agent, to brief him on the situation. The plan, as Fall laid it out, was to have Chase meet McKinney in Cleveland so the two of them could get their stories straight regarding the loan. From there Chase would proceed to Washington, tell the committee where the money had come from, and hopefully get Walsh off Fall's back once and for all. In the meantime, Fall wired Chase's boss, Treasury Secretary Andrew Mellon, with whom Fall had served in the cabinet, requesting a leave of absence for Chase "to leave for Washington immediately on business important to me personally. . . . He will call on you at Washington regarding matter."

This hastily devised scheme began to unravel almost immediately. Chase spent several days trying to contact McKinney, who was, he learned, away on business. When Chase finally got hold of McKinney, the industrialist said he was ill and at home recovering. Even so, he invited Chase to drop by the Italian Renaissance–style mansion he owned on Cleveland's East Boulevard. When Chase broached the subject of the loan, McKinney had his answer ready. Of course, he'd seen the papers and was well aware of the downside of having his name linked with Fall at this juncture, old friend or no. "I have not made him a loan and I could not say that I have," McKinney told Chase.

The next afternoon, December 4, Chase wired Fall from Chicago, where he was staying at the Blackstone Hotel. CLEVELAND MATTER NOT SATISFACTORY. CAN POSSIBLY BE WORKED OUT. Now Fall had no choice but to come east. MRS. FALL AND SELF LEAVING THIS AFTERNOON TRAIN, he wired back the same day. By the time the Falls arrived in Chicago, Chase had checked out of the hotel. Gone where? To Washington? Back to New Mexico? Fall hadn't a clue. This was rapidly turning into a nightmare. Increasingly desperate, Fall made a second attempt to persuade McKinney, asking him in a cable to come to Washington and help him deal with the Magee matter: KINDLY ANSWER AND DO YOU KNOW WHEREABOUTS OF CHASE?

On the same day, December 5, he also cabled Smoot, assuring the Utah senator that he was having copies made of court records pertaining to the Harris sale and making other preparations to dispel the charges against him. He expected to leave Chicago the following day, Thursday. IF REACHING THERE FRIDAY MORNING WILL BE PREPARED TO FACE THE COMMITTEE FRIDAY AFTERNOON, he said. THE PUBLIC WILL HAVE ANY HEALTHY OR DISEASED CURIOSITY SATISFIED AND WE WILL SEE THE UTTER FRIVOLITY AND PARTISAN ATTACKS TO WHICH I HAVE BEEN EXPOSED BEFORE CONCLUSION OF THE HEARING.

The Falls never left for Washington. Instead, they departed for New York, summoned there by Ed Doheny.

AT THE TIME, Doheny was in Manhattan launching a new subsidiary, Pan American Western Co. The last thing he needed was the publicity that would ensue if Albert Fall told the committee who had loaned him the Harris ranch money. Such a revelation would jeopardize Doheny's ability to raise the $20 million he needed to fund this new venture through a stock offering that was being carried out by Blair & Co. Second, he was creating Pan American Western to incorporate all his California oil holdings under a single entity. At this point, his California holdings consisted largely of Naval Reserves No. 1 and No. 2, which were, of course, the subject of the hearings in Washington.

Which was why Doheny asked the Falls to come to New York instead of going to Washington. Almost as soon as they arrived, Doheny visited them at the Waldorf-Astoria, where the Falls always stayed in New York. Ill, obviously severely distraught, and drinking excessively, Fall rather resembled a road company King Lear. Doheny got right to the point. He wanted Fall to understand that if Tom Walsh asked him about the loan, he'd deny having made it. Doheny also had a helpful suggestion. Why not say that Ned McLean, the newspaper publisher, had loaned Fall the money? McLean was rich. He thought the world of Fall, was a little slow on the uptake, and was lacking in judgment. In short, he was the perfect patsy. Besides, at one point two years earlier,

McLean had actually been interested in buying a third of Three Rivers and raising racehorses there. He had a credible reason to give Fall money.

Increasingly desperate, Fall decided to follow Doheny's advice, arranging to met McLean in Atlantic City and once again delaying his arrival in Washington. To his increasingly anxious friends on the committee, he apologized profusely for the delay, explaining to Lenroot that he had been ill. His doctor in New York recommended several days of sea air. Thus, Atlantic City, where the Falls were staying at the Ritz-Carlton and where McLean had agreed to confer with Fall. The newspaper owner arrived on December 20 in his private railroad car, the *Enquirer*. Emma greeted him. Apparently thinking this was only a social call, she was reluctant to awaken Albert. He'd had a bad night, she explained.

McLean explained that the matter was important. He had only an hour, as he was on his way to his winter home in Palm Beach. To connect the *Enquirer* with the train going south, he had to get back to Washington. Fall appeared in a dark red smoking jacket, looking like death warmed over. "Ned, do you remember the transactions and negotiations we had in '21?" Fall asked, referring to a discussion he and McLean had regarding McLean possibly buying into Three Rivers. Ned remembered. "Would you mind saying that you loaned me that money in cash?" Fall continued. "Some of my political enemies are deviling me, and it would be of great assistance."

A loyal friend, McLean agreed. He said his good-byes to Albert and Emma and started for Florida, unaware at the time that Fall, as part of his strange, desperate odyssey, would soon follow.

THE FALLS FINALLY arrived in Washington a few days before Christmas, checking into the Wardman Park. Fall's health had worsened. Visitors, of which there were many, noticed that he was perspiring profusely and talked rather incoherently about going to Havana. This was most unsettling to Smoot and Lenroot, who stopped by on December 23 in the late afternoon. "Senator Smoot and I were taken to Mr. Fall's room and found him in a dressing gown and a nurse present," Lenroot later recalled. "When the nurse left, and after some conversation with Mr. Fall regarding his health, I stated to him that I had insisted on his coming to

Washington to explain certain transactions that had come before the committee and particularly with reference to where he had procured the money he had bought the Harris ranch."

After considerable cajoling and browbeating on the part of Smoot and Lenroot, Fall said he'd be willing to tell them in confidence the name of the man from whom he had procured the money. "I told him I didn't want the name in confidence, but I wanted him to tell the committee who had provided the money," Lenroot responded.

"Edward B. McLean," Fall said, blurting out the name just as Smoot and Lenroot were putting on their overcoats to leave. It was Ned McLean who had loaned him the ranch funds. He couldn't reveal McLean's name to the committee, however, not before wiring him in Palm Beach and getting his permission. He'd do that right away.

We have no record of Lenroot and Smoot's reaction to this revelation, but it likely was one of profound relief. By evoking McLean's name before the committee, Fall would totally undercut the case Walsh had been trying to build, magically expunge the taint of oil and graft from the hearings, and likely bring the investigation to an abrupt halt just as it was gathering dangerous momentum. One problem, though. Even if McLean gave his approval, Fall didn't want to testify. He was far too ill, he claimed. Likely, too, he realized that on this occasion, unlike his first appearance before the committee, he'd be under oath. Either way, he informed Lenroot and Smoot that he wasn't going to appear before the committee as scheduled on December 27.

There are two versions of what happened next. On the night after Christmas, Fall had five visitors: Smoot, Lenroot, Harry Sinclair, a Sinclair lawyer named G. T. Sanford, and Will Hays. A brief refresher on Hays. This was the jug-eared former RNC chairman who'd served as postmaster general under Harding. He'd resigned his post in March 1922 to head up the Motion Picture Producers and Distributors Association of America. At the time, Hollywood had been the scene of a number of scandals: the death of actress Virginia Rappe at an orgy hosted by Roscoe "Fatty" Arbuckle; the murder of bisexual director William Desmond Taylor; the drug-related death of matinee idol Wallace Reid. Concerned about the industry's image, the studios brought in Hays to clean up "sin city." He was now living in a penthouse apartment in Manhattan, drawing a princely salary of $150,000 per annum plus a big expense account. Life had been good to Will Hays, though he still looked like a weasel.

Though Hays was no longer RNC chairman, he'd met with Harry Sinclair in November and persuaded the oilman to chip in $260,000 to help get rid of that tiresome 1920 campaign deficit. Unfortunately for Hays, the RNC, and Sinclair, the oilman submitted the payment in Liberty bonds from the Continental Trading deal, but we'll get to that later. As to the matter at hand, Hays wanted to ensure that the committee believed Ned McLean had been Fall's moneyman for reasons that are likely self-evident. If McLean was the source, then no one could disparage the GOP or point an oil-smudged finger at Sinclair, who, you'll remember, was also a client of lawyer Hays.

According to Lenroot's later testimony, this little group embarked on a collaborative effort to draft a letter of explanation about Fall's finances. Said letter, Hays claimed, would suffice to end the hearings. Hays said later he had been assured of this by key members of the committee, two of whom were present in Fall's suite. Again, according to Lenroot, there was much discussion that night at the Wardman Park about what exactly the letter would say. Calls were made to Doheny in New York and McLean in Florida for their input. The latter agreed to give a deposition in Florida to verify that he was the source of the loan, but there was no way he was going to come to Washington to testify in person. Like Fall, he was sick. A sinus infection.

In the end, according to Lenroot, Fall himself, feverish and slightly delirious, possibly a little *borracho*, dictated the letter from his sickbed as Lenroot, Smoot, Sinclair, lawyer Sanford, and Hays looked on, offering words of encouragement and suggestions here and there. Mixing elements of righteous indignation and piety, Fall noted that "some evil-minded" persons had concluded that because Sinclair had visited Three Rivers shortly after Fall acquired the Harris place, Sinclair had supplied the funds. Not so. "It should be needless for me to say that in the purchase of the Harris ranch or any other purchase or expenditure I have never approached E. L. Doheny or anyone connected with him or any of his corporations, or Mr. H. F. Sinclair or anyone connected with him or any of his corporations, nor have I received from either of said parties one cent on account of any oil lease or upon any account whatsoever."

As for the Thoroughbred stallion and the other livestock Sinclair had given him after his visit to Three Rivers, Fall said that he insisted on repaying the oilman in full for the gift. "So long as I was in official position, I did not feel I could accept any gift of any kind," he concluded.

The second version of this story, as later recounted by Fall and Doheny, differs in one important respect. Fall did not dictate the letter. In fact it had been drawn up by Hays before he came to the hotel. Fall merely signed it—as ill as he was, did he know what he signed?—and Lenroot read it to Walsh and the other committee members the following morning, the day Fall had been scheduled to appear. In either case, by signing the letter, Fall set himself up—or more likely was set up—to take the fall for Teapot Dome.

And, yes, Albert Fall was the embodiment of the term *fall guy*.

33

THE PALM BEACH STORY

Even many of Walsh's strongest supporters assumed he would abandon the hearings after Lenroot read Albert Fall's letter to the committee. Ned McLean as the source of the loan? To those in Washington who knew the often eccentric McLean, knew of his close friendship with Fall and his extravagance with money, the story made perfect sense. Tom Walsh had been following the wrong trail. The hearings had been largely a waste of time and money. Time to close shop and get back to the day-to-day business of the Senate.

Walsh wasn't done, however. He wanted McLean to appear before the committee personally and was prepared to subpoena him. Lenroot responded that a mere request should be sufficient. Fine. Walsh said he'd request that McLean appear, telegraphing him on January 2, 1924, asking him to return to Washington right away. Walsh's insistence on continuing the hearings drew fire even from some of the Democrats on the committee and was seen by many as excessive. "Much of Washington thought him obsessed, a reformer become fanatic," Mark Sullivan said. "Throughout the country the oil investigation as a spectacle teetered toward the status of a comedy; in the newspapers there was a trace of jeering."

Walsh had learned something, though, about Ned McLean that made Fall's claims highly suspect, something about him personally that gave the lie to Fall's tale of McLean's wanting to buy a third interest in Three Rivers and raise racehorses. Not that Walsh, who didn't drink and rarely attended dinner parties of the kind frequented by the McLeans, traveled in the same circles or was privy to the secrets of the rich. But the woman Walsh had been seeing for several years, Mrs. Borden "Daisy" Harriman, was as plugged into Washington society and political gossip as anyone in the city.

One of the country's most prominent Democrats, Daisy Harriman was born Florence Jaffray Hurst on July 21, 1870, in New York. She grew up in the privileged, aristocratic world that her contemporary Edith Wharton portrayed. As was typical of young women of her class and time, the gracious, blue-eyed, athletic, five-foot-nine Daisy summered in Newport, made her debut at Delmonico's, went to finishing school, and at nineteen married Borden "Bordy" Harriman, a well-to-do cousin of the late W. Averell Harriman. Energetic, exceptionally bright, and a born political activist, Daisy eschewed the life of a New York society matron after marriage to campaign against child labor and promote women's rights. In 1903, as an alternative to exclusive all-male clubs in Manhattan such as the Union and the Century, Daisy cofounded the Colony Club, the first women's social club in New York. In 1906, she was appointed manager of the New York Reformatory for Women. Three years later, Daisy lent her financial support to the shirtwaist workers strike and later helped organize a strike meeting of the Women's Trade Union League at the Colony Club.

Although a lifelong Republican, she became a fervent Wilson supporter after attending the 1912 Democratic convention as a spectator, joined the Democratic Party, and formed the Women for Wilson organization (she also later cofounded the Woman's National Democratic Club in Washington). Early on in the Wilson administration, the Harrimans moved to Washington, where President Wilson appointed Daisy the only female member of the U.S. Commission on Industrial Relations. After her husband died the following year, she continued on with the commission until 1916. At the start of World War I, she organized the Red Cross Women's Motor Corps, at one point leading 350 uniformed women to a field hospital in France. "We had a wonderful

time," she later recalled, "and under the circumstances we did a beautiful job."

Daisy first met Tom Walsh and likely his wife, Elinor, who was also
active in getting women to vote for Wilson, during Wilson's 1912 campaign. After both Harriman and Walsh lost their spouses within a year
of each other, the Montanan and the New York socialite began seeing
each other. By the 1920 Democratic convention in San Francisco,
Walsh and Harriman, both strong backers of William McAdoo for the
presidential nomination, were more than casual acquaintances. "Senator
Walsh asks me to take a walk and we stroll about outside for an hour. It
is a relief to get into the fresh air for a little and not to hear that contin-
ual repetition of 'Alabama, Arizona, Arkansas,' etc. I shall dream of that
roll call for weeks," she noted in her July 3, 1920, journal entry. That
night, Walsh took her to the Fairmont for drinks. "I began asking him
about Vice-Presidents, he said, 'Let's get McAdoo nominated first,' "
Daisy later recalled.

The dynamic Harriman—"the heroine of the Democratic party," as
The Washington Post once called her—and Walsh, the intellectual lion of
Washington, seemed a well-matched couple, despite their vastly different social backgrounds. Certainly they were on the same page politically. By 1923, they were seen in each other's company constantly in
Washington. Walsh was a regular at her spirited Sunday night dinner
parties, to which Daisy would ask both Republican and Democratic
leaders and encourage them to debate the issues of the day.

The relationship was not without its hitches, however, one of them
being Walsh's disproportionately large and ungainly Yosemite Sam
mustache, a holdover from his days as a frontier lawyer. Daisy insisted
that Walsh trim it. The story circulating in Washington at the time was
that he did so on the condition that she marry him. The belief generally
was that Walsh was more smitten with Harriman than she with him, although H. L. Mencken had a different take on the relationship. He recounted a train trip to New York in which he encountered Daisy going
from car to car searching for Walsh and later came upon Walsh hiding
out in the caboose. Daisy was initially among the few who encouraged
Walsh to continue to pursue the investigation, often inviting him over
to the Woman's National Democratic Club, where she was the organization's first president. There Walsh discussed Teapot before Daisy and

club members, a number of whom, including Eleanor Roosevelt, began attending the Teapot hearings. Though Walsh never identified his source, it was likely Daisy who provided him with a key piece of information about Ned McLean that led Walsh to believe Fall was lying about the loan's source. At the time, Daisy and the Republican Evalyn McLean were the two reigning social hostesses of Washington, vying to attract the most interesting and influential guests to their table. Each knew everything about the other, down to what they had served the previous night at dinner and what gossip was exchanged over brandy and cigars. Each knew the other's secrets, one of which related directly to the supposed McLean loan. At the time Fall claimed McLean gave him the ranch money, the high-living newspaper publisher was vastly overextended financially. Ned McLean didn't have $100,000 to loan Albert Fall or anyone else. He was broke.

Two days after Fall had failed to testify before the committee, asserting he was too ill to make an appearance, he and Emma took off for Palm Beach, checking into the Breakers Hotel, where the McLeans had a cottage. He registered under an assumed name, Howard Pardee. Mind you, this was one of the most powerful and recognizable political figures in the United States—a man whose picture had appeared repeatedly on the front pages of the nation's newspapers—using an alias. Ned had asked the Falls down the previous day. WHY DON'T YOU COME DOWN FOR A REST, he wired. THE WEATHER IS PERFECTLY WONDERFUL. EVALYN JOINS ME IN LOVE TO YOU BOTH. Evalyn McLean, who hadn't seen Albert Fall in almost a year, was shocked at his appearance. "For the first time in my life, I saw a man crumble right before my eyes," she later wrote.

In Washington, Walsh continued to press for McLean's appearance despite the publisher's assertions that he was too ill to travel north. As a compromise, McLean, through his lawyer, Wilson's former attorney general A. Mitchell Palmer, agreed to testify in writing from Florida to having made the loan. Walsh said that wouldn't do. He wanted McLean to show up in person, noting that a sinus infection, McLean's alleged malady, wasn't exactly a life-threatening illness. A simple operation could resolve the problem. In fact, Walsh said he'd undergone the same procedure a few weeks earlier "without any disastrous results."

The majority of the committee differed with Walsh, voting to let McLean remain ensconced in Palm Beach and answer Walsh's queries from there. At this point, Walsh shared his information with Lenroot that McLean, as Lenroot would later note, "did not have anything like that amount [$100,000] on deposit in the banks in Washington." Lenroot, who had just taken over from Smoot as committee chairman, then suggested that Walsh go to Florida on his own to take McLean's deposition there.

With the hearings seemingly taking on a new life, a number of powerful people in Washington and Palm Beach were growing increasingly nervous. Walsh was relentless. Nothing seemed to stop him. Coolidge, who hadn't commented on the hearings in the press in accordance with Taft's advice, abruptly decided that his secretary, former Virginia congressman C. Bascom Slemp, needed a vacation and sent him—where else?—to Palm Beach. There, every night of his two-week stay Slemp had dinner with Fall and McLean.

In Palm Beach, McLean had begun to realize that he had painted himself into a nasty little corner on behalf of Albert Fall. As the owner of the *Post* and *Cincinnati Enquirer*, however, he still wielded enormous power and influence despite his declining fortune. McLean enlisted a number of his employees at the *Post*, including its editor, Ira E. Bennett, and its hard-nosed police reporter, John Major, to keep him apprised of what was going on in the hearings and moonlight as lobbyists on his behalf if needed. Between them, they worked to persuade as many Democratic senators as possible to try to get Walsh to back off making McLean testify.

To this task force, McLean added several Department of Justice informants, including an agent, Mrs. W. O. "Jesse" Duckstein, who was married to McLean's longtime confidential private secretary, W. O. Duckstein. They too were asked to tip off McLean regarding developments with the investigation that might adversely affect the publisher. This little group worked in tandem with McLean's high-powered legal team, headed up by Mitchell Palmer, to keep McLean from having to face the committee—and, worse, possibly go to jail.

McLean also had been enlisted by Harry Daugherty to serve as a

$1-a-year G-man. This entitled him to certain resources, including various Bureau of Investigation codebooks. On learning that Walsh wanted him to testify, McLean had a private wire set up between his Palm Beach cottage and the *Post* headquarters in Washington so that he could send and receive sensitive information in the privacy of his own living room. To assist with this project, John Major enlisted the help of the White House. TO EXPEDITE MATTERS AND THE ASSURANCE OF GETTING YOUR MESSAGES ABSOLUTELY CORRECT, HAVE ARRANGED WITH SMITHERS AT THE WHITE HOUSE TO HAVE OUR END OF THE PRIVATE WIRE OPENED AT 6 O'CLOCK TONIGHT, the resourceful Major cabled McLean on January 3. With E. W. Smithers, the White House's telegraph operator, receiving and decoding the incoming messages from Palm Beach, McLean and Bascom Slemp could keep Coolidge in the loop regarding the goings-on in Palm Beach relating to the investigation and the increasingly erratic behavior of Albert Fall, aka Howard Pardee.

As far as McLean was concerned, being a G-man was a lot more exciting than publishing a couple of stodgy newspapers. One of the best things about it was making up names for the players in the Teapot drama. For himself, McLean chose the name "the Big Bear" and later "the Chieftain." John Major, the police reporter, was "the Little Bear." At first, Fall was dubbed "the Man at the Wardman Park," but that was too transparent, since Fall was directly identified with the hotel where he had lived for so many years. McLean changed the name to "Apple." Aptly enough, Walsh, whom the jittery McLean viewed as stalking him, was dubbed "Jaguar." On and on it went, until just about everyone McLean knew in Washington had been given a code name, sometimes two or three depending on which codebook he was using. This all became quite confusing, especially since McLean was sending and receiving as many as three hundred cables a day and sometimes confused the code names.

On January 9, McLean learned that "Jaguar" was leaving for Palm Beach to question him. McLean received the following cable from one of his secretaries at the *Post:*

ZEV HOCUSING IMAGERY COMMENSAL ABAD HOSIER LECTIONARY, CLOT PRATTLERN LAMB JAGUAR ROVED TIMEPIECE NUDITY, HOCUSING LECTIONARY CHONCILLA PETERNET BE-

DRAGGLED RIP RALO OVERSHADE QUAKE . . . JAGUAR BAPTISCAL
FITFUL HUFF, WAXWORK PAINLESS CASCADE WIPPEN, WOB

Decoded, this read, ZEVELY THINKS TREND OF INVESTIGATION FA-
VORABLE TO YOU. NOT IMPRESSED WITH WALSH AS CROSS-EXAMINER.
THINKS YOU NEED HAVE LITTLE APPREHENSION ABOUT FORTHCOMING
INTERROGATION . . . WALSH LEAVES SEABOARD TONIGHT. DUE FRIDAY
MORNING.

Walsh wanted to interview McLean on the morning he arrived, but
McLean asked that the questioning be delayed until after lunch. In the
meantime, he and several lawyers conferred with Fall, who was coming
completely unglued, vacillating between saying he was going to testify
and get the matter over with and then harrumphing that Walsh had no
right to inquire into his personal business. Just before McLean was to
meet with Walsh, Fall warned Doheny of what was transpiring in a
telegram: WALSH AUTHORIZED TO TAKE TESTIMONY . . . WILL EXAMINE
MCLEAN AND PROBABLY MYSELF. FACTS WILL BE DEVELOPED, POSSIBLY
NAMES NOT DISCLOSED.

On the afternoon of January 10, Walsh interviewed a visibly nervous McLean at his cottage, "Ocean Front," getting directly to the
point. "Mr. McLean, did you loan $100,000 to Mr. Fall?" Walsh asked.

McLean: "I did, yes, sir, in checks."

Walsh: "Whose checks?"

McLean: "My own checks."

Walsh: "Have you got the checks?"

McLean: "I don't think so—I am not positive."

Walsh: "Were they returned? What became of them?"

McLean: "Senator Fall returned them to me."

Walsh: "When?"

McLean: "In the last part of December 1921, sir—the last week—I
am not positive as to day."

Walsh: "So that so far as you are concerned you did not give him
any cash?"

McLean: "Cash? No sir."

Returned checks, no cash, added up to no loan, at least not from
McLean. Walsh, who was expecting further subterfuge, was "dumbfounded" as much by the confession as by the ease at which it was obtained. After the deposition, he summarized his interview with

McLean in a letter to Fall, asking if Fall wanted to respond in person or in a written statement. Contacting Fall, however, was another matter. The hotel manager refused to deliver the letter. In recent months, Walsh had been stonewalled by oil barons, batteries of high-priced attorneys, and his own colleagues in the Senate. Now, the manager of the Breakers, as resolute as a Swiss guard at the Vatican, was obstructing the investigation.

"Senator Fall is not registered here," the manager said.

"I understand he is not registered here," Walsh responded, "but I know as well that he is in the hotel, and I very respectfully ask you to hand the letter to him."

"Well, I do not want to hand him the letter," the manager said.

At this, Walsh threatened to bring in the sheriff to search the hotel room by room, thereby aggravating the hotel's high-society guests. Only mildly intimidated, the manager proposed a compromise: He would give the letter to Ned McLean and let him deliver it to Fall.

According to one account of what happened next, McLean delivered Walsh's letter to Fall's suite, where he found him composing a second telegram to Doheny, telling the Californian that he was going to name him as the source of the $100,000. "I'll be damned," McLean said on learning for the first time that Doheny had been Fall's backer.

Fall, it seemed, really was finally ready to at least talk with Walsh, but at 5:22 that evening he grasped at one last straw, wiring Lenroot to ask if the committee chair "had given to Walsh authority to subpoena me as a witness?"

Two hours later, Lenroot wired back saying that there was "no such intention. Walsh stated he might wish to examine McLean's secretary or other employees who might be there." This was untrue. The committee had authorized Walsh to act as a one-man subcommittee to depose both McLean and Fall, but for whatever reason, Lenroot chose to be less than candid on this matter, thereby providing Fall with the out he needed. Instead of meeting Walsh the next day as he'd agreed, he and Emma again skipped town, this time bound for New Orleans. When reporters later asked Fall why he'd ducked Walsh, he responded that Walsh only had the authority to question McLean and his secretary. He also wanted it "thoroughly understood that the source from which I obtained the money . . . was in no way connected with Mr.

Sinclair or in any way involved in any concession regarding the Teapot Dome."

Fall, of course, was indulging in a little semantic hairsplitting. The loan in fact had nothing to do with Teapot or Sinclair. It had come from Doheny. It was altogether a different "loan" Fall had received from Sinclair relating to the Teapot concession.

34

TRUE CONFESSIONS

With McLean having been ruled out, Tom Walsh was almost certain that Harry Sinclair had been the source of the Harris loan, plus another $130,000 or so that had gone toward ranch improvements and back taxes. Then, on January 20, a Sunday, Assistant Navy Secretary Theodore Roosevelt contacted Walsh with a request. Roosevelt's younger brother Archie had some important information to relate to the committee about his employer, Harry Sinclair, Ted said. Ted wanted to bring Archie down to Washington to testify as soon as possible. Walsh said he'd make time for the younger Roosevelt the following day.

On Monday morning, Walsh began the committee meeting by reading a report of his interview with McLean and his unsuccessful attempt to get a response from the former interior secretary. Fall had claimed he was far too ill to endure a deposition. This prompted Senator T. H. Caraway, a Democrat from Arkansas, to note on the Senate floor, "I have known more robust constitutions to be ruined by criminal courts than all the plagues put together."

Fall was now in New Orleans, staying at the Hotel Roosevelt, Walsh explained to the committee. He was again talking about leaving the country, maybe going to Havana. Walsh and Lenroot had asked

Louisiana governor John M. Parker to have state law officers keep Fall under surveillance. In addition, Department of Justice agents were keeping tabs on Fall with orders not to permit him to leave the country "under any conditions."

With Ned McLean's admission that the loan story was bogus, the hearings were suddenly the hottest ticket in Washington. Indeed, room 210 in the Senate Office Building was packed with reporters and on-lookers, among them a large contingent of the Roosevelt clan who had gathered to offer Archie—"Archikins," as he had been called as a child—moral support. Among them were brother Ted; Archie's wife, Grace; and his sister, Alice, with her husband, Congressman Nicholas Longworth, Harding's old golfing chum. Archie had been a war hero, receiving the Croix de Guerre from the French government after being wounded so severely that he had been discharged from the army with full disability as a captain. He had also served as vice president of one of Harry Sinclair's many subsidiaries, Union Petroleum, but had resigned abruptly over the weekend. With his wife and brother, he had taken the early-morning train down Monday from New York to testify.

To observers, it was evident as Archie took the witness stand that he had never fully recovered from his wounds. He walked with a cane and seemed frail, nervous, and slightly disoriented. When Walsh asked him when he had begun working for Sinclair, he responded, "In August—let's see, when was the war?"

It began in 1917, Senator Smoot volunteered.

Roosevelt: " '18, '19. I think it was August 1, 1919, I went with the Sinclair company."

As he continued to testify, young Roosevelt—he was not yet thirty—grew more confident, explaining that the previous day he'd sub-mitted his resignation because he felt he could no longer give his loyalty to his employer for reasons he enumerated to the committee. "Firstly, [because of] the amazing testimony that has been turned up by your committee. Secondly, I learned some things in the office that . . . corrob-orated my suspicions. Thirdly, I noticed that two of the people most concerned with the naval leases had left the United States in a great hurry."

According to Roosevelt, Monday last he had just finished reading about Walsh's interview with Ned McLean in the newspaper when Harry Sinclair summoned him abruptly up to his office. Sinclair "asked me to get him a ticket on the Steamship *Paris*," Roosevelt recalled. It was the next boat departing New York for Europe. Sinclair had asked Roosevelt to make the reservation because he knew that Archie and Ted's brother Kermit was associated with the steamship line. He also had additional requests. "Mr. Sinclair asked that his name was not put on the passenger list; nor was I to tell anyone in the office [he was leaving]," Roosevelt said, adding that he was connected with all Sinclair's foreign work. As far as he knew, "there was absolutely no reason which would require the immediate presence of Mr. Harry Sinclair in Europe at the present time."

One more thing: Roosevelt mentioned that he was friendly with G. D. Wahlberg, Sinclair's private secretary. Soon after Sinclair sailed for Europe, Wahlberg came to see Roosevelt in his office. According to Roosevelt: "He shut the door and he said to me first he had some advice. He said that he wished I would resign from the company. I had a name and a reputation that I should guard very zealously. As a friend, Mr. Wahlberg said he was extremely unhappy with Mr. Sinclair."

Roosevelt asked Wahlberg if Sinclair had bribed Fall. Wahlberg hesitated momentarily before responding "that somebody might have lent Mr. Fall some money." Now, with his boss out of the country, Wahlberg was worried that he might be asked to explain certain financial transactions, including a $68,000 payment Sinclair had made to Fall's ranch foreman, he told Roosevelt. As to why Sinclair had left the country, Wahlberg said: "Well, it must be . . . on account of the findings of Senator Walsh's trip down at Palm Beach."

At the request of Archie, Wahlberg had also come down from New York to testify. As soon as Roosevelt stepped down, Walsh called Wahlberg to the stand and asked him about his relationship with Sinclair. Wahlberg said he had been Sinclair's private secretary since 1916, but he intended to forward his resignation at the end of the day. Before he did so, he wanted to clarify one thing Roosevelt had said, however. Roosevelt had quoted him as saying Sinclair had given Fall's ranch manager $68,000. That should have been "six or eight *cows*," Wahlberg explained.

Six or eight cows. This provided a moment or two of comic relief among the reporters. Walsh, however, didn't miss a beat. "What induces you to resign?" he asked. Wahlberg said that after Roosevelt's testimony and his own appearance before the committee, it was unlikely he could continue working for Sinclair. Besides, he was extremely unhappy and overworked.

When had his state of unhappiness begun? Walsh asked.

"It has gone on for two or three years," Wahlberg said. When Walsh and Smoot pressed him as to why he was resigning so abruptly after all this time, Wahlberg would say only that he anticipated Sinclair would be angry he had testified against him. Wahlberg went on to state that before sailing for Europe, Sinclair had ordered all his financial ledgers, journals, cash, and checkbooks removed from his office. Sinclair attorney G. T. Sanford had come to collect them. Further, Sinclair had loaned Bill Zevely $25,000 worth of Liberty bonds without requiring a receipt. His boss had also turned over additional Liberty bonds to a man Wahlberg didn't know named Hays. "There were suspicions that these loans had some relationship to the matters now under investigation," Wahlberg said. This was the first time Liberty bonds had been mentioned in the course of the investigation, the first time Will Hays's name had come up, although no one on the committee or in the press immediately made the connection to the former RNC chairman, perhaps because the newspapers had spelled the name Hayes.

Once Wahlberg stepped down, Archie Roosevelt again took the stand and stressed that he could not possibly have misunderstood Wahlberg on the matter of the $68,000. In fact, Wahlberg had repeated the allegation in a telephone conversation that very morning with Archie, he said. Ted had been listening in and backed up his brother's assertion.

For Walsh, it had been a productive day. The committee was closing in on Harry Sinclair, or so the Montana senator believed until he reached his office late that afternoon. There, Walsh's assistant handed him a telegram from the St. Charles Hotel in New Orleans, signed by a well-known California lawyer named Gavin McNab. McNab said he'd been trying urgently to reach Walsh by telephone. He asked Walsh to postpone the hearings until he and his client reached Washington and could give the committee some "important facts" regarding the Fall loan. His client was Ed Doheny.

IN NEW ORLEANS, Fall's health seemed to have improved. He appeared on several occasions in the lobby of the Roosevelt Hotel, where he and

Emma were staying, and willingly answered questions from the press despite Emma's assertions that her husband was too ill to talk to reporters. "You can say emphatically that Harry Sinclair has never loaned or given me a penny," he stated.

Tired of running and concerned now about Emma's health—the last few months had taken a terrible toll on her—Fall decided finally to confront the inevitable, knowing full well what awaited him. "I knew that if I disclosed that Doheny had loaned me the money, an avalanche of political abuse would be loosed against the Republican administrations, against Doheny and against me," he later said. "I knew that under these conditions my reputation would be defamed and that I would be unable to adequately meet in the public press the charges against me." Not that he had much choice in the matter. On one of his ambles through the Roosevelt lobby, he was served with a subpoena by a U.S. deputy marshal.

On arriving in New Orleans, Fall asked both Sinclair and Doheny to meet with him there. Bill Zevely, who Archie Roosevelt mistakenly thought had also left the country with Sinclair, arrived in Sinclair's stead and was also served with a subpoena. This was on January 21, the same day Roosevelt and Wahlberg had testified. The following morning, Zevely and Fall conferred in Fall's suite. They decided to account for the $25,000 in Liberty bonds Wahlberg had mentioned to the committee by saying it was a loan to Fall from Sinclair by way of Zevely. They would also concede that Fall had received $10,000 as an advance against expenses for the Russian trip. As for the additional $233,000 Sinclair had given Fall in Liberty bonds and $36,000 in cash, there was to be no mention.

Doheny arrived in town soon after, aboard his private railroad car, the *Empire*. With him was wife Estelle, much put out that her husband had been dragged into this mess by his old "pard" Albert Fall; Fall's former law partner, W. A. Hawkins, whom Doheny had picked up en route; and the aforementioned Gavin McNab. A burly Scot who towered over Doheny, McNab—he pronounced his name "Gahvin Mucknob," with a thick Scottish burr—boasted a client list that included Doheny, Mary Pickford, Charlie Chaplin, and Roscoe "Fatty" Arbuckle. It had been McNab who had successfully defended Arbuckle in the sensational Virginia Rappe murder case—and, ironically, Will Hays who soon after banned Arbuckle from the movie industry in his first act as supreme film czar. McNab, Mark Sullivan said, "carried a suggestion of force and charm that made him one of the great lawyers of his generation."

Now Doheny was bringing McNab to New Orleans and then Washington to deal with the problematic Albert Fall and the committee. On Doheny's arrival at the Roosevelt, Fall insisted that Doheny wire Coolidge and ask the president to cancel all the naval leases. This request McNab promptly nixed, though as an alternative he suggested, on behalf of his client, of course, that Coolidge establish a committee to study the lease.

Fall also reiterated his request that Doheny tell the committee about the loan. To this Doheny agreed, reluctantly. There was a slight problem, however. Doheny had ripped off Fall's signature from the IOU that Fall had given to Ned Doheny when he received the $100,000. McNab, a longtime Hollywood studio "fixer," had Fall make out a new, postdated IOU with special ink and paper after assuring him that no expert would be able to tell the difference. Though Fall, according to his biographer, considered this "a damn fool idea," he reluctantly complied.

Business concluded, Fall and the others returned to Washington, the Dohenys and McNab in the *Empire*, and Fall and Zevely, who had remained in New Orleans but hadn't been included in Fall's meeting with Doheny, following in a later train. Fall had wanted to travel with Doheny in the private car, but the media-savvy McNab pointed out that for his client to arrive together with Fall, already a pariah in Washington, was ill advised.

Despite having agreed to testify about the loan, Doheny was still looking for wiggle room. Like Fall, he realized that his admission would have far-reaching consequences. He, Estelle, and Ned, whom he had enlisted as his bagman, would all be tarnished with negative publicity. In December, Doheny had tried to compromise Walsh and his investigation by offering the Montana senator and his brother John a piece of a lucrative oil deal. Likely unaware he was skirting a trap that could later damage his career and reputation, Walsh had turned him down politely. "The business of a corporation such as you would organize . . . would almost of necessity acquire leases from the government and while I am in the official position I hold, it seems to me unwise . . . to engage in any business dependent in any appreciable degree on government favor. This may be squeamish on my part, but I prefer to be thought oversensitive than to be under suspicion of having utilized the position to which my people have elevated me for my own profit." Now, as Doheny was heading back to Washington, he and McNab cabled Walsh urging him to drop the probe. Walsh didn't bother to respond. The oilman and McNab also made an eleventh-hour effort to get another of the oilman's attorneys and currently the leading Democratic presidential candidate, William McAdoo, to pressure Walsh to halt the investigation. Like Walsh, McAdoo refused. As a result, by the time he finally reached Washington, Doheny was reconciled to appearing once more before Walsh and the Teapot panel. And this time, he had no choice but to tell the truth.

By the time Doheny reached Washington on January 23, Walsh was aware that Albert Fall had received money from both recipients of the naval leases. He arranged for Doheny to appear before the committee at 3:00 p.m. on January 24. By then, the big committee room as well as the corridors outside were jammed with reporters, onlookers, and almost the entire U.S. Senate, whose members had deserted the Senate chambers to witness Doheny's testimony. Among them was the old lion La Follette, who sat, arms crossed, just behind Doheny. Walsh began. "I asked the committee to meet this afternoon because I was informed that Mr. Doheny desired to come before the committee to make a statement," he said. "We would like to have him now."

Doheny began by reading a prepared statement. He then responded to the committee's questions. Indeed, he had made the $100,000 loan. As proof there was no direct connection between the payment to Fall and the naval leases, he emphasized that the loan had been made on November 30, 1921, more than a year before he had been awarded the California fields. As before, he insisted that his interest in the leases was strictly patriotic, while conceding that he stood to make upward of $100 million from the Elk Hills and Buena Vista fields.

Doheny explained that in claiming the loan had come from another source, his old "pard" Fall had "been making an effort to keep my name out of the discussion for the reason that a full statement might not be understood." Much against his wishes, of course. He had, he asserted, urged Fall to disclose the full facts about the transaction all along.

Doheny hadn't mentioned the loan during his first appearance because "no such statement was pertinent in answer to any of the committee's questions." Besides, the loan was strictly a personal matter, drawn from Doheny's own funds, made to a friend he had known for thirty years. In what one reporter called "homely" terms, Doheny described the adventures he'd shared with Fall in the mining camps, the bonding they'd experienced enduring hardships and ever-present "danger from Indians." Toward Fall he'd felt "deep sympathy" because of the ex–interior secretary's many business adversities and family tribulations. "Mr. Fall had invested his savings . . . in his home ranch in New Mexico, which I understand was all that was left to him after the failure of mining investments in Mexico and nine years of public service in Washington, during which he could not properly attend to the management of his ranch," he said. "His troubles had been increased in 1918 by the death of his daughter and son, who up to then had taken his place in the management of the ranch."

Subsequently, Doheny continued, Fall had become increasingly set on acquiring a neighborhood property controlling the water that flowed through his home ranch. It "was a hope of his amounting to an obsession. His failure to raise the necessary funds . . . had made him feel like he was a victim of untoward fate. Fall's heart seemed set on that business enterprise, and I told him that if he wanted it I would loan him the money to purchase it."

Walsh wanted to know how the negotiations for the loan had been carried out, how he'd transmitted the money.

"In cash," Doheny said.

"How did you transport the cash?"

Doheny: "In a satchel."

Walsh: "Who acted as your messenger in that matter?"

"My son," Doheny responded.

Walsh: "You are a man of large affairs and of great business transactions, but . . . was it not an extraordinary way of transmitting money?"

Doheny shrugged off the question, explaining that the sum was "a mere bagatelle" to a man of his great wealth. "Certainly a loan of $25 or $50 from one individual to another would not be considered at all extraordinary, and a loan of $100,000 from me to Mr. Fall is no more extraordinary."

Walsh said he could appreciate Doheny's perspective but noted that "from Fall's side it was quite a loan."

"It was indeed," responded Doheny. "There is no question about that.... And I am perfectly willing to admit that it probably caused him to favor me, but under the circumstances he did not have a chance to favor me. He did not carry on these negotiations ... because the negotiations were carried on by men not under his control." This assertion elevated a few eyebrows. If Fall and his subordinates in the Department of the Interior hadn't doled out the leases, who had? Doheny insisted the whole matter had been handled and approved by bumbling old Ed Denby and the Navy Department.

At the outset of Doheny's testimony, Walsh had noticed that the Californian and Smoot were passing notes like schoolboys in the back of the classroom. When Walsh asked about the contents, Doheny reached into his pocket and pulled out what remained of a badly shredded piece of paper. Taunting Walsh, he said with a smile, "I will have to tell you what was on it unless you are very painstaking in reading."

Smoot explained that the note was regarding some oil fields in California that he had asked Doheny to check out on behalf of a friend. Reed Smoot wanted the target of the Teapot investigation to check out *oil fields in California*? Walsh was speechless at this revelation, but another committee member, Clarence Dill of Washington, asked, "Was this on the naval reserve?"

At this, Smoot puffed up in anger, countering that he had never handled an inch of public ground in his life and never would. To Walsh, the incident was yet another indication of Smoot's hostility toward the investigation—and Doheny's seemingly cavalier attitude toward the proceedings.

Asked by Lenroot whether he thought there was any impropriety in loaning "money to an officer of the government with whom you had very large business transactions," Doheny responded: "No, sir, I did not.... I do not lend except to those I'm associated with.... And I lend money in quantities that would surprise some of you gentlemen here."

Aware that in the past Doheny had employed several high-level Interior Department officials, including Fall's predecessor, Franklin K. Lane, who recently had died, Walsh asked if Doheny had any men who had served in the Department of the Interior under Fall in his employ. At this Doheny drew a blank. "I don't believe we have," he responded. "I think I have something like fifteen thousand employees, and I do not know them all."

The cross-examination lasted for two more days, with Doheny continuing to present himself as the folksy, if fabulously rich, old-timer with a heart of gold. "There is nothing extraordinary about me," he said at one point. "I am just an ordinary, old-time, impulsive, irresponsible, improvident sort of prospector."

In the end, his biographer noted, committee members began to view Doheny as "a slippery witness." In view of some of his dubious assertions—Fall's total lack of involvement with the leases, for one—and Lenroot's reminder that the Californian "had greatly misled" the committee during his earlier appearance, some also questioned his integrity. Walsh, who continued to "entertain a warm regard" for his friend, didn't go that far, but he regretted "that Doheny had permitted himself to become involved in so shady a transaction," he later said.

Later, after Doheny had been indicted, Walsh wrote to a friend, "One gathers from the [newspaper reports] that the case hinges on whether the $100,000 paid to Fall was received by him as a bribe or loan. To my mind it is of no consequence which view is taken. I venture to say that even if it were a loan, a contract made under such circumstances would, if justice prevailed, be adjudged void as against public policy."

35

DAMAGE CONTROL

On Sunday, January 27, the president and Grace Coolidge attended the morning services at Washington's First Congregational Church. With them were several friends, including the William M. Butlers. Butler was a conservative Boston textile manufacturer who served as Coolidge's campaign manager and chairman of the RNC. He and his wife were guests at the White House for the weekend. Theirs wasn't a social visit, however. After a week of explosive testimony before the Walsh committee, Teapot boiled over, producing the biggest political scandal the nation had seen since Grant's second term. Butler and many of the other party politicos wanted the lid put back on pronto.

As a United Press reporter noted in an article that appeared on the front page of newspapers around the country on January 24, "The Teapot Dome scandal, which for a long time was 'just' another senate investigation . . . has become almost overnight a throbbing drama of politics, high finance and intrigue." Even *The New York Times*, which, Walsh complained, had shown only nominal interest in Teapot since the investigation started, began devoting banner, front-page headlines to the hearings. The Sunday, January 27, edition carried a full two-page story headlined TEAPOT DOME CASTS A BROAD SHADOW, with photos of Sinclair and Doheny flanking Fall like bookends.

Of course, with the elections now ten months away, the Democrats eagerly seized upon the scandal as a means of striking out at the GOP. Democratic National Committee chairman Cordell Hull called Teapot "the greatest political scandal of this or any other generation" and asserted that the case was a product of the "Ruthless Reactionaries" in the administration. Even some Republicans chimed in. Congressman Hamilton Fish III from New York labeled Teapot "the greatest conspiracy to defraud the government that had ever been conceived in this country." Doheny, Sinclair, and Fall should proceed immediately to prison, Fish insisted.

Meeting in Cleveland over the weekend of January 26–27, Democratic women from seven midwestern states voted to make the scandal their rallying cry in getting out voters. Meanwhile, prospective presidential candidates such as California senator Hiram Johnson were already seeking to get maximum mileage from the investigation. "The Teapot Dome scandal has made Calvin Coolidge an impossibility as a Republican candidate," said George Henry Payne, Johnson's campaign manager.

Under intense fire, worried Republicans needed to exert damage control as quickly as possible. Not only was Teapot potentially a major campaign liability, but it had stalled the president's political agenda. Everything from Secretary of the Treasury Mellon's tax reduction package to the administration's efforts to aid farmers in the drought-ridden Northwest was on hold as Senate and House got caught up in the Teapot debate.

President Coolidge and William Butler had their own reasons for wanting Teapot to go away. In November, in preparation for the upcoming 1924 elections, the RNC had decided to clear off its remaining debt from the 1920 election. To accomplish this, our old friend Will Hays, the former RNC chairman—and the Hays that G. D. Wahlberg had recently mentioned in his testimony—had gone once again to Harry Sinclair. In response, Sinclair had given two contributions, one for $75,000 and another for $175,000, both in Liberty bonds from the Continental Trading deal. For Hays, this presented a problem since the bonds had traceable serial numbers, meaning they could lead back to Sinclair—not a good idea given Sinclair's prominence in the investigation.

The resourceful Hays, however, decided to have a number of wealthy Republicans "launder" the bonds. He'd give $25,000 or $50,000 in bonds to one of the party's big backers, who in turn would provide Hays and the RNC with a check for the same amount. Thereafter, the bonds, if traced through the serial numbers, would lead to some rich Republican, not the RNC. The punch line of this little story is that the new RNC chairman was William M. Butler, the president's campaign manager. Butler was one of those asked to launder $25,000 in Liberty bonds—bonds that were the product of a crooked oil deal, no less—for brother Hays in exchange for a $25,000 check.

Of course, Walsh and the Democrats would have a field day if this came out. As for "Silent Cal," since taking office, the president had met in secret several times with two of the investigation's main targets, Fall and Doheny, Fall most recently right after his initial appearance before the committee and Doheny only three weeks before the Californian testified a second time. Granted, the meetings had to do with Mexico and Doheny's loan to Obregón, not Teapot. In December 1923, Adolfo de la Huerta, a minister of Obregón's cabinet, led a counterrevolution against the Obregón government. Not only was Doheny's $10 million loan to Obregón at risk as a result, but the Bucareli Agreement, under which Obregón promised not to expropriate American oil holdings in Mexico in exchange for U.S. recognition of his government, was in jeopardy. Though there's no proof that the two events were directly linked, the Coolidge administration agreed to sell $1.28 million worth of armaments, including 11 airplanes, 24 machine guns, and 250 demolition bombs—largely on credit—to Obregón only a few days after the president met with Doheny in Washington.

During the hearings, Walsh learned about Coolidge's confab with Doheny, which the Californian described as purely social, but he knew nothing about the $10 million loan to Obregón, or Fall's role in acting as a middleman between the president and Doheny. Like the Sinclair-Hays-Butler connection, this information, if uncovered and made public, would likely not advance the president's future political aspirations or benefit the Grand Old Party.

THE REPUBLICANS WHO'D gathered aboard the presidential yacht *Mayflower*—and indeed many other influential members of the party— were eager to have Coolidge preempt the committee and specifically

Walsh before the Democrats demanded the White House take action against Fall, Doheny, and Sinclair. Being proactive was not the cautious president's style, however. Since the hearings began, Coolidge had done his best to ignore or minimize the Teapot investigation and distance himself from the hearings as ex-president Taft had advised. In October when reporters had queried him about the investigation, Coolidge had responded, "There is no action that could be taken by the President relative to it." A week before Archie Roosevelt testified, the president told newsmen that the oil leases were "under investigation, I think, by a senatorial committee, and of course no action is contemplated by any other arm of the government so far as I know." Finally, the day after Doheny testified for the second time, Coolidge said he believed prosecution in the case now "warranted criminal investigation." At this Harry Daugherty, still the nation's top lawman, promptly announced he was going to Florida on vacation.

Despite advice to the contrary from Butler and the others, the president wanted to wait until Fall had testified a second time before acting on Teapot. Aboard the *Mayflower*, however, Coolidge received a radio call from one of the committee members—Lenroot, it was later learned—with news that caused him to do an abrupt about-face. In a private, closed-door session Saturday morning, Walsh had informed the committee that first thing Monday morning he intended to appear before the entire Senate to present a resolution asking the president to cancel the leases and prosecute where necessary with specially appointed counsel. According to what Lenroot told the president, Walsh also intended to demand that Coolidge fire Navy Secretary Denby immediately.

After Coolidge shared with his guests the news regarding Walsh's intentions, he, Butler, and the others aboard the presidential yacht—including Arthur Prentice Rugg, chief justice of the Massachusetts Supreme Judicial Court, and George W. Pepper, a Republican senator from Pennsylvania—quickly came to a consensus. Walsh's demands could prove enormously damaging and put the White House on the defensive. Coolidge, it was agreed, must seize the initiative with a statement of his own. At 7:00 p.m. from the *Mayflower*, the president radioed Bascom Slemp, his secretary, telling him to go to the White House at once. He also summoned the chairman of the investigating committee, Lenroot, and Augustus Seymour of the Justice Department. Since Daugherty was in Florida, Seymour was the acting attorney general.

Two hours later, Coolidge arrived back at the White House accompanied by Butler, Rugg, and Pepper. There the president conferred with Acting Attorney General Seymour and the others, then drafted a concise five-paragraph statement basically covering the same points that Walsh intended to lay out before the Senate, including the need for special counsel: "If there has been any crime with the naval leases, it must be prosecuted," Coolidge asserted. "If there has been any property of the United States illegally transferred or leased, it must be recovered." He went on to stress that this was not exclusively a Republican scandal. Members of both parties were involved, he claimed. Having been so advised by the Justice Department, he proposed to "employ special counsel of high rank, drawn from both political parties, to bring such actions for the enforcement of the law."

Slemp then alerted the media that the president was preparing to issue an important statement. Normally, a statement from the White House would be mimeographed and then handed out to reporters, but in this instance there wasn't enough time. With Coolidge standing at his side, Slemp read the statement to reporters over the White House telephone at midnight, giving most of the nation's major newspapers time to run it on page one in their late Sunday morning editions. In one cool, calculated move, "Silent Cal" had managed to upstage Tom Walsh.

On monday morning, January 28, the U.S. Senate convened to debate the resolution that Walsh intended to present. "Not since the . . . League of Nations debate has such a crowd packed itself into the Senate galleries," a *New York Times* reporter noted. "Nor have so many Senators been on the floor. There was no effort at camouflaging the gravity of the situation." Among the crowd were Daisy Harriman, Eleanor Roosevelt, and a group of other prominent Democratic women who'd been following the hearings regularly.

Promptly at 10:00 a.m., Walsh took the podium. For more than six hours, he laid out the facts of the case in what one journalist characterized as his "dryly desolating" style. The Montanan started out by read-

Oklahoma oilman Jake Hamon had his eyes on the prize: the White House. He wanted a president who would give him the secretary of interior post—and with it the key to rich naval oil reserves in Wyoming and California.

Clara Hamon had been Jake's mistress for ten years. When she found out Jake wasn't going to take her with him to Washington, she shot and killed him.

Ohio political operative Harry M. Daugherty thought Warren Harding would make "a great-looking president." With Jake Hamon's backing, and bankroll, he put Harding in the White House.

AP IMAGES

Going into the 1920 Republican Convention, Harding, an obscure Ohio senator, was given little or no chance to win the nomination.

U.S. SENATE ARCHIVES

With Jake Hamon dead, Albert Fall was given the
secretary of interior job.

Jess Smith kept the books and acted as the bagman for the Ohio Gang. Even though he wasn't on the Justice Department payroll, Jess's desk was strategically situated just outside Attorney General Daugherty's office. To get to Daugherty you had to go through Jess. AP IMAGES

Frank Hogan (left) and Edward Doheny. Doheny said that he and Albert Fall were old "pards," and he had lent Fall $100,000 out of friendship. Later, Hogan, Doheny's one-million-dollar lawyer, would represent both men. AP IMAGES

Nan Britton, Harding's longtime mistress, would visit the White House for afternoon trysts.

AP IMAGES

Harry Sinclair started out as a soda jerk in his father's Lawrence, Kansas, drugstore and ended up one of the world's biggest oilmen. Along the way, Albert Fall gave him the keys to Teapot and the even richer Salt Creek fields.

AP IMAGES

President Harding and his wife, Florence, leave for Alaska. They had been looking forward to the Alaskan trip for several years. He would die in San Francisco on his return. AP IMAGES

President-to-be Calvin Coolidge and his wife, Grace. Coolidge's strategy was to distance himself from the ongoing investigation.

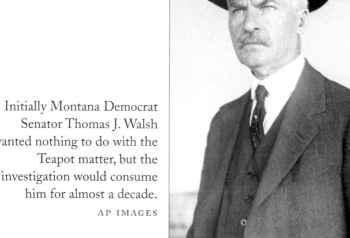

Initially Montana Democrat Senator Thomas J. Walsh wanted nothing to do with the Teapot matter, but the investigation would consume him for almost a decade.

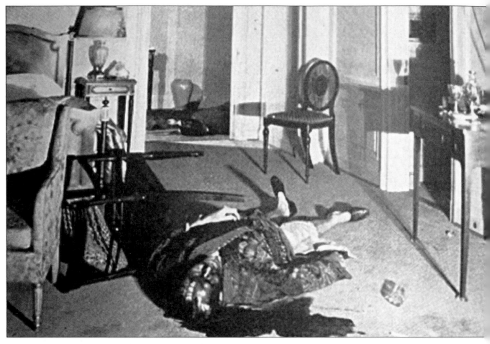

Wearing a dressing gown, young Ned Doheny's corpse is sprawled in the foreground. Hugh Plunkett can be seen lying in the doorway in the background.

ing letters and documents written by Harding and Fall that clearly indicated the entire cabinet and the vice president had conferred and approved the leases, thereby countering Coolidge's assertion that he knew nothing about Teapot. Referring repeatedly to giant maps of Teapot and the California fields that his staff had hung on the chamber walls, Walsh explained the step-by-step process by which the reserves had been transferred from the Navy Department to Interior; the fallacy of the leakage argument; how Fall had given the leases out secretly and without competitive bids to Sinclair and Doheny; and how the oilmen in turn had rewarded him. His was a brilliant summation of everything the committee had learned thus far. In conclusion, Walsh responded to questions about the investigation, demanded that the leases be canceled, and chastised the president for not acting sooner. He was merciless in his attack on Denby, stressing that the navy secretary had signed away oil reserves worth several hundred million dollars and as his defense could say only that the wool had been pulled over his eyes. Denby's "ineptness and stupidity" had made Teapot possible, Walsh charged. Unless Denby's resignation was on Coolidge's desk by sundown, Walsh promised "to ask action by this body appropriate to the occasion."

As the debate continued over the next few days, virtually every senator who spoke after Walsh, Republicans included, favored passing the Walsh resolution. Some Republicans such as Peter Norbeck, a committee member, even went so far as to pay tribute "to the earnestness and very great ability of Senator Walsh. The investigation lasted for months . . . some members of the committee had other duties . . . but one man stayed on the job at all times. I think he has performed a very great public service." Several senators, including Democrats J. Thomas Heflin of Alabama and T. H. Caraway of Arkansas, wanted Congress to cancel the leases outright. "Why should we pay fat salaries to go into the courts?" Heflin demanded. Walsh counseled that the matter was better left to the special prosecutors.

Heflin also lashed out at Coolidge for having done nothing to prosecute those who had "pillaged and plundered" the public domain and for his claim that the scandal involved men from both parties. It was strictly a Republican affair, Heflin said. "This whole arrangement was made prior to the election of 1920. I believe Fall was to be made secretary of the interior and Denby secretary of the navy. I believe Sinclair got what was promised him before the election . . . and Doheny what was promised to him. I think certain interests that contributed to the Republican Party knew they would get the oil in due time."

On the matter of Denby, the Senate passed a resolution on February 11 asking the president to dismiss him from the cabinet. In response, Coolidge reminded the Senate that "the dismissal of an officer of the government . . . other than by impeachment, is exclusively an executive function." He wouldn't budge.

WHILE THE CONGRESSIONAL debate raged on in both houses, the Committee on Public Lands and Surveys got an unexpected visitor. Ed Doheny reappeared at the behest of Senator James A. Reed, a Missouri Democrat with presidential aspirations. With the Democratic presidential convention only four months away, the party had all but settled on a candidate: William Gibbs McAdoo, who had served as secretary of the Treasury under Wilson, his father-in-law, was the clear frontrunner. Although Walsh was mentioned as a possible contender as well, McAdoo's only real competition was Reed of Missouri, who seized upon the hearings as a means of removing his rival, McAdoo.

On January 31 on the Senate floor, Reed asked that Doheny be recalled before the Teapot committee. Privately, Reed told Lenroot that the committee should ask Doheny what former public officials and cabinet officers he had on his payroll. Many of them, Reed asserted, were Democrats. Smelling blood, Lenroot immediately subpoenaed Doheny after assuring Reed that "if no one else asks the questions he [Reed] desires, the chairman [Lenroot] will do so."

On this occasion Doheny, who was prepped by Reed before the hearings, was only too happy to appear. He was still fuming that, in his view, Walsh and the Democrats, members of his own party, had betrayed him. After a few exchanges between Doheny and Walsh in which the Californian tried to explain why the $100,000 IOU he'd produced from Fall wasn't signed or even written in Fall's handwriting, Lenroot began his questioning. Aside from his relationship with Fall, did Doheny employ any former cabinet members or high-level government officials? Lenroot asked. "Yes, sir," Doheny responded, listing the names, as one journalist put it, "like a parvenu art collector calling the roll of his Rembrandts."

Among those whom Doheny had put on his payroll were the late Franklin K. Lane, former secretary of the interior; former attorney general Thomas W. Gregory; former secretary of war Lindley Garrison; and George Creel, former chairman of Wilson's wartime Committee on Public Information. All were Democrats, as was the last and most important name Doheny produced: Willam McAdoo. McAdoo had been representing him as a lawyer since the end of the Wilson administration, Doheny explained, and to date had received $250,000 in legal fees. Asked why he'd hired these men, Doheny responded, "I paid them for their influence." As Mark Sullivan noted, if some Republican lawyer had sought "to put the most damaging words into Doheny's mouth, he could not have done more than that."

At the revelation that Doheny employed McAdoo and the others, the reporters fell over themselves rushing to the nearest phones to call in the latest of the sensational stories emanating from the Teapot hearings. Doheny had given McAdoo, the Democrats' presidential hopeful, more than twice the sum Fall received. That McAdoo's work as an attorney for Doheny's oil company had absolutely nothing to do with Teapot was immaterial, at least to the pro-Republican newspapers. They promptly tarred McAdoo with the same brush that had tarnished Fall.

For the Democrats, Doheny's testimony was devastating. Walsh immediately protested that Lenroot's question was entirely beyond the bounds of the committee's charter, but the damage had already been done. Though he would fight gamely to save his reputation, McAdoo's political aspirations had been substantially dashed by Doheny. Nor could the Democrats use Teapot Dome as their battle cry in the upcoming elections. Both Walsh and McAdoo knew that this was Doheny's payback. Not long after the incident, McAdoo wrote Walsh, saying he believed Doheny had deliberately tried "to injure me by the interjection of my name into the oil inquiry . . . in retaliation for his refusal" to pressure Walsh to stop the investigation. Had Walsh agreed to participate in Doheny's Montana oil deal, he too would likely have been pilloried.

Since his arrival in Washington, Fall had been holed up in Zevely's home. He had been scheduled to appear before the committee on January 25 but again claimed to be too ill to endure the questioning. An attorney he'd engaged when he'd reached Washington told the committee Fall "was on the verge of having a nervous breakdown." In response, the committee appointed several doctors to examine him. In reaction, Republicans claimed that the committee was invading the ex–interior secretary's sickroom. Senator Heflin then reminded the Senate that Fall hadn't hesitated to invade President Wilson's bedroom in the White House after he had suffered a stroke.

After the doctors diagnosed the former cabinet member to be in an "anxious" state but fit to testify, Fall finally showed up at the Senate Office Building on February 2, entering the committee room with Senate attendants and his lawyer running interference. Again the corridors in the Senate Office Building leading to the committee room were lined with hundreds of men and women hoping to glimpse the elusive ex–interior secretary. Fall's cane, once an ornament of virility, as Mark Sullivan noted, was now indispensable. Even with it, he seemed scarcely mobile. Wearing a blue serge suit that looked as if it hadn't been pressed since he'd left New Mexico and in need of a haircut, Fall read a statement to the committee in a clear, almost disembodied voice: "I decline . . . to answer any questions on the ground that it may tend to incriminate me. . . ."

Of course, Fall, who was forever trying to use the law to justify his own ends, couldn't be satisfied simply by invoking the Fifth Amendment. He followed his initial statement with a complicated and largely incomprehensible legal argument in an attempt to show that the committee "has no further authority to question me."

His appearance lasted perhaps ten minutes. Walsh, who had records of earlier hearings beside him in preparation for a cross-examination, asked no further questions. Nor did the other committee members. "That was one of the most tragic spectacles Washington ever saw," Mark Sullivan, who was present, later wrote. "A former Senator appearing before his former associates under what amounted to a charge of crime; a former Cabinet-officer already plainly guilty of a lie and by all appearances guilty of having accepted a bribe. . . . Concluding, he did not look at his fellow Senators or any one else. The crowd, turning to watch him, was so silent that the tapping of his cane could be heard as, with shuffling feet, he moved slowly down the corridor."

On February 18, Edwin Denby sent his resignation to President Coolidge. In a press statement, he defended the leases. A cartoon that appeared in a number of newspapers the following day showed the former navy secretary being catapulted from the deck of a battleship into the water. "Did he jump instead of being fired for the good of the country?" the caption read. That same night, Walsh boarded a train for Pinehurst, North Carolina, where he planned to take a well-earned but brief rest. "I have just gone through a campaign that has made unusual demands upon my physical vigor and reserve nervous force, and I find before me a great accumulation of work imperatively demanding my attention," he later wrote to a friend.

At his hotel, Walsh was called by a reporter from the *Raleigh News & Observer* and told that Denby had resigned. Walsh described the resignation as "a consummation devoutly wished for." He declined further comment.

36

THE CONSPIRACY

Tom Walsh had been at Pinehurst only two days when he learned that Harry Sinclair had arrived back in the United States aboard the *President Harding*. Departing from Southampton, the ocean liner had been scheduled to arrive in New York on the morning of February 20, but because of heavy seas and a blizzard, it had to lay off Sandy Hook for five hours. As soon as it finally docked in Hoboken, where it was subject to a quarantine inspection, a dozen or so reporters swarmed aboard. They'd been tipped off that Harry Sinclair was a passenger, back in the United States after five weeks abroad.

They found Sinclair on deck, where he greeted the members of the press with a big smile and handshakes all around. When the reporters asked what he had to say about the Teapot affair, Sinclair told them he'd see them in a few minutes in the ship's tearoom—appropriately, the tearoom of the *President Harding*. In case anyone had missed the significance of the setting he'd chosen, Sinclair said with a wink, "Get that . . . in the tearoom."

They caught up with him a few minutes later lunching with his wife, Elizabeth, who was recovering from the flu, and several business associates. In response to the outpouring of questions, Sinclair was evasive but jovial, even cocky, his mood likely buoyed by President

Coolidge's decision to turn over the Teapot investigation to the special counsel the president had handpicked. No doubt they would be easier to deal with than the Inspector Javert–like Walsh. Meanwhile, the Public Lands and Surveys Committee hearings were ongoing, but with the appointment of the special counsel, they would soon wind down.

Sinclair hadn't really been following the investigation closely, he told reporters. The newspapers in France hadn't given Teapot much attention. He'd returned "not entirely familiar with what has happened in connection with the investigation." A photographer asked him to go up on deck to pose for a picture. Sinclair happily obliged, posing with one of his engineers, Walter S. Morris, the two of them playing horseshoes. "Get closer to the stake," the photographer urged.

"I know they'll think I'm cheating," Sinclair, who was clearly enjoying himself, said with a wink.

"And that will need an investigation," quipped Morris.

"Look serious," said another photographer.

"I'll give you my committee face," Sinclair answered, thumbing his nose at Walsh and the committee. After returning to the tearoom, Sinclair refused to respond to questions about Teapot, though he did say he'd happily testify again if asked. He seemed more interested in horse racing than oil. The previous year, his horse Zev—named in honor of Bill Zevely—had won the Kentucky Derby. Now, after visiting France, he predicted that Zev would meet the French champion Epinard in a few months. The French were "strong for it," he said, adding that Epinard hadn't a chance against his horse.

As he was leaving the ship, a reporter mentioned the "million-dollar slush fund" report that had been circulating in Washington. "I haven't heard about that," Sinclair said with a big smile. "How much of that am I supposed to have furnished?"

On the pier, Sinclair was met by family members, friends, and Zevely, all of whom went on to the Sinclair town house at 975 Fifth Avenue, where Sinclair was throwing a modest welcome-home party for himself.

WALSH WAS BACK in Washington on February 23, determined to develop a new line of inquiry in the oil hearings. He wanted to focus the investigation on what he believed had been a well-orchestrated effort by

Big Oil to co-opt the Harding administration in order to gain control of the naval reserves. "I am seeking to get at what I conceive to have been the original conspiracy," he wrote to an old friend. That meant going after those Walsh believed had been at the center of the conspiracy, starting with Harry Sinclair. But he had to move quickly. The two counsel appointed by Coolidge, former Ohio senator Atlee Pomerene, a Democrat, and Republican Owen J. Roberts, were preparing to begin their own investigation of the leases.

Walsh was not happy with the choices, in part because Coolidge had not bothered to consult him on either selection. The president, he complained privately, had treated him "contemptuously," an assessment with which many of his colleagues concurred. Nebraska Republican George Norris said on the Senate floor that he was "amazed" and "humiliated" that Coolidge had failed to consult Walsh regarding his choices. Moreover, Walsh didn't think either man was up to the job. He had served on several committees with Pomerene, a rotund, florid-faced, balding sixty-year-old Cincinnatian with big basset hound brown eyes. More conservative than most of his Democratic brethren, Pomerene, now in private practice, had proven an effective debater during his tenure in the Senate. He was noted for going directly for his opponent's jugular and took special delight in goading Albert Fall. Still, he would never be mistaken for Oliver Wendell Holmes, or Tom Walsh, for that matter.

The Republican Owen J. Roberts, forty-nine, was a practicing Philadelphia lawyer, a Greek scholar, and something of an oddball. He had a goofy but engaging smile and a shrewd, tenacious intellect, had entered the University of Pennsylvania at sixteen, and had studied law there as well. At his Valley Forge farm, he raised Guernseys and as a hobby collected Revolutionary War–era clocks, which he was trying constantly to synchronize. Senator George Pepper had suggested Coolidge appoint him. "The fighting Welshman," Pepper had called him. Pepper had been aboard the *Mayflower* when Coolidge decided to claim Walsh's proposal to appoint special counsel as his own. Pepper had also dismissed the Teapot hearings "as a ridiculous circus," which, in Walsh's view, made his support of Roberts suspect. Further, neither Roberts nor Pomerene was nationally known, and neither had experience in public land laws or a grasp of the extraordinarily complex issues involved in the investigation. The battery of highly paid, highly experienced attorneys that Doheny and Sinclair had on their payrolls would steamroll them, Walsh believed. Nonetheless, both nominees were confirmed by the Senate on February 17 and would soon launch their own probe. This meant Walsh would likely get only one more crack at Sinclair. He wanted to make the most of it. He wanted, he told a reporter from the United Press, to "establish the facts that would lead to a conviction."

Starting with the unexplained and unsecured $25,000 loan to Fall, Walsh had been amassing evidence against Sinclair while the oilman was in France. Walsh, in fact, now had so many investigative lines out, so many sources and so much information coming in, that it was almost impossible to corroborate even the most promising tips and sort out rumors from facts. In mid-March, Walsh began receiving reports that the former president of the First National Bank, Muskogee, Oklahoma, Frank Hubbard, a close friend to both Zevely and Sinclair, had attended a weekend party at Zevely's home in Garden City, Long Island, in the spring of 1923. Present, according to Hubbard, were Sinclair, Fall, Daugherty, Senator Charles Curtis of Kansas, Denby, and Zevely. The party, Hubbard said, "had a Dutch lunch wherein everything from champagne on down could be had" and centered around a marathon poker game in which Sinclair by prearrangement lost "fabulous sums" to Fall, Daugherty, Denby, and Curtis. A few months later on a visit to Los Angeles, Hubbard told several people about the party, including an old friend, Thomas A. Sanson of the Merchants National Bank and a former Oklahoma judge. Sanson, in turn, related the story to several California lawyers, two of whom wrote to Walsh with the story.

On receiving this information, Walsh wrote one of the California attorneys, James L. Allen, on March 19, 1924: "Information has come to me . . . that you know something about what passed as a poker party at the home of Bill Zevely at which Sinclair lost very considerable sums there to Fall and possibly Denby, the assumption being that they got theirs in that way. I shall be glad to have a letter from you about this matter and shall treat it as entirely confidential until you direct otherwise." This would not be the only time in the investigation that Walsh would hear tales of Sinclair using poker losses to enrich those whose influence he wished to secure.

Allen responded ten days later, confirming the story as Hubbard had relayed it. The Muskogee banker would likely tell all he knew about the party, Allen said—that is, if Walsh could find him. As the hearings began probing how the RNC and the oil barons influenced the 1920 election and the oil policies that ensued, witnesses became increasingly scarce. Unbeknownst to just about everybody but Harry Sinclair and their immediate families, two of Sinclair's cohorts in the Continental Trading swindle, Harry Blackmer—Blackmer with $10 million—and Prairie Oil's James O'Neil had skipped the country to settle in France. And unlike Sinclair, they had no plans to return.

In February, Jim Sloan, Harding's former bodyguard and currently Washington manager of the brokerage firm Ungerleider & Co., with whom Harding and Daugherty had dealt, told Walsh's assistant that "members of the former Republican National Committee were scattered and scared to death." On February 14, Miguel Otero, former governor of New Mexico Territory, wrote Walsh to tell him that four or five men who had been involved in Bonfils's successful efforts to blackmail Harry Sinclair were hiding out on the Navajo Reservation to avoid being served subpoenas. It was Otero who had been the source of the story that President Harding had instructed Sinclair to pay Bonfils and the others the million dollars. At the time—and without the additional information that would come out later—Walsh had viewed this tale as too far-fetched to pursue, though he would later have second thoughts.

Never one to be intimidated, Bonfils appeared voluntarily before the committee on February 8 and 9. In response to questions from Walsh, the *Denver Post* publisher charged that there was a conspiracy among Doheny, Sinclair, and the Standard Oil–affiliated companies to let Sinclair have Teapot Dome and Doheny the California reserves. "They [Sinclair and Standard Oil] having no antagonistic interests in California," Bonfils stated, "had no objection to letting Mr. Doheny have the naval reserve there, and they went into the agreement along those lines and the leases were granted."

In this assessment, Bonfils was essentially correct. Doheny got California, while Sinclair and Robert Stewart's Standard Oil of Indiana got Wyoming. Bonfils had a credibility problem, however, because by now the committee was aware that Bonfils, Tammen, and young Leo Stack had received $1 million from Harry Sinclair in exchange for dropping the *Post*'s exposé of Teapot. Lenroot took up the questioning on this matter. Didn't Bonfils believe the lease was a proposition that represented graft? he demanded.

"I believed it represented a lot of money to a lot of people," Bonfils responded. "Call it graft if you wish."

"You thought it was a rotten commercial transaction, yet so long as you got your fee out of it, $1 million, you were willing to stand upon this rotten deal and contract," Lenroot continued.

"I did not," Bonfils responded.

This brought Lenroot to his feet. He began to wave a copy of Bonfils's contract with Sinclair in front of the witness's face. "This whole deal was for the purpose of purchasing your silence in your newspaper. Once you had your money, the attacks ceased."

"No," responded Bonfils. Now he was leaning threateningly across the table toward Lenroot. "They did not cease. They have not ceased! They will never cease."

Lenroot then read a telegram from the *Post*'s editor stating that no article had appeared on Sinclair or the leases since the contract had been signed. Bonfils remained defiant. "I came here voluntarily," he stated. "One would think from the way you talked I was the criminal." At this, the witness was excused so that he could proceed to Charleston, South Carolina. There Bonfils was going to board the naval transport *Henderson* to cruise to the Panama Canal as the guest of Navy Secretary Denby, who was nine days short of resigning.

IN PROBING WHAT Walsh called "the conspiracy," the committee and Walsh in particular were venturing into what would prove to be dangerous territory. Some of the boys on the opposing team played dirty, notably Harry Daugherty and his old Ohio Gang enforcer, redheaded Billy Burns, both of whom were still in office. In late January, one of the committee members, likely Walsh, informed D.C.'s chief of detectives, Clifford L. Grant, that he had reason to believe an attack might be made upon him. Thereafter, the Washington, D.C., Police Department assigned Detective Arthur Scrivener to attend the hearings and keep a sharp watch for any untoward incident.

Walsh and other senators who were hammering away at the Republicans—even some like Arkansas's T. H. Caraway and old Bob La Follette, who weren't members of the committee—were frequently followed. Their offices were broken into; their files were ransacked. Walsh believed that both his office phone and his home phone were tapped;

his mail, he discovered, was being opened. His secretary reported that two unfamiliar women were often in the ladies' room and seemed unduly interested in office gossip. From colleagues and constituents in Montana, he learned that federal agents were snooping around in an obvious attempt to find something incriminating in his past. On one occasion, Walsh's daughter, Genevieve Gudger, who was visiting from the Philippines, was out walking with her three-year-old daughter in a stroller when she was stopped by a stranger. He threatened her with harm if she did not force her father to drop the investigation.

Meanwhile, the Republicans mounted a campaign to smear Walsh—"show him up as a public enemy," he said. On March 11, Senator Lenroot resigned as chair of the committee. He supposedly had suffered a nervous breakdown and committed himself to Southern Pines, a private sanitarium in North Carolina. At the news of his resignation, Frederick Bonfils, still nursing a grudge against the former committee chairman for having impugned his journalistic integrity, wrote Walsh, suggesting Lenroot might have had an ulterior reason for quitting. "I think it ought to be brought out very clearly that Mr. Lenroot secretly visited Mr. Fall a good many times before and during the Senatorial investigation, and that he made no report of such visits to the Committee of which he was chairman. It was Mr. Lenroot's indulgence that enabled Mr. Fall to testify without being placed under oath— Why?" Bonfils claimed Lenroot had been in the pocket of a pro-leasing Wyoming oilman, Frank G. Curtis, who had financed Lenroot's earlier political campaigns.

Clearly, Bonfils was well plugged in to the Washington scene. This information was on target. Given the publisher's proclivity for blackmail, it is well within the realm of possibility that he may have even hastened Lenroot's exit from politics by threatening to expose his connection with Curtis. That, however, wasn't Walsh's concern. The important thing was that Lenroot, whose primary focus on the committee had been, Walsh said privately, "protecting his political friends," was gone. Moreover, the man who replaced him, Senator Edwin F. Ladd of North Dakota, the ranking Republican on the committee, had largely been supportive of Walsh. That was the favorable news. The negative was the new man on the committee, Selden Spencer, a Republican "sniper" from Missouri, who immediately began to impugn Walsh's methods and motives. Spencer went so far as to subpoena Walsh's brother John and question him about his work as an attorney for oil companies in Montana, none of which had anything remotely to do with Teapot. Walsh charged angrily that Spencer was "seeking to cast some suspicion on me."

More accurately, the Republicans from the White House on down were seeking to shut down the hearings altogether before more damaging information came out—and before Harry Sinclair and Will Hays had to testify again. Both had been subpoenaed to appear by the committee. Both were scheduled to appear on the same day, March 22.

WILL HAYS CAME down from New York a day early. His first stop was the White House, where presumably he had a little chat with the president. That same day, Edwin F. Ladd, a former chemistry professor and college president, was summoned to 1600 Pennsylvania Avenue as well. Upon arriving at the White House, the new committee chairman likely expected to meet President Coolidge, but Coolidge preferred to remain deep in the shadows in matters regarding the oil hearings. The president didn't show his face. Instead, the sixty-three-year-old Ladd was surprised to find former RNC chairman and Harding's ex–postmaster general, Will Hays, there to greet him. Hays's choice of a meeting place sent a message to the committee chairman that couldn't have been clearer. Even though he was officially out of politics, Hays had summoned Ladd to the White House on behalf of the president.

On Ladd's arrival, Hays suggested the two men take a taxicab ride so they could talk in private. Hays wanted to speak with Ladd on a matter of some delicacy, he explained. He was hopeful he could persuade the new Public Lands and Surveys Committee chairman to join with other Republicans on the committee in calling an immediate halt to the hearings. With the Walsh investigations dominating the headlines, the party was in disarray, Hays stressed. A week earlier, Walsh had summoned Coolidge's assistant, Bascom Slemp, before the committee and established that both he and Ned McLean had been communicating with the president by code while Walsh was questioning the newspaper publisher and Fall in Palm Beach. The Democrats were using this disclosure to link Coolidge to the scandals, *The New York Times* reported on March 30, 1924.

At the same time, Republicans in the Senate as well as the president were being criticized by members of their own party for not taking a stronger stand in defending themselves. Retired Indiana senator Albert Beveridge, one of the party's senior statesmen, had recently complained, "Republicans have . . . shilly-shallied, sidestepped, dilly-dallied, etc., until members of our party think that we are all in the wrong." This kind of criticism and internal bickering was highly damaging in light of the upcoming election, Hays reminded the North Dakotan. "The inquiry had become merely a political one," Ladd would later quote Hays as telling him. The Democrats were seeking simply to "cast odium on the Republican Party in connection with the leasing" of Elk Hills and Teapot. Now that Fall's involvement had been uncovered, there was no point in continuing on, Hays stressed, or in recalling the same witnesses again and again and raking over old ground. Walsh had gone too far, Hays continued. He was relentless. The investigation had to be stopped before it got completely out of hand. The special counsel could carry on ably from here.

Hays and Ladd cruised around Washington for almost an hour while Hays did his best to win Ladd over. At first, Ladd listened politely, he later said. After all, this was one of the most powerful members of his party sitting beside him in the cab, the man who as president of the Motion Picture Producers and Distributors Association of America was cleaning up Babylon, whose name would later be attached to the motion picture moral code (popularly called the "Hays Code"). But as Hays continued, Ladd became increasingly irritated and uncomfortable. He reminded Hays that his request was at best inappropriate and probably illegal. Finally, he made it bluntly clear to Hays that he intended to do his duty as committee chair regardless of the consequences and asked to be dropped off at the Senate Office Building.

Hays obliged him, then continued back to the White House, where Ladd had no doubt he would inform the president that Ladd had refused his request.

ACCOMPANIED BY ATTORNEY Martin W. Littleton, Harry Sinclair settled his ample frame into the witness chair on the morning of March 22. He was, as usual, exquisitely tailored and looked as if he were preparing to step into the winner's circle at Churchill Downs to receive the gold Kentucky Derby trophy. Ed Doheny's well-cultivated public persona was that of the kindly old Irish uncle with a twinkle in his eye and a good-luck gold piece hanging from his vest chain. Sinclair presented himself as the high-rolling robber baron, a sport who always picked up the bar tab and who—unlike the somber Walsh, whom he enjoyed chiding—never took himself too seriously. He winked at his own good fortune and enjoyed every minute of it. The press loved him.

On his previous visits, Sinclair had sailed through the hearings as easily as his racehorse Zev—aka "the Brown Express"—a nineteen-to-one shot, had wired the field in the Derby, winning by a length and a half. Walsh was determined that wasn't going to happen again. He had his questions ready: What had been the purpose of the $25,000 loan to Fall? Why had he given $1 million to Bonfils? What about the $68,000 he was supposed to have given to Fall's ranch foreman? Sinclair's secretary, G. D. Wahlberg, had been scheduled to testify the day before about both the $25,000 loan and the $68,000 supposed gift, but like so many others involved in the case, he had gotten suddenly ill. With his boss testifying, Wahlberg was recuperating in Havana.

Of paramount interest to Walsh, of course, was Sinclair's role in putting Warren Harding in the White House. As early as December 1923, he had begun hearing stories about Sinclair's role in electing Harding, stories that he would eventually corroborate. "Recurring to the talk we had in New York concerning the rumor . . . that Sinclair had raised a million dollars to elect Harding upon an understanding that Fall was to be made Secretary of the Interior, I am . . . assured upon what seems an altogether reliable authority that the rumor is founded in fact," he wrote an associate, Scott Ferris, on December 13. More recently, *New York Times* reporter Harold Vivian had run a story, based on a source from Hays's office in New York, Joseph O'Neil, saying that Sinclair had given Hays $1 million in stock to wipe out the 1920 campaign debt.

There was more: copies of telegrams proving that Fall had been visited at Three Rivers by Sinclair and the other participants in Teapot, Harry Blackmer and Robert Stewart; Sinclair's reported large poker losses to Fall, Denby, and others; and the trading in Mammoth stock by various government officials, including Harry Daugherty.

As soon as Sinclair was sworn in, Walsh began: "Mr. Sinclair, I desire to interrogate you about a matter concerning which the committee had no knowledge or reliable information at any time when you had heretofore appeared before the committee and with respect to which you must then have had knowledge. I refer to the testimony given by Mr. Bonfils concerning a contract that you made with him touching the Teapot Dome. I wish you would tell us about that."

To the committee's great surprise, Sinclair refused to answer. He didn't bother evoking the Fifth Amendment, because, he explained, "there is nothing in any of the facts or circumstances of the lease of Teapot Dome which does or can incriminate me." He just flat out refused to answer. Walsh asked eight more questions and got the same response each time: "I refuse to answer on the advice of counsel."

Sinclair, who remained cordial throughout, even cheerful, then read a long statement saying in effect that the committee had officially been supplanted by the special counsel and as a result hadn't the authority to question him any longer. Certainly, Sinclair and his attorney knew the risks they were incurring with this defiant legal strategy—an almost certain citation for contempt of the U.S. Senate. This, however, they apparently viewed as preferable to Walsh's continuing questioning, especially in light of the new and potentially damaging information the committee had uncovered.

When Sinclair had finished, Walsh excused him. "Gentlemen, I thank you," Sinclair responded with his trademark smile.

HAYS WAS UP NEXT. Though he eventually told his assistant, Douglas H. McArthur, and at least one other committee member, Alva B. Adams of Colorado, about Hays's visit, Edwin Ladd hadn't mentioned to Walsh his recent taxi ride with the former RNC chairman. Had he done so, the hearings might have taken an altogether different turn. For all his tenacity, Walsh could sometimes be too trusting. That had been the case in his dealings with Hays. Prior to Hays's appearance, Walsh had received a number of tips that Hays had been involved with the Teapot transaction from the get-go; that he had personally been given a large block of Sinclair stock for services he'd rendered Sinclair; that he had received a personal donation of $100,000 in cash from Sinclair in the 1918 election and subsequently $1 million from the oilman to cover the 1920 election costs.

Appearing before the committee, Hays conceded that his law firm, Hays and Hays of Sullivan, Indiana, "had for many years been the law firm for Mr. Sinclair." Yes, Sinclair had contributed to the 1920 Harding campaign, but no more than $75,000. The *New York Times* story that Sinclair had given $1 million in stock to the RNC "is as false in content as it is libelous in purpose," he stated. With equal certitude, he denied knowing anything about the oil leases until he read about them in the paper "a month or more after his resignation." When Walsh asked him if he was the Hays who G. D. Wahlberg testified had received Liberty bonds from Sinclair the previous summer, he said he wasn't sure. Wahlberg might have been referring to Hickle Hays, his brother. In any case, the transaction had been purely personal, Hays assured the committee. He'd be glad to have a committee representative examine his books if Walsh liked. What he didn't say was more important than what he volunteered. He never mentioned to Walsh and the others that the $75,000 had been only a fraction of what he'd received from Sinclair in Liberty bonds. Nor did he discuss how he'd used wealthy Republicans to launder the bonds.

As his testimony continued, Hays's memory faltered. His responses seemed to meander on endlessly, were difficult to follow and confusing. Which was Hays's intent, obfuscation being one of his special talents. Years later, his ghostwriter Raymond Moley marveled at "how he could talk at great length without seeming to say anything, Finally I learned that he [Hays] used language mainly not to reveal but to conceal thought." Sinclair had refused to answer questions. Hays's answers were largely unintelligible, on occasion reverting to inspired gibberish. Eventually, Walsh and the other frustrated committee members excused the witness.

Less than a month later, Walsh learned that Hays had visited Albert Fall in December at the Wardman Park Hotel and may have authored the famous Ned McLean letter. He realized he had let the former RNC chairman off too easily. "When you were on the stand, on your assurances that the loan of stock to you and your brother by Mr. Sinclair was a purely private matter and you expressed willingness to have your books examined . . . I felt obliged to respect your desire that the transaction should not be inquired into and refrained from further interrogating you about it," Walsh wrote Hays on April 17, 1924. Now, Walsh said he and Edwin Ladd might need Hays to return to the hearings to discuss the loan. First, however, he and Ladd wanted to hear exactly what had gone on in Fall's hotel room during Hays's visits. "I shall

be obliged if you will write me what the facts are concerning your reported visits to him [Fall] at the hotel, and as to any talk you had with
him," Walsh wrote Hays.

ON MONDAY, March 24, Walsh spoke on the floor of the Senate, asking
that the body cite Sinclair for contempt of the Senate on the grounds
that the witness had defied and flouted the Senate's authority. "This is
one of the gravest matters that can possibly have the attention of this
body, affecting as it does, the power to proceed in an orderly way to secure such information as it may need to aid it in the all-important task
confided to this body by the Constitution and by the people," he said.
"A contempt of court, however humble that court may be, is always a
matter of supreme importance. A contempt of this high tribunal cannot
be measured by any words." Within less than a half hour, the motion di-
recting the president of the Senate to refer the matter to the Washington, D.C., district attorney was passed by a vote of 72 to 1. Walsh
recommended that Sinclair be given the maximum sentence allowable
if convicted.

With his usual restraint, Walsh refused to comment further on the
matter, but the Alabama Democrat Senator J. Thomas Heflin had no
such reservations. "If something isn't done here in a week, I serve notice
that I am going to have Mr. Sinclair brought in here and turned over to
the sergeant at arms," he threatened. "Crooks are going unwhipped by
Justice and nothing is done."

37

THE REDHEAD, THE RADICAL, AND THE
ATTORNEY GENERAL

During the second week in March, while Tom Walsh was preparing to question Messrs. Sinclair and Hays, Roxy Stinson, the redhead who was briefly married to the late Jess Smith, was staying under an assumed name in the Hotel Washington across the street from the White House. With her was Maude Mitchell, whose job it was to answer the phone, keep Roxy from venturing out—and keep away all would-be visitors.

That Roxy should be in the nation's capital at the height of the oil hearings had nothing to do with Teapot—not directly, at least. Three weeks earlier, on February 20, 1924, Burton K. Wheeler, the ambitious freshman senator from Montana, rose in the Senate to introduce a resolution to investigate Harry Daugherty on the grounds that the attorney general had done nothing "to arrest and prosecute" Fall, Doheny, Sinclair, and the rest of the oil crowd. "We find the Department of Justice, instead of trying to detect the greatest crooks and those guilty of the greatest crimes against the nation that have ever been perpetuated . . . protecting them all during this time; we find them protecting them tonight because I am reliably informed that only last Sunday night the attorney general of the United States held a conference with Ed McLean," said Wheeler.

Wheeler, a Progressive Democrat, was Walsh's protégé and a close friend. The Montana senators had summer houses only about a hundred yards apart on Lake McDonald in Glacier National Park. Walsh had helped Wheeler rise in Montana politics and had encouraged him to go after Daugherty, providing him with much of the information he needed to pursue his investigation. Walsh believed that Daugherty had been one of the unseen architects of the oil scandals. His name had popped up on numerous occasions during the Teapot hearings. Two of his former special assistants testified that Fall and Daugherty had worked in concert to ensure that Standard Oil of Indiana retained control of certain rich oil lands in the Elk Hills reserve (not those taken over by Doheny). They also quashed a federal investigation of Standard Oil of Indiana, which enabled that company to move into the Salt Creek fields adjacent to Teapot and circumvent antitrust constraints. Throughout the period when Fall was preparing to dole out the leases to Sinclair and Doheny, Daugherty, Ned McLean, and Fall met secretly once or twice a week in Daugherty's house on K Street. Walsh remarked that this was apparently "a kind of rendezvous" and suspected the three of conspiring together. If Denby was utterly inept, Daugherty, in Walsh's view, was an outright crook. "Harry Daugherty has his hand in every dirty piece of business that came out of the Harding administration," he said.

Yet Walsh's committee didn't really have the resources or time to go after the sitting attorney general of the United States, having already cast perhaps too wide a net. But Wheeler, who had complained earlier to Walsh that the Senate wasn't providing him "with the action" he was accustomed to in Montana, was primed to go. Walsh pointed the way. Harry Daugherty and his buddy Billy Burns, who headed up the Department of Justice, would give the new boy all the action he could handle and then some.

ON MARCH 1, by a vote of 66 to 1, the Senate passed Wheeler's resolution. By this time, Washington was rife with rumors that Daugherty, as Wheeler put it, "was up to his neck in massive graft." With the exception of the president, the Republicans were as eager to oust him as the Democrats, perhaps more so given that the attorney general was proving a major embarrassment to the GOP in an election year. The day after the Wheeler resolution passed, a Republican senatorial delegation led by Henry Cabot Lodge marched to the White House to ask the president to drop Daugherty. Coolidge refused.

The forty-two-year-old Wheeler was chosen as counsel for the newly formed Senate subcommittee that was to investigate Daugherty. Unlike the methodical, intensely focused, and invariably well-prepared Walsh, the junior senator from Montana often shot from the hip and assiduously cultivated favorable publicity. He projected the image, he later conceded, of being the "natural product of Montana's brass knuckle era." In reality, Wheeler was a New England Yankee from Hudson, Massachusetts. He'd studied law at the University of Michigan. On graduation, he planned to practice in Seattle but got waylaid in rough-and-tumble Butte, Montana, losing his last dollar in a poker game there. In Butte he hung his shingle, initially making a name for himself defending labor leaders, a number of whom were Socialists. As a conse-quence, when he initially came to Washington, Wheeler was branded, he said, "as something of a radical."

As soon as the Wheeler resolution had been approved, Wheeler, like Walsh, became the target of Daugherty's own "brass knuckle" tactics. And Daugherty had far bigger brass knuckles. "Harry Daugh-erty was a defiant and vengeful man who was ready to strike back with all the considerable resources of the Department of Justice," Wheeler later noted in his autobiography. Self-cast now in the role of an interrogator, Wheeler also began to draw flak from some of his con-gressional colleagues as well as the press. "In the Senate even a lot of the Democrats were not friendly to me at that particular time and practi-cally every paper in the country was opposed to me," Wheeler later re-called. "But Senator Walsh said to me, 'Don't let that worry you. When you get your facts before them, they'll begin to change their opinion somewhat.' "

Privately, Walsh acknowledged that much of the flak that had been directed at him since the Teapot investigation was now being tar-geted at his colleague from Montana. "The Republican National Com-mittee . . . seems to have abandoned its effort to show me up as a public enemy to direct its guns against my colleague, Senator Wheeler," he wrote to a friend.

At the outset of the investigation, Wheeler began getting letters and calls from both outside and inside the government telling him of Daugherty's illicit activities. A number of these sources, Wheeler later said, "urged me to contact a Miss Roxy Stinson, divorced wife of Jess Smith, Daugherty's close friend who had committed suicide in 1923." At the time, Roxy was about forty. She lived in Columbus, Ohio. In the nine months since Jess's death, she was still feuding bitterly with the Daugherty brothers, Harry and Mal. They had taken $11,000 from an account at Ungerleider & Co. that Jess had opened for her, claiming the money had to go into Smith's overall estate. For the Daugherty boys, that would prove a big mistake. Roxy got mad, *and* she got even. The $11,000 was by rights her money. She needed it to pay for a house she was building. To get it back, she sued in probate court, informing Mal that if the case wasn't settled in her favor, she might be forced to reveal some potentially incriminating information about the Daugherty brothers—to wit, large sums of cash her ex-husband used to deposit in the Midland Bank in Washington Court House, Ohio, on their behalf every month. Mal Daugherty was the bank's president. Investigators might also be interested in exactly where this money had come from, Roxy suggested.

At this, Harry Daugherty reverted to his usual bully-boy tactics, assigning Bureau of Investigation operatives to follow Roxy, tap her phones, read her mail, record her comings and goings. At one point, some of the attorney general's friends, including Sam Ungerleider, lured her to the Hollenden Hotel in Cleveland, where they told Roxy she was going to prison unless she promised not to say anything about Harry Daugherty. When Roxy refused to be intimidated, one of the would-be blackmailers, A. L. Fisk, said, "You know, Harry Daugherty is a pretty stubborn man."

"So am I, and he is not going to strong-arm me," Roxy responded. "I am not Jess Smith, and there is not going to be a convenient bullet in my head."

IN EARLY MARCH, Wheeler boarded a train to Columbus, Ohio, to meet with Roxy. When he told her the committee needed her testimony, she balked. "I promised her national publicity, but she said that was the one thing she wished to avoid," he later recalled. Finally, Wheeler handed Roxy the Senate subpoena calling for her appearance "forthwith." Reluctantly, Roxy packed a bag and started back to Washington with Wheeler, who questioned her on the train. What she told him, he later said, "was enough to convince me she could blow the case against the attorney general wide open."

At the Hotel Washington, Wheeler left Roxy with Maude Mitchell, his sister and also his secretary. Roxy begged to call Ned McLean, an old friend. Absolutely not, Wheeler said. He wanted to get her on the stand "before Daugherty's friends could scare her into silence." The hearings weren't scheduled to begin until March 13. Wheeler moved them up twenty-four hours. "I sprang my glamorous surprise witness," he said. "I could hardly have found anyone more ideal to get the hearings rolling full tilt. The press—which was scribbling furiously from the open gavel—noted that Miss Stinson was fashionably dressed, and attractive. Sitting with a sealskin coat draped over her shoulders, she talked in a low voice. Though she was obviously under tension, I believe she came through as an utterly credible witness."

For three days in front of Wheeler's committee, Roxy, with frequent outbursts of tears, told what *The New York Times* described as "an amazing story." Wheeler's first questions probed her dealings with her late ex-husband, Jess Smith, Harry Daugherty's "intimate friend," as Roxy characterized the relationship between the two men; she explained how she and Jess had remained close after the divorce. Jess, she said, would spend three weeks a month in Washington and then come to Ohio to see her and take care of business on behalf of Daugherty. When Smith was in Washington, Roxy testified, he would communicate with her every day by either letter or telegram.

Jess told Roxy everything about the graft in which he, Daugherty, and the other members of the Ohio Gang were involved. She detailed the often enormous deposits Smith made each month at Daugherty's bank in Washington Court House and remembered Smith once counting out $75,000 in thousand-dollar bills. Roxy explained how Daugherty and Smith had pocketed $180,000 by illegally showing the Dempsey-Carpentier fight around the country; about large sums collected by the Ohio Gang from bootleggers; and about a mysterious, crooked oil deal that netted its participants $33 million. She was likely referring to the Continental deal but refused to divulge the names of those involved, and the committee didn't press her on this point. This caused *Time* magazine to speculate that somehow Harding had been involved in this transaction. As for the late president, Roxy said she'd met him many times in Ohio as well as in Washington and had once been his dinner partner. At the dinner, "the president was very attentive to me," Roxy recalled.

Roxy also told of the now famous "little green house of K Street," where the Ohio Gang did much of its business. She had been present at secret conferences at the Daughertys' "shack" in Washington Court House after the 1920 Republican convention when both Daugherty and the late Jake Hamon had bragged to her about getting Harding nominated—and Hamon's plans to take over the Interior job. She'd been there as well after the election, when, she said, Daugherty and her late husband had each given oil operator James G. Darden $2,400 to invest in oil speculation in naval fields, which at the time had not been taken over by Interior. This was the same James Darden whom the marines, on Fall's orders, ran off Teapot. Finally, she spoke of the last few days of Smith's life, how he thought strangers were following him, how he refused to walk at night in Washington County except in the middle of the street, and how he cautioned her not to go out after work.

Throughout her testimony, Daugherty lashed out in interviews at Roxy, calling her a "malicious, angry woman." At one point when she was testifying, Mal Daugherty was standing only a few feet from the witness stand. He seemed to be giving Roxy the evil eye. Unfazed, Roxy asked Daugherty to verify a statement she had just made, which immediately brought an objection from Wheeler.

The newspapers couldn't get enough of Roxy. Her picture adorned the front pages of the national newspapers. With her as the star witness, the hearings quickly captured the country's interest. As a *Washington Times* reporter noted, these sessions "had all the atmosphere of a murder trial, combined with the bated breath excitement of the opening of King Tut's tomb—the King Tut in this instance being poor Jess Smith."

When Roxy finally stepped down, Wheeler called on others, including Gaston Means, to corroborate her statements, but as much as anything, it was Roxy's sensational testimony and the national exposure it received that brought down the attorney general. On March 28, Coolidge finally ousted Harry Daugherty from office, after the attorney general refused to turn over departmental papers to Wheeler's committee. Soon after, Billy Burns, the last member of the Ohio Gang, also resigned. Before departing, however, both prepared a nasty surprise for Burton Wheeler that was intended to wreck his career before it really got started.

WALSH'S OWN HEARINGS began to wind down soon after. He had, he wrote to a friend, "uncovered corruption without parallel in the history of the country." Still, he sensed that he had only scratched the surface of a larger conspiracy that had originated with the 1920 election and was the bedrock of much of the corruption that had prevailed during the Harding administration. "He had not exhausted all his leads but found himself at last circumvented," Walsh's biographer wrote. "Republicans were secretive, or uninformed about the alleged 1920 conspiracy, and Sinclair escaped further investigation at this time by refusing to show his books."

On May 6, 1924, in response to attacks on him as well as on his colleague Burton Wheeler from Senator Selden Spencer and others claiming their respective investigations were politically motivated, Walsh spoke to the nation in a statement broadcast by the Radio Corporation of America in Washington. "Corruption in public life is a vice that eats into the very structure of our system," he said. ". . . Exposure of it is a service of the highest order and . . . swift, certain, and condign punishment is the only cure for it outside of moral regeneration."

On that same day, for the first time since the hearings began, not a single spectator was present in room 210. A week later, the Committee on Public Lands and Surveys suspended its hearings. By then, much of the country's attention had turned elsewhere. Few seemed to appreciate what Walsh had accomplished and the extraordinary obstacles he had encountered. A distinguished exception: Harvard law professor Felix Frankfurter. In the May 1924 issue of *The New Republic*, Frankfurter wrote, "For nearly two years the efforts to uncover wrong doing in the disposal of our public domain were hampered by every conceivable obstacle on the part of those in office and those influential out of office. . . .

Governmental machinery, prestige, wealth, and agencies of publicity—all were for covering things up. No one who has not had some experience of the power the government can exert is able to realize the tremendous pressure against which both Walsh and Wheeler were contending. Both the hostile resources and the inertia which they had to overcome were incredible."

38

STATE OF DENIAL

Soon after he was approved by the Senate on February 18, forty-nine-year-old Owen Roberts, one of the recently appointed special counsel, paid a courtesy call on Tom Walsh. For both men the meeting, at least initially, was uncomfortable owing to their preconceptions about each other. Still annoyed that Coolidge had snubbed him in making the counsel appointments, Walsh suspected the Philadelphia lawyer, who with Atlee Pomerene would be taking over the Teapot investigation, was likely in the pocket of the president. In turn, Roberts had bought the Republican Party line that Walsh's probe had been driven primarily by partisan politics.

According to one account of the meeting, Roberts told Walsh that the president had assured him he was working for the United States government, not the Republican Party and not the White House. Coolidge had given him and Pomerene the green light to pursue the investigation wherever it led—and promised all the help he could give. Given that in Walsh's view the president to date had done nothing to further the investigation, he was a mite skeptical of this pronouncement. Still, he told Roberts that if the counsel were running for office, "on that ticket you would have my vote."

At the time of this meeting, Daugherty was still attorney general. He'd been lobbying Coolidge to help with the special counsel's investigation. At all costs, Pomerene and Roberts should prevent this from happening, Walsh told his visitor. "I have only one piece of advice," he said. "I wouldn't depend on the Justice Department for investigative purposes, nor would I approach the attorney general's office for information if I were you." He went on to say that he believed Daugherty "would go to any length to protect himself and his friends—and make no mistake about it, the people we are after are friends of the attorney general . . . the Department of Justice and the Bureau of Investigation are handpicked by Daugherty and rotten to the core." Walsh then enumerated the various attempts that had been made by Daugherty and friends to obstruct the investigation and intimidate him, including the threat to his daughter while she was out walking his three-year-old granddaughter in a stroller.

At the conclusion of what would prove the first of many meetings between the special counsel and Walsh, Walsh told Roberts that he and Pomerene could rely on his support as needed. Despite his initial concerns, both counsel "impressed him favorably, and all three worked surprisingly well. In part they simply shared information relating to the oil cases and congratulated each other when the decisions went their way," Walsh's biographer noted. "Walsh, however, was in a position to help the prosecutors appreciably. Besides giving advice, he pressed for the passage of laws, and even the negotiation of a treaty, that would facilitate their task of bringing alleged criminals to justice. Walsh was determined to do everything in his power to substantiate his own findings in the Senate probes."

In subsequent meetings with Senator Pepper, his sponsor, and the president, Roberts reported that he had been impressed with Walsh, though he was not sure he'd dispelled whatever mistrust the Montanan felt toward him. When Roberts and Pomerene visited the White House on their first day of work, Roberts also told Coolidge how Daugherty's bunch, according to Walsh, had tried to impede the Senate investigation and had threatened Walsh's daughter. Coolidge was sufficiently alarmed to secretly assign a team of Treasury Department Secret Service agents to the investigation. The Secret Service had a well-deserved reputation for incorruptibility and would prove invaluable to the special counsel and later Walsh.

Assigned offices in the Transportation Building at 17th and H streets, Roberts and Pomerene began their investigation by studying the Senate record, boning up on the government leasing laws, and wading through tens of thousands of pages of records and documents, including the transcripts of the Walsh and Wheeler hearings. In briefing Roberts and Pomerene on the files, Walsh pointed out some important gaps. He told the special counsel how both Florence Harding and Daugherty had burned many of Harding's papers after the president's death (the Daugherty brothers would soon burn their bank records to prevent Wheeler from perusing them). Also, some of the key figures in the investigation, most notably Sinclair, had refused to turn over their bank and business records, Walsh noted.

On March 11, Roberts and Pomerene traveled to Cheyenne, Wyoming, to file an application before Judge T. Blake Kennedy in the United States District Court for an injunction to restrain Mammoth from operating Teapot while they sought a decision to cancel the lease. Cheyenne had been chosen as the site of the Teapot trial since it was the capital of the state in which the Teapot fields were situated. They then went on to California to take similar action against Doheny's company regarding the Elk Hills and Buena Vista fields, filing in the United States District Court in Los Angeles before Judge Paul McCormick. The plan, as put forth by Roberts, was to pursue the civil suits first on the grounds that the leases had been given as the result of bribery and conspiracy. If they won these cases in the civil courts, Pomerene and Roberts could then go after Doheny, Sinclair, and Fall in criminal courts on charges of conspiracy and bribery. As Roberts would later acknowledge, they were essentially adhering to Walsh's earlier recommendations that the government first regain the reserves and then pursue Fall and the others in the criminal courts.

On the train ride west, Roberts was joined in the club car by one of Sinclair's battery of lawyers, G. T. Stanford. Stanford queried the special counsel on his career plans after the Teapot investigation and waxed enthusiastically about the benefits of working for Sinclair Oil. For a man of Roberts's talents, such a job could be the ticket to wealth, happiness, and the good life. When Roberts later told Walsh about the none-too-subtle effort to compromise him, Walsh responded, "What a pity you didn't get it in writing."

CLEVELAND, OHIO, JUNE 1924

Four years after the GOP selected Warren G. Harding as their presidential candidate, the Republicans held their national convention in the new horseshoe-shaped Cleveland Public Auditorium. At the time, the country's economy was booming. The American public seemingly had its fill of political infighting and corruption, or so Coolidge believed. In early December 1923, shortly after his State of the Union address, Coolidge had announced he was going to seek the Republican nomination and promptly began locking up delegates. "If they did not commit [to Coolidge] they would lay themselves open to retribution," a Coolidge biographer noted. As a result, the president secured the nomination well before the convention—and before the fallout from the Teapot hearings could jeopardize his chances. The move had been orchestrated by his campaign manager and the RNC chairman, William M. Butler.

The convention itself has since been called the dullest in American history. "Keep Cool with Coolidge" was the Republican slogan. This was the first convention ever broadcast on the radio, but the national audience heard nothing about the oil scandals, the resignations of Denby and Daugherty, or any Republican plans to ensure that this kind of malfeasance wouldn't recur. Daugherty, in fact, was present at the convention with Coolidge's blessing, there to help ensure Coolidge's nomination. No one objected. The administration had other priorities: the secretary of the Treasury's tax cuts; the Reed-Johnson bill restricting immigration that Coolidge had signed a few months earlier. The only acknowledgment of the Harding years came in a ceremony honoring the many presidents from Ohio: Grant, Hayes, Garfield, McKinley, Taft, and, yes, Warren Harding.

Remarkably, Coolidge didn't even bother to attend but remained in Washington. Once he was nominated, Charles G. Dawes, a banker from Illinois and author of the Dawes Plan, which was used as the basis for restructuring the German postwar economy, was selected as his running mate. Nor did "Cool Cal," the conservative, businessman's hero,

bother to campaign aside from a few set-piece speeches. He left the political stumping largely to his running mate after the Coolidges'
younger son, Calvin Coolidge Jr., died unexpectedly in July.

THREE RIVERS, NEW MEXICO, MAY 1924

While Walsh was defending the findings of the Public Lands and Surveys Committee and preparing for Wheeler's case, the special counsel
and their team of Secret Service agents were trying desperately to
gather the evidence they needed to present their arguments to the federal judges in Los Angeles and Cheyenne. The Los Angeles trial was
scheduled to commence in October 1924, the Cheyenne trial in March
1925.

In New Mexico, one of the Secret Service agents assigned to help
the special counsel, Thomas B. Foster, covered much of the same
ground that the *Denver Post* reporter D. F. Stackelbeck had traveled two
years earlier in investigating Fall. In visiting banks Fall used in both
Carrizozo and Alamogordo, New Mexico, Foster discovered that beginning in late March 1923, just a few weeks after he resigned from the
cabinet, Fall had made substantial deposits in each, including a $50,875
sum on March 29. Foster also talked to some of the workers on the
Three Rivers renovation projects who told him that the work had cost
Fall anywhere from $50,000 to $100,000. The power and irrigation
projects, Foster learned, were supervised by engineers in the Office of
Indian Affairs who were paid by the government, not Fall.

As he was traveling to Pueblo, Colorado, from Alamogordo
overnight by train, Foster's briefcase was stolen. This was no random
theft. Awaiting him at his hotel in Pueblo was a letter from Thomas
Moran, who headed up the group of agents assigned to help the special
counsel. Moran warned Foster that agents of the Burns Detective
Agency, plus operatives from both the Justice Department and the Bureau of Investigation, were on his trail. Moran instructed him to be
careful how he sent back his reports, to keep no copies, and to burn the
letter he was reading.

In New Mexico, Foster had learned that Fall and his son-in-law at
the Three Rivers ranch, Mahlon T. Everhart, used the First National
Bank in Pueblo for their ranching business. A helpful assistant teller,
L. T. Rule, told Foster that on May 22, 1922, Everhart deposited $90,000

worth of Liberty bonds to Fall's account and subsequently another $140,000. Foster noted that the serial numbers of these bonds all fell within two groups. Foster immediately contacted Moran with the recommendation that Pomerene and Roberts check with the Treasury Department to find out who had acquired these bonds originally. Liberty bonds had been used by Sinclair in the $25,000 payment to Fall for the Russian trip. Hays had testified that Sinclair had given him $75,000 in Liberty bonds to help bail out the RNC. It figured, then, that the Pueblo bonds had come from the same source, Sinclair. Proving this, however, would not be easy, especially since Mahlon Everhart had made himself extremely scarce.

In May 1924, Foster finally tracked down the elusive Everhart back in El Paso and served him with a subpoena. Appearing before a grand jury in Washington on June 2, the lanky rancher took the Fifth Amendment, refusing to say a word about the mysterious Liberty bonds he had turned over to Fall's bank in Pueblo. Meanwhile, over the summer and into early autumn, the Secret Service scoured through account files and dusty ledgers in banks and brokerage houses from New Mexico to Toronto, interviewing anyone who might have knowledge of the source of the bonds. The trail eventually led them to the Dominion Bank of Canada in Toronto and a prominent, socially well-connected Canadian barrister named H. S. Osler.

By now, the Secret Service operatives had established that the bonds had been purchased by the bank on behalf of something called the Continental Trading Company Ltd. At first Osler, who the Secret Service learned had been Continental's president, claimed the company had been organized solely by him for the purpose of settling an estate. Unfortunately, he informed the Americans, all Continental's records had been destroyed. He couldn't remember any of the names of the owners who had received the bonds. Harry Sinclair? Osler had heard the name, of course, but had never met the man.

In New York, Sinclair's former personal assistant, G. D. Wahlberg, back in the city after his extended recuperative stay in Havana, had a different story when the agents questioned him. Yes, Osler knew Sinclair. Osler had called on the oilman at his Rockefeller Center offices several times and had extensive correspondence with him. Armed with this information, the agents returned to Toronto to confront Osler once more. This time, Osler conceded some of his "oil clients" had organized

Continental and that the company had acquired a large amount of oil from Colonel A. E. Humphreys in Denver. He refused to reveal who these clients were, though he now admitted that indeed he had met Harry Sinclair.

Interviewed by Foster in Denver, Humphreys related the details of the transaction nearly three years earlier at the Vanderbilt Hotel in New York. Humphreys had sold 33,333,333 barrels of oil to Continental. At the meeting were Osler and Continental's four owner-partners, Harry M. Blackmer, chairman of the board of Midwest Refining Company; James O'Neil, president of Prairie Oil and Gas Company; Colonel Robert W. Stewart, chairman of Standard Oil of Indiana; and Harry Sinclair. These men had purchased Humphreys's oil at $1.50 a barrel, Humphreys confirmed, then promptly resold it to their own oil companies at $1.75 per barrel, creating a one-day profit of just over $8 million. A little more than $3 million of this sum, Humphreys believed, had then been converted by Osler into Liberty bonds and divided among the four Continental partners: Sinclair, Blackmer, O'Neil, and Stewart. Osler, who handled the paperwork and acted as president of the dummy Canadian company, took a 2 percent cut off the top.

This was a shocking revelation. If Humphreys was telling the truth—and there was no reason to believe otherwise—four of the country's leading oilmen had used a dummy company to defraud their own shareholders out of millions of dollars, converted the booty into Liberty bonds, divided it four ways, then used at least some of the money to pay off Fall and the RNC. At least some of these bonds, the government agents quickly ascertained, had serial numbers that were consistent with those Everhart had deposited in Pueblo.

Foster immediately wired the news of his discovery to Roberts and Pomerene. It couldn't have come at a better time. The special counsel had been working on the Los Angeles and Cheyenne cases for months without pay, since the $100,000 appropriated for their investigation had been held up in Congress, and paying expenses out of their own pocket. With the Cheyenne trial coming up, they seemingly had no real case, no hard evidence. Now that had abruptly changed. With Humphreys's affidavit, they had established a link between Sinclair and the Liberty bonds that Fall had used to refurbish Three Rivers.

Thanks to the Secret Service, they had also uncovered another blockbuster, the possible involvement of Colonel Robert W. Stewart.

As head of the largest and most successful of the Standard Oil companies, Stewart was one of the most powerful and influential oilmen in the world, certainly one of the most respected. He had been a hero in the Spanish-American War. His portrait had appeared on the cover of *Time*. As Standard Oil of Indiana's chairman, he had made a fortune for himself and his shareholders, the most prominent of whom were old John D. Rockefeller and his son John D. Rockefeller Jr.

It was almost inconceivable to Roberts and Pomerene that someone of Stewart's stature would be involved in a sordid swindle of this sort. But both Humphreys and Osler named him as one of Continental's principals. With these revelations, the government needed more time to prepare its case. They wanted to talk to Sinclair, and they needed to corroborate Humphreys's assertion that Continental's ill-gained profits had been converted into Liberty bonds and divvied up among the company's principals. In Cheyenne, however, Judge T. Blake Kennedy refused to delay the case. It would begin as scheduled the first week in March.

NEW YORK, JUNE 1924

The Democrats convened three weeks after the Republican convention at New York's Madison Square Garden. This was the Garden that Stanford White had designed in 1890—and where he was later murdered by Harry Thaw, husband of one of White's many young mistresses, Evelyn Nesbit. The Moorish-like structure with its thirty-two-story minaret-like tower, capped by a distinctly non-Moorish statue of the huntress Diana in the altogether, took up the entire block between Fifth and Madison and 26th and 27th streets. This was where John Ringling, Jake Hamon's onetime partner, brought his circus every spring with its high-flying acrobats, trumpeting elephants, and so-called Congress of Freaks. Here in 1916, the Garden roof, now decked with American flags and red, white, and blue bunting for the Democrats, had resounded with cheers when Jess Willard successfully defended his heavyweight title against Pittsburgh's Frank Moran, when Jack Dempsey had pummeled Bill Brennan four years later, finally knocking him out in the twelfth round. The Democratic convention was to be the Garden's last hurrah. The Metropolitan Life Insurance Company, which held a mortgage on the property, planned to tear it down in a few months. Nothing in its thirty-four-year history, however, would match the spectacle of the contentious, prolonged fracas that characterized the 1924 Democratic convention.

On June 21, Walsh departed Washington for the convention in New York. He had been named permanent chairman of the convention based on his prominence as the fearless oil investigator. The convention began officially on the afternoon of June 24. Cordell Hull, chairman of the Democratic National Committee, called the gathering to order. There followed a blessing from Patrick Cardinal Hayes. The keynote speech by Senator Pat Harrison of Mississippi, an impassioned attack on the insidious political influence of Big Oil, was postponed to 7:30 p.m. because of better nighttime radio reception. "Oil has become the open sesame of power," Harrison said. "It gained admittance to the robber's cave and participation in the plunder. It has been the inspiration of this administration's foreign as well as domestic policy. The magic significance of its flow has awakened the State Department to an interest not only in Mexico and . . . Colombia, but away off in the Near East. . . . Show this administration an oil well and it will show you a foreign policy." At this, the 1,446 delegates and 12,000 onlookers cheered wildly, not quieting even when Cordell Hull fainted for the third time that day from the intense heat and had to be carried off the stage.

Dressed in an elegant black cutaway coat despite the lingering heat—since taking up with Daisy Harriman, the Montanan had become quite the Beau Brummel—Walsh took the podium the next morning to a resounding ovation. Harrison introduced him as "a real Democrat and the greatest investigator in the history of our country." In his measured speech, Walsh, no match for Harrison as an orator—went after the president for ignoring Teapot and challenged the American public to assert itself at the polls in reaction to the scandals. "I cannot admit the people of America are indifferent to the corroding influence of corruption in office, high or low," he said. "But we shall see. They are on trial. If, notwithstanding what has transpired, the party now in power is continued in control by the people of the United States . . . what judgment may be passed on them by the people of the world?"

With the convention fully under way, Walsh set about trying to keep order in what quickly evolved into one of the ugliest brawls in American political history. "Walsh's slight figure moved with quick steps on the speaker's platform to and from a lectern banked with four large microphones," his biographer noted. "He talked, he shouted, he pounded with his gavel trying to bring order to the disorderly mob."

When the delegates more or less ignored a long-winded speech by ex-senator James D. Phelan nominating McAdoo, talking and shouting among themselves and wandering about the arena, Walsh erupted. He rapped his gavel furiously, demanded order, and directed the sergeants at arms to clear the aisles. A *Times* reporter wrote that Walsh was so angry that his gray mustache actually seemed to bristle. He literally barked at offenders. "What does he think, we are witnesses?" one wisen-heimer standing near the podium said, drawing a laugh from the crowd and a scowl from Walsh.

At the outset of the convention, McAdoo, who favored Prohibition and had regained some of his political momentum since Doheny's dev-astating revelations, was the leading candidate. Right behind him was New York governor Al Smith, like Walsh a Catholic, but "wet." The Californian McAdoo had the backing of the South and the West, "the happy warrior" Smith had the support of the urban East Coast. Smith had been unblemished by the oil scandals. "There ain't no oil on Al," his backers chanted. Walking now with crutches as the result of polio, Franklin Delano Roosevelt served as his floor manager, while Eleanor Roosevelt spoke fervently on Smith's behalf, traveling around the city in an automobile with a giant papier-mâché teapot mounted precariously on its roof to remind voters of the scandal.

McAdoo came under fire because of Doheny's charges. He also had the support of the Ku Klux Klan, which was still a political force in both the South and the West. McAdoo hadn't sought KKK backing, but he hadn't renounced the Klan, either. His many detractors in New York shouted, "Ku, Ku, McAdoo and oil, too!" every time McAdoo's name came up.

For two weeks (a record), Walsh presided over multiple, increas-ingly heated conflicts: north versus south, east against west, Klan sup-porters against Catholics, farmers clashing with city slickers, drys against wets, and above all, McAdoo and Smith followers flailing away relentlessly at each other. Teapot got lost in the din. Night after night, Americans listened on their radios to the Democrats self-destruct. In his efforts to retain some semblance of order and parliamentary proce-dure, Walsh banged so loudly and often on the podium with his gavel that it frequently shattered and bounced into the delegate space below.

At one point, he became so frustrated, he uttered what likely was the first profanity—a "goddamn"—ever broadcast nationally. At the convention's end, one delegate rose to propose that all his colleagues who hadn't been hit by Tom Walsh's gavel gather in a telephone booth to give thanks.

The ballots came so fast and furious that at one point humorist Will Rogers was fifteen minutes late for one session and discovered on his return three ballots had been cast in his absence. In all, there were 103 ballots, a record at the time. With both Smith and McAdoo refusing to give ground, and both at loggerheads in terms of votes, the delegates eventually settled on a compromise candidate, John W. Davis, a respected Wall Street lawyer from West Virginia. Lacking in charisma and largely unknown, Davis intended to make Teapot the touchstone of his campaign and sought Walsh to serve as his running mate. Cries of "Walsh, Walsh, Walsh!" resounded through the Garden, but prudently Walsh declined the offer, after a number of his colleagues, including Burton Wheeler, asserted that Davis hadn't a prayer in hell of winning. Instead, Walsh returned to Montana in an effort to regain his Senate seat. Governor Charles W. Bryan of Nebraska was selected as the vice presidential nominee.

In the national campaign, the Democrats as well as the newly formed Progressive Party, which put forth La Follette and Walsh's protégé Burton Wheeler as its presidential and vice presidential candidates, respectively, hammered away at Teapot and the Republicans without much effect. Davis, Al Smith, Walsh, and others (the showman Wheeler debated an empty chair on which he asked his audience to imagine President Coolidge was seated) tried to get Coolidge to respond to charges about the scandal, but "Silent Cal" remained entirely mum, refusing to take the bait.

In Montana, conservatives from outside the state sent large, unreported contributions to defeat the Teapot investigator, "black money" that could have come from any number of Walsh's enemies. On October 20, Walsh wired Frank P. Walsh (no relation), a member of the special Senate Committee on Campaign Expenditures: RUMORED THAT $100,000 COMING TO MONTANA TO BE USED AGAINST ME, NOT PASSING, HOWEVER, THRU EITHER NATIONAL COMMITTEEMAN OR CHAIRMAN REPUBLICAN COMMITTEE. KINDLY QUESTION CAREFULLY REGARDING REMITTANCES TO THIS STATE.

Despite the outside funding and threats from the KKK, which was active in Montana, Walsh nonetheless was reelected by a majority of 10,000 votes out of 170,000 cast. With the victory, the positive exposure he received from Teapot, and his role in the convention as a voice of reason and restraint amid persistent bedlam, Walsh emerged as a national figure and one of the undisputed leaders of the minority party.

Nationally, the Progressives garnered a respectable 4.8 million votes, the Democrats 8.3 million, and Coolidge 15.7 million. "Silent Cal" had survived Teapot unscathed. Subsequently, historian William E. Dodd wrote Walsh, saying that the one Democrat who could have beaten Coolidge, William McAdoo, had been done in by Doheny's implication of him in the scandal. That was "the greatest calamity" in the entire Teapot story, Dodd said. Walsh disagreed. The greatest calamity in his view was the seeming indifference of the voters, or at least 15.7 million of them, to the corruption he and the committee had uncovered. "I am amazed . . . at the people who seem for the first time in history to contemplate graft in high office with resignation," he said.

LOS ANGELES, JULY 1924

On July 1, after the sixth ballot at the Democratic convention, it was announced from the platform, "Former secretary Fall, Harry F. Sinclair, E. L. Doheny, and E. L. Doheny Jr. have been indicted, due to the excellent efforts of your Permanent Chairman." In what was the first of the government's criminal cases against the oil operators and Fall, criminal indictments had been returned against them for fraud. Based largely on evidence uncovered in the Public Lands and Surveys Committee hearings, the two Dohenys were accused of inducing Fall on behalf of the Pan American Petroleum and Transport Company to commit an unlawful and felonious act in exchange for a $100,000 bribe.

These were difficult times for the Doheny clan. At the same time the Feds were coming after him, Edward Sr. was being investigated for bribing a harbor commissioner in Los Angeles. The matter had to do with two choice leases Doheny had secured at Los Angeles Harbor for his oil tankers and an extended vacation the oilman had provided gratis to the former president of the Board of Harbor Commissioners, Edgar McKee. Soon after the leases were granted, McKee was on his way to Honolulu aboard the Doheny yacht, *Casiana.*

Ned Jr., whom Doheny père had identified in his testimony as the bearer of the now famous black bag, was particularly upset by the legal actions targeted at him. Likely neither father nor son had expected Ned to be indicted. He had simply been his old man's errand boy. Still, both he and his father each had to post $5,000 bonds on July 19, a pittance to the Dohenys but a huge embarrassment, especially to Ned, who with his wife, Lily, was among the young elite of Los Angeles society, forever turning up at charity balls and black-tie dinners. Ned, whose name appeared far more often in the society section than the business pages, sat on half a dozen civic boards. Now there was gossip about Ned, whispers behind his back. In September, he learned that the board of directors of the Methodist Church, one of the controlling factions at the University of Southern California, had voted to boot him as a USC trustee if any of the charges against him proved valid. Soon after, he gave $200,000 to the university to solidify his standing on the board.

Ned could end up in jail—all because he'd done a seemingly harmless favor for his father. The elder Doheny assured him that all would be well, advised Ned to carry on just as if nothing had happened. Ned's response, according to a Doheny biographer, was to travel more and more on business, always taking Hugh Plunkett with him for companionship, and to spend more time in his town house at 15 East 84th Street in New York. Plunkett was now in his employ full-time. Lucy and the Dohenys' five young children stayed behind in their estate in Chester Place, next door to Ned's parents.

Doheny Sr.'s instinct was to fight with every resource at his disposal. In July, he hired a new legal team headed up by Frank J. Hogan, a slight, cocky, forty-eight-year-old Irishman who'd been born churchmouse poor in Brooklyn, put himself through Georgetown University Law Center, and quickly established himself as one of the greatest trial lawyers of his generation, a kind of Houdini of the courtroom whose greatest trick was to make the charges against his clients disappear. "The best client," Hogan used to say, "is a rich man who is scared." Doheny was both. He gave Hogan $1 million as a retainer with the promise of more if Hogan succeeded in getting father and son acquitted.

Over the summer, Doheny and his legal team cooked up a legal and public relations strategy that hinged essentially on two arguments: (a) Doheny had leased the reserves because he was a concerned patriot; and

(b) Albert Fall had little or nothing to do with leasing the reserves to Doheny. It had all been Edwin Denby's doing.

Later Doheny, with Hogan at his side in the comfort of his Chester Place den, would expound on the patriotic nature of his deed and Denby's part therein to a *New York Times* reporter. EDWARD L. DOHENY'S OWN STORY OF THE ELK HILLS OIL LEASES, TOLD FOR THE FIRST TIME, was how the *Times* played up the story, which ran in excess of fifteen thousand words, no questions asked, just Doheny expounding on his version of the case. Doheny explained that he had agreed to the leases and the related building of an oil storage facility only because his old friend Admiral Robinson had secretly informed him "that an invasion of the Pacific Coast of the United States was probable unless the Pearl Harbor base was built without a moment's delay."

He also explained to the *Times* that the whole naval lease policy of the Harding administration had originated not with Fall, but solely with the secretary of the navy and his department. All this had been extensively documented, Doheny claimed, in a series of telegrams "which so mysteriously disappeared from the government files that were ransacked by representatives of the Senate investigating committee." Unfortunately for Fall and the Dohenys, these documents hadn't been seen since.

CHEYENNE, WYOMING, MARCH 1925

A few weeks before the Cheyenne trial commenced, the participants began gathering in Wyoming's capital city. Every bar, barbershop, restaurant, and hotel in town was overrun by oilmen, witnesses, reporters, and lawyers who had arrived by the trainload. Not even Cheyenne's fabled annual "Frontier Days" attracted this big a gathering or generated as much excitement. Harry Sinclair's entourage took up the entire fifth floor, some forty rooms, in the Plains Hotel and even included several beefy security guards from Sinclair's Rockefeller Center headquarters. In uniform, they stood sentinel outside Sinclair's suite.

On the floor below, Roberts, Pomerene, and their far smaller retinue occupied six rooms. In the view of local oddsmakers and pundits, the government men seemed badly outmanned, outgunned, and vastly outlawyered. Several months earlier, Roberts and Pomerene had presented their case to a federal judge in Los Angeles to argue that Doheny's lease for the Elk Hills reserves should be canceled. The atmosphere in Los Angeles, where Doheny was a popular, powerful figure, had been hostile, but nothing like what the government lawyers encountered in Cheyenne.

The judge in the Teapot trial, T. Blake Kennedy, had headed up the Wyoming Republican delegation to the 1920 Chicago convention that nominated Harding. Harding had subsequently appointed Kennedy to the federal bench on the recommendation of Harry Daugherty. Sinclair was represented by a team of nine lawyers, including his New York attorney, Martin Littleton, and his in-house legal staff, headed by Bill Zevely. To co-represent him in the trial, Sinclair had also hired the leader and éminence grise of the Wyoming bar, J. W. Lacey. The seventy-seven-year-old Lacey was highly regarded in a state where Big Oil was venerated and easterners, especially agents of what was seen as a meddling federal government, were suspect. While not a local boy, the flamboyant Kansan Harry Sinclair was no outsider. Thanks to Albert Fall, he and Robert Stewart of Standard Oil of Indiana controlled both Teapot and the adjacent Salt Creek field roughly two hundred miles to the north. Together, these fields constituted the world's largest reserve of light crude oil and provided employment for a sizable percentage of the state's workforce.

In this oil-dependent state, Sinclair was a popular figure. He would come into a bar in Cheyenne's Cherokee strip and buy rounds for everyone in the place until closing time. With his fortune Harry Sinclair could, and did, buy just about anything or anyone he wanted. He also doled out cash and concessions to many of Cheyenne's most influential people, including Harry P. Hynds, owner of the Plains Hotel and Judge Kennedy's closest friend.

Before the trial, a Sinclair executive, A. E. Watts, took Hynds and his wife on a Caribbean cruise aboard Sinclair's yacht, *Sinco*. According to the society pages of the Cheyenne paper, Sinclair and his agents wined and dined the Hynds several times a week prior to and during the trial. In return, Sinclair frequently was a guest of the Hynds at their residence. There, Sinclair and the hotel owner played poker, with Sinclair often losing large sums. In one game, Sinclair managed to drop $40,000 to Hynds, news that traveled like a prairie fire through Cheyenne.

Clearly, though, Sinclair believed he would recoup his losses many times over in the courtroom. With the trial starting, he seemingly had absolutely nothing to worry about. A few days after the opening arguments, *The New York Times* described Sinclair as "the most unconcerned man in Cheyenne." Fall, who'd come up from New Mexico, was so cocky that he couldn't contain himself. Running into Roberts and Pomerene in the Plains lobby, he boasted, "I'm surprised you people turned up at all. Don't you know you're licked before you start?"

The trial got under way on March 15 with the reporters in Cheyenne filing stories that the special counsel had uncovered some startling new information regarding a mysterious dummy company, Continental Trading. Problem was that most witnesses that could shed light on the activities of Continental were out of reach. After the Canadian courts had ruled that Continental's president, H. S. Osler, had to answer all the Americans' questions, Osler promptly departed for a prolonged big-game hunting trip in Africa. The special counsel subpoenaed Standard Oil's Robert Stewart, only to discover that Stewart had also left the country. No one at his home office seemed to know his whereabouts. Roberts had also tried to force Harry Blackmer and James O'Neil back from France for the trial without success. Four of the five principals in the shadow entity that had spawned Teapot were half a continent and an ocean away. Meanwhile, Fall and Sinclair wouldn't testify because of protection afforded by the Fifth Amendment.

At least Roberts and Pomerene had Sinclair's former assistant, G. D. Wahlberg, and A. E. Humphreys on tap. Wahlberg testified that there was a long-standing link between Sinclair and Osler. Humphreys, a flamboyant wildcatter, explained what had transpired at those Vanderbilt Hotel meetings at which Sinclair, Blackmer, Stewart, and O'Neil had acquired his oil. By far the more able of the special counsel, Roberts, who argued the government's case, was shrewd and persistent, but from the start it was evident where Judge Kennedy's sentiments lay. He ruled that Roberts could not introduce Fall's bank accounts into evidence as proof that Fall had received Liberty bonds. Despite vehement objections from Roberts, Kennedy allowed Everhart, Fall's son-in-law, not to testify based on his Fifth Amendment rights not to incriminate himself. How could Everhart incriminate himself? Roberts demanded. He didn't work for the government, and he'd had nothing to do with dispensing the oil leases to his father-in-law. Like Ed Doheny's son, Ned, he'd simply been a bagman.

Without Everhart's testimony, the government couldn't establish the critical link between Harry Sinclair, the Liberty bonds, and Albert Fall. Without Everhart, the government essentially had no case. The trial had been projected to last six weeks to two months, but the government and defense concluded their final statements by March 26. Kennedy announced that it would be several months at least before he would hand down his decision.

Early in April, Stewart returned from Colombia, where he had traveled on oil business. He hadn't known anyone was looking for him, he told reporters. The same week, Osler got back from Africa with a few new trophy heads to mount in his Toronto mansion. On June 19, 1925, Kennedy announced he was ruling against the government on every point. There had been no collusion or fraud. The Teapot leases were to remain in effect. At the news, Sinclair stock soared. Soon after, Judge Kennedy, his wife, Harry P. Hynds, and his spouse departed for an extended Mediterranean cruise aboard Sinclair's yacht with Sinclair's man A. E. Watts again serving as host. In Cheyenne, several prominent Democrats, including Joseph C. O'Mahoney, city editor of the *Cheyenne State Leader* and later a U.S. senator for Wyoming, wrote Tom Walsh that Harry Sinclair was footing the bill for the judge's vacation.

GREAT FALLS, MONTANA, APRIL 1925

One of the last things Harry Daugherty did before departing Washington was to indict Burton Wheeler on a trumped-up influence-peddling charge. In the indictment, Daugherty claimed that Wheeler was in the pocket of one Gordon Campbell, a small-time oilman. Aware that Wheeler's wife was pregnant, the Department of Justice scheduled the trial at what for the Wheelers was the worst possible time. "They set it down in April . . . at the time they knew Mrs. Wheeler was going to have a baby, thinking I'd have to ask to postpone it," Wheeler later recalled. He'd discovered the date only by reading about it in the newspaper.

Tom Walsh was outraged at the Wheeler indictment. In a private meeting with the new attorney general, Harlan Fiske Stone, he argued that the charges should be thrown out at once. Stone assured him that Wheeler would be treated with all possible fairness but refused to drop the case. That wasn't good enough, Walsh said. The charges should never have been filed. On the Senate floor, he called the indictment "a plain case of political reprisal."

Walsh volunteered to serve as Wheeler's defense attorney. The trial was held in Great Falls, Montana, beginning on April 15, 1925, a full year after the indictment had been returned. Financier Bernard Baruch, Harvard Law School professor Felix Frankfurter, and Josephus Daniels, former secretary of the navy, were among those who organized a defense fund on Wheeler's behalf, raising $15,000.

As its mystery witness, the government produced a New York lawyer named George B. Hayes. Hayes claimed that on the evening of March 16, 1924, between the hours of 5:00 and 7:00 in the evening, Wheeler had met him at Peacock Alley in New York's Waldorf-Astoria in an effort to persuade him to front an illegal oil deal. Walsh cross-examined Hayes with his usual surgical incisiveness, quickly establishing that the government witness had four federal income tax violations against him and was facing disbarment proceedings at the time the Justice Department asked him to testify against Wheeler. As it happened, Walsh continued, Wheeler had in fact been in Manhattan with his wife on March 16. However, the Wheelers had spent the evening having cocktails, eating dinner, and attending the opera with a party of prominent friends, including the famous Colonel Edward M. House, President Wilson's former right-hand man, and Walsh's friend Daisy Harriman. Wheeler hadn't been anywhere near the Waldorf that night. "There is nothing whatever in this on which you would condemn a jailbird or streetwalker," Walsh said in summation, nearly shouting in anger, according to one of the reporters present.

The jury was out a little over two hours and took two votes—the first to go to dinner on the government's tab, the second to acquit Wheeler. Later, at a celebratory dinner with Walsh and a couple of lawyers and newspaper reporters who had been covering the trial, Wheeler was handed a telegram from Washington. His wife had delivered their first child.

The larger issue that had concerned Walsh and Wheeler's many supporters was spelled out in a congratulatory telegram Senator Robert La Follette sent to Walsh after the trial. CONGRATULATIONS ON YOUR MAGNIFICENT WORK, La Follette wired him. YOU HAVE ADDED ANOTHER GREAT SCORE TO YOUR GREAT RECORD. OUR FIRST CONCERN WAS

TO SEE WHEELER EXONERATED. BUT BACK OF THAT AS YOU CLEARLY
PERCEIVED WAS THE INTEGRITY OF THE PUBLIC SERVICE WAS AT STAKE.

Two months later, La Follette was dead, felled by a heart attack at
the age of seventy.

WASHINGTON, D.C., SEPTEMBER 28, 1926

Fourteen months after Judge Kennedy's ruling in Cheyenne, the United
States Circuit Court of Appeals reversed his decision and declared the
Teapot Dome lease invalid because it was negotiated and executed
under fraudulent circumstances. The court agreed with every charge
that Walsh had spelled out in the committee report on Teapot. Doheny's lead attorney, Frank Hogan, announced immediately that he was
appealing the ruling.

Following the court of appeals decision, an elated Owen Roberts
wrote Walsh, "I think you are entitled to congratulations as well as
counsel, because the decision is a vindication of your legal judgment as
well as ours." Five months later, the U.S. Supreme Court handed down
a decision that represented the ultimate vindication for Roberts,
Pomerene, and their staunchest ally in Washington, Walsh. The highest
court in the land overturned Doheny's appeal, finding that the naval
leases at Elk Hills were illegal and "tainted with corruption." It also let
stand California judge Paul McCormick's ruling, which Hogan had also
appealed, that the Elk Hills contract was null, void, and fraudulent because of Doheny's $100,000 payment to Fall.

After four years, the U.S. Naval Reserves were once again property
of the U.S. government. "Very naturally I rejoice in the result," Walsh
wrote an acquaintance, James J. Flaherty, on November 1, 1927.

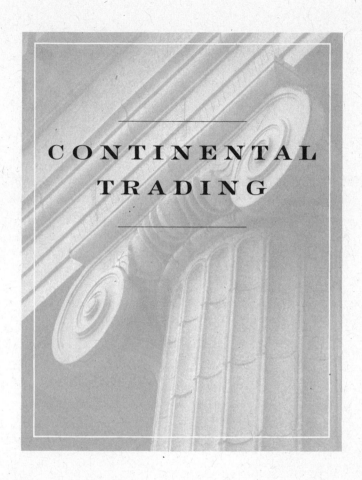

CONTINENTAL
TRADING

39

THE UNSEEN HAND

In the fall of 1927, a thirty-four-year-old *St. Louis Post-Dispatch* reporter named Paul Y. Anderson met with Thomas Walsh in Washington. Anderson had been covering Teapot almost exclusively since 1923. He had interviewed Walsh several times, admired him, and, like the senator, believed much about the Teapot scandal had yet to be revealed.

By now, it had been established that Albert Fall had received at least $300,000 in Liberty bonds. These had been traced back to the Continental Trading Company. In their various investigations, the special counsel had also learned that Fall's bonds were part of a much larger windfall, over $8 million in illicit gains, more than $3 million of which Continental's partners had converted into Liberty bonds. What had happened to the remaining funds—the bonds that hadn't been given to Fall? That was the question Anderson posed to Walsh.

At least some of the funds had been used as a slush fund for corrupt purposes involving the Republican Party, Anderson believed. Walsh concurred. He remained certain Sinclair had established a slush fund of $1 million and had been pursuing this line of inquiry when the 1924 hearings had come to an abrupt halt after Harry Sinclair refused to testify. However, without Everhart's testimony, Pomerene and Roberts had been unable to link Sinclair or his Continental associates directly to Fall. Now, Anderson and his legendary managing editor, O. K. Bovard, urged Walsh to reopen the Teapot investigation, this time focusing exclusively on the Continental funds.

Walsh was reluctant. He was now sixty-eight years old, in good health, but still he knew all too well how exhausting, all-consuming, and thankless a task this was. Besides, these were boom times. "In the domestic field there is tranquillity and contentment . . . and the highest record of years of prosperity," Coolidge reminded the country in his State of the Union address. Lindbergh had soloed across the Atlantic in May. The stock market was at an all-time high. America was fixated on its boundless future. Revisiting Teapot would not play well politically in this climate. Still, Walsh was willing to pursue a Continental inquiry, with one important stipulation, he told Anderson. He couldn't be the one to introduce the resolution in the Senate.

Walsh had been criticized in the past as using the Public Lands and Surveys Committee probe to further the Democratic political agenda and his own ambitions. Determined to seek the Democratic presidential nomination in the upcoming election, he couldn't be seen as using the renewed probe toward that end. If the investigation was ordered, he assured Anderson, he would "prosecute it with such vigor as he could command." But someone else would have to get the Republican-controlled Senate to reopen the inquiry.

Encouraged, Anderson began writing what would prove to be a Pulitzer Prize–winning series of articles and interviews pressing for an inquiry into the still mysterious Continental affair. As Walsh had suggested, he also sought to enlist someone to champion a Senate resolution to reopen the investigation. Anderson's first choice, Owen Roberts, turned him down on the grounds that such a probe went beyond his brief as special counsel. Not knowing Anderson had already talked to Walsh, Roberts suggested Anderson approach the Montanan.

Anderson and Bovard also sought backing from the attorney general and seventy-two-year-old Andrew Mellon. Mellon had continued on as Treasury secretary under Coolidge, emerging as the real force in the administration, more powerful, many believed, than the president. Aside from providing the small Secret Service unit to help the special counsel with their various probes, neither Treasury nor Justice had offered the slightest assistance to Roberts and Pomerene in the course of their three-year effort to bring Fall, Sinclair, and Doheny to justice. No surprise, then, that neither Justice nor Treasury saw any need to probe Continental. At least they had responded to Anderson and Bovard's request. President Coolidge remained mum after Anderson appealed to the White House.

Ultimately, Senator George Norris, the Progressive Republican from Nebraska who had supported Walsh's efforts in the initial hearings, declared he would bring the matter before the Senate when Congress reconvened. On January 9, 1928, at Norris's urging, the Senate passed a resolution initiating a new investigation, one that would again be conducted by the Committee on Public Lands and Surveys. That Walsh, who was still a committee member, would lead the probe was a given.

40

A BRIBE AS BIG AS THE RITZ

In October, as Paul Anderson began his campaign to investigate the disposal of the Liberty bonds, Harry Sinclair and Albert Fall were being tried for criminal conspiracy in the criminal branch of the District of Columbia Supreme Court. In previous trials, Sinclair had presented himself as the embodiment of the swashbuckling oil tycoon. This was the self-made multimillionaire whose racehorse Zev had won the Kentucky Derby, who wagered hundreds of thousands of dollars a night at baccarat in Arnold Rothstein's casino in Saratoga. On this occasion, however, his handlers presented an altogether different Harry Sinclair. This Sinclair was a conservative family man and good corporate citizen who lay awake nights agonizing about the fate of his seventeen thousand employees should the courts rule against him.

When the trial began on October 17, Sinclair appeared with his wife, children, and eighty-year-old mother in tow. Reporters who had been covering the various civil and criminal actions against Sinclair couldn't remember having seen any of the family members in court before. The former secretary of the interior also arrived en famille. His wife, Emma, two daughters, and personal physician accompanied Fall. Even though Fall had been vigorous enough to announce a few months earlier that he intended to run again for the U.S. Senate, he arrived in

Washington appearing far older than his sixty-five years. He was drawn, frail, and disheveled. His doctor said the former interior secretary was in poor health. At the outside, he had maybe three or four months to live. This was not the first or last time during Fall's prolonged tribulations that doctors had pronounced him at death's door, only to have him rally as soon as the legal hurdle was cleared.

When the trial began, both he and Sinclair seemed uncharacteristically nervous, understandably so. Earlier in the year, the U.S. Supreme Court had reclaimed Teapot from Mammoth Oil. In announcing its decision, the Court harshly criticized Sinclair and Fall, characterizing the latter as a "faithless public servant."

Fresh off their success in the nation's highest court, Pomerene and Roberts were seemingly in a strong position to prosecute the criminal conspiracy trial. But the special counsel were having difficulties of their own, most notably a lack of funding. Roberts, Pomerene, and their associates hadn't been paid since June. Roberts was so discouraged that he wanted to resign, though Walsh had urged him to stay on. While Congress again dragged its heels at appropriating a second $100,000 desperately needed to pursue the conspiracy litigation, the special counsel, neither of whom was a wealthy man, again funded the government's efforts out of their own pockets.

As the trial got under way, the government encountered many of the same obstacles it had confronted in Cheyenne and in other trials— the refusal of Everhart as well as Fall to testify, the absence of Blackmer and O'Neil, both still in France, Blackmer comfortably ensconced in Paris with a Norwegian opera singer. And, of course, the Canadian Osler had embarked on yet another African safari. Unbeknownst to Roberts and Pomerene, they were also contending with Sinclair's behind-the-scenes efforts to rig the jury. Having suffered defeat in the nation's highest court, the oilman was leaving nothing to chance this go-round.

Immediately after the jury had been sworn in on October 18, Sinclair directed Henry Mason Day, his international troubleshooter, to engage the William J. Burns International Detective Agency—after leaving the Bureau of Investigation, Burns had returned to his old trade—to spy on the jurors and "lock up" one or two through bribery or intimidation in order to bring about a mistrial. This wasn't the first time Burns had taken on such an assignment. In 1912, the future director of the Bureau of Investigation tampered with a jury in Oregon in order to ensure the conviction of a man named Jones. Jones was subsequently pardoned by President Taft, who characterized Burns's activities as "the most barefaced and unfair use of all the machinery for drawing a jury."

The sixty-seven-year-old Burns had put his son W. Sherman Burns in charge of the agency's day-to-day operations, but for an important client such as Sinclair he didn't mind getting his hands dirty if necessary. On October 12, he visited Washington to meet with Sinclair in his Mayflower Hotel suite about the upcoming trial. Subsequently, Burns obtained a false affidavit from one of his operatives claiming that a juror named Glasscock had been seen talking to a U.S. attorney. This was later presented to the trial judge in an attempt to show the government wasn't playing by the rules.

Burns's operatives shadowed all the jurors from early morning through much of the night, creating an extensive dossier on each and reporting daily to Burns, who then briefed Sinclair. Singling out three jurors whose finances were shaky, Sinclair decided to offer them substantial payoffs if they held out for acquittal. Unfortunately for the oilman, one of his would-be benefactors, Edward Kidwell, a streetcar motorman and chronic gambler, bragged to some of his co-workers that he was going to get "an automobile as long as a block" from that "fine fellow" Sinclair if there was a mistrial. Over drinks at a local tavern, Kidwell made the same boast to a reporter from the *Washington Herald*.

At about the same time, one of the Burns agents, a recently hired operative named William J. McMullin, began to have second thoughts about what he was doing. The suddenly conscience-stricken McMullin went to Pomerene and Roberts with his story. They immediately called a meeting in their offices. Joining them were McMullin, several of the Secret Service agents, and United States attorney Peyton Gordon. Quickly the assembled team worked out a plan to ensnare Sinclair. McMullin would work as a double agent, staying on the Burns payroll and gathering proof of what Sinclair was up to while secretly reporting back to the government.

By October 31, Roberts and Pomerene had the information they needed. In the courtroom that morning, Sinclair seemed to have regained his old jaunty confidence. He chatted amicably with Colonel Robert Stewart, who was scheduled to testify that morning about the Humphreys oil purchase. Fall chomped away on his usual unlit black cigar. As the judge approached the bench, Pomerene stood, saying he had a matter of the gravest importance to discuss. Sinclair blanched, apparently guessing what had transpired. In the anteroom, Pomerene and Roberts presented reports to Judge Frederick L. Siddons from the Burns detectives that had been seized that same morning in a raid of the Burns headquarters at the Wardman Park Hotel. They also gave the judge affidavits detailing the bribery attempts and even a scheme to blackmail one of the jurors.

Of course, as soon as court was adjourned, all of Washington was speculating wildly as to what had transpired in chambers. The following day, Judge Siddons declared a mistrial. Two weeks later, he ordered Harry Sinclair, Burns, his son Sherman, and half a dozen Sinclair executives to appear before him on December 5 and show cause why they shouldn't be held for criminal contempt for jury shadowing. Fall had nothing to do with the scheme. Old and bewildered, he seemed unable to grasp what had happened.

41

THE LINK

The renewed Public Lands and Surveys Committee hearings resumed on January 24, 1928. Again, the nation's newspapers devoted much of the front pages to the scandal. The hearings were held in the Senate's minority caucus room. On this go-round, the committee chairman was Gerald P. Nye, a Republican from North Dakota and former newspaper editor who was prone to issuing inflammatory, publicity-generating statements. On learning that Sinclair had tried to bribe jury members in the criminal conspiracy case, Nye told reporters that both the oilman and Fall should be subjected to the death penalty.

Nye could say whatever he liked, but from the outset it was clear this was going to be largely Thomas Walsh's show. Again, he would act as prosecutor—his enemies would characterize him as "the grand inquisitor"—select witnesses, and drive the investigation. To date, not a single figure in what was the largest political scandal in American history had gone to jail. There were still vast gaps in the public knowledge of what had transpired—gaps Walsh and his fellow committee member intended to fill.

Confident that the Senate would pass the resolution, Walsh sought to eliminate many of the impediments that had hindered the special counsel's investigation. In the conspiracy case, Everhart had again refused to testify. On December 11, 1927, almost a full month before the Senate voted to renew the investigation, Walsh wrote Senator Norris asking for his support in dealing with the Everhart matter. "I am planning to go to the Senate tomorrow in order to introduce a bill, copies of which I am asking my secretary to show you," Walsh explained. The legislation would reduce the statute of limitations for defrauding the United States government from six years to three. If it passed, Everhart would no longer be protected by the Fifth Amendment. "On introducing the bill I shall ask unanimous consent for its immediate consideration without reference to a committee, hoping it will go through the House before the Fall-Sinclair trail is resumed."

By the time the Public Lands and Surveys Committee hearings kicked off, Walsh's bill had cleared Congress and had been signed by President Coolidge. As a result, on the opening day of the hearings, Walsh's first witness was M. T. Everhart. Before confronting Fall's son-in-law, though, Walsh placed into the record the copy of the contract between Colonel Humphreys and the Continental Trading Company that Pomerene and Roberts had uncovered in their investigation. He also had testimony from the Cheyenne trial read into the record.

Everhart was the next order of business. The tall, lanky rancher was clearly uncomfortable settling into the witness chair. For four years, he had been repeatedly subpoenaed to testify against his father-in-law, each time refusing. Walsh, however, didn't believe Everhart had played even a minor role in the fraud. Fall had used his son-in-law as a bagman just as Ed Doheny had deployed his only son, Ned, the only difference being that Ned had carried a black valise filled with cash while Everhart had transported a parcel of Liberty bonds.

After Everhart was sworn in, he stated he was an involuntary witness and wished to be formally subpoenaed. Walsh promptly accommodated him, ordering the assistant sergeant at arms to produce a subpoena. Sitting directly across the table from Walsh, Everhart answered each of the questions that were being put to him by the senator. Both men spoke in such hushed tones that Walsh might have been Everhart's priest hearing his confession. Reporters crowded around the hearing table so they could follow the exchange. Nye finally asked that the two men move away from each other and speak louder so that others could hear.

In early 1922, Everhart conceded, he and his father-in-law had talked about ways to come up with fresh capital so they could pay off substantial outstanding debts on the Three Rivers ranch and make long overdue improvements. In May 1922, a date fixed by Walsh as a month after the Teapot lease was signed, Everhart came east to attend his mother's funeral. Fall asked him to stop in Washington, where in Fall's offices at the Interior Department, Everhart, his father-in-law, and Harry Sinclair discussed the ranch. It was Everhart's recollection that Sinclair and Fall had already agreed to some sort of deal prior to his arrival in which Fall was to receive $233,000 in Liberty bonds.

How did Everhart collect the bonds? Walsh inquired. Everhart explained that he had met Sinclair in his private railroad car and waited while Sinclair gathered $198,000 in Liberty bonds. After turning over $2,500 of these bonds to Fall, which the then interior secretary wanted for his own use, Everhart had traveled to New York to collect an additional $35,000 in bonds from Sinclair. Fall had also asked Everhart to hit up Sinclair for an additional $36,000 loan, this in cash. On other occasions, Everhart recalled Sinclair giving Fall yet another $35,000 loan.

What had he done with the bonds? Walsh inquired. Everhart said he'd shipped them to the First National Bank, the ranch bank, in Pueblo, Colorado. Had he or Fall given Sinclair a receipt or IOU for the bonds? No, nothing. Had any of the money been repaid? Everhart didn't know. He had distanced himself from the scheme, and from his father-in-law, some time ago.

Everhart said he hadn't received any of the money himself. Nor had he had anything to do with its distribution. Rising from the witness chair when Walsh finished, Everhart seemed immensely relieved. He shook hands with Walsh and with Senator Kendrick from Wyoming, an old friend and still a member of the committee. Everhart had been "through hell" and now felt as though a great weight had been lifted from his shoulders, he told a friend who had accompanied him to the hearings. On the first day of the hearings, Walsh and the committee had uncovered what the special counsel had been trying vainly to establish for four years—an irrefutable link between Fall, Sinclair, and the Liberty bonds.

42

ABOVE THE LAW

Ideally, Walsh and the committee would have liked to grill Harry Sinclair immediately pursuant to Everhart's testimony, but Sinclair was sequestered a few blocks away on trial for criminal contempt along with Sherman and Billy Burns, and the loyal Henry Mason Day, pursuant to the discovery that they'd attempted to rig the jury in the conspiracy case. Sinclair would have to wait. In his place, Walsh summoned Colonel Robert Stewart to the stand. Large and imposing, the imperious Stewart, like Walsh, had grown up in the Midwest and come from modest circumstances. After excelling at little Coe College in Iowa, Stewart graduated from Yale Law School, then practiced law for several years in South Dakota. There, his path had crossed with Walsh's. On one occasion, they were combatants in a bitter lawsuit. In 1913, the highly ambitious Stewart had been hired as general counsel for Standard Oil of Indiana, rising expeditiously to become its chairman.

In their various investigations, Pomerene and Roberts had established that Stewart had been one of Continental's organizers but hadn't gotten Stewart to testify. The oilman conveniently managed to be out of the country on important business every time the special prosecutors tried to get him into the witness chair. In the new Public Lands and Surveys Committee hearings, Stewart had been scheduled to testify immediately following Everhart's appearance. He had been subpoenaed almost two weeks earlier, but when Walsh called his name, Stewart's personal counsel, L. L. Stephens, informed the committee that, unfortunately, Stewart was absent. Walsh demanded to know why. Colonel Stewart was in Havana, where he was "very, very busy on matters of great import—matters which I would prefer not to divulge," Stephens explained in a tone that implied somehow the national interest was at stake. In all likelihood, Colonel Stewart couldn't get back to Washington much before March 1.

This, of course, was the same evasive tactic Stewart had taken successfully with the special counsel, but Walsh was fully prepared to deal with it. He produced a small stack of Havana newspapers from the previous week and proceeded to read aloud from them. Like Sinclair, Stewart was a horse-racing aficionado. The Havana papers reported him as frequenting the racetrack's Jockey Club nearly every day. There were photographs of the colonel at luncheons, cocktail parties, dinners, and even a ball at the Havana Yacht Club. When Walsh finished his account of Stewart's whirlwind social schedule, he stared silently at Stephens for several moments. Under such intense scrutiny, the Standard Oil attorney seemed to shrink in his chair. He reminded one reporter of a culpable schoolboy who had been dragged before the principal. "I think that without further discussion you had better cable Colonel Stewart that the Senate Committee on Public Lands expects his prompt appearance before it," Walsh said. "Is that understood?"

Stephens nodded. It was understood.

While the committee awaited Stewart's arrival, Walsh put Edward G. Seubert, president of Standard Oil of Indiana, Stewart's second in command, on the stand to respond to questions about the oil company's part in the Continental deal. Seubert testified that Stewart had returned from New York in November 1921 with what he termed "a great contract." It called for Standard Oil of Indiana to buy thirty-three million barrels of oil from Continental Trading at $1.75 a barrel. Directors of the company had rubber-stamped the deal after Stewart assured them $1.75 represented the best price they could get.

Had Seubert or any of the Standard board ever heard of Continental Trading Company prior to this transaction? Walsh asked. No. Didn't Seubert and the board question why Continental had been able to buy a quarter share of the same thirty-three million barrels from

Colonel Humphreys at $1.50 a barrel, 25 cents below what Standard Oil had paid? They hadn't asked, Seubert conceded. Later, however, it had dawned on him that someone must have made a pretty penny on the deal. Never had he imagined that someone had been Stewart. "We had implicit confidence in Colonel Stewart," he told the committee.

Stewart showed up on February 1, looking tanned and rested from his Cuban stay. For a few minutes, he and Walsh exchanged pleasantries and war stories about their salad days in the Dakotas. As soon as Walsh brought up Continental Trading and the Liberty bonds, however, Stewart became truculent. He wanted his old adversary to know he wouldn't stand to be treated in the brusque manner with which the senator had just dealt with Seubert.

"Do you know, Senator, what I would have told you, had you talked to me as you did those other witnesses?" he asked.

"No," replied Walsh, "but I shall know pretty soon, for I am going to put those very same questions to you."

When Walsh asked about the oil transaction, Stewart responded, "I never got a dollar out of the deal personally. Further than that I decline an answer." He then challenged the right of the Senate committee to examine the dealings of Continental at a time when Fall and Sinclair were under indictment. The courtroom, not a Senate caucus room, was the proper venue for such questions, he insisted. Of course, Stewart hadn't deigned to appear at any of the earlier Teapot-related trials, let alone testify, but Walsh let that slide. He explained that Stewart was required to respond to the committee's questions despite the proceedings against Fall and Sinclair. Perhaps, he suggested, the Colonel would like to rethink his position and return to the hearings the following morning. If he again failed to respond, however, contempt proceedings would be initiated against him, and he likely would face prison, Walsh warned.

When Stewart returned twenty-four hours later, he again refused to answer questions. Had he conferred with Harry Sinclair about the deposition of the bonds? Walsh asked. "That is none of your business, Senator, nor is it any business of the committee." No sooner had Stewart gotten up from the witness chair than Walsh, Nye, and the other committee members proceeded to the main Senate chambers. With them the committee members brought a four-page typewritten report summarizing Stewart's refusal to answer their questions. The room quickly filled with reporters, who sensed a major story in the offing.

Within a few minutes, Walsh was recognized and took the podium. He asked for a resolution that the report be read. The move was granted unanimously. As soon as the Senate clerk had finished his reading, Walsh asked for a second resolution. He wanted the Senate to cite Stewart for contempt. "Is there an objection?" asked Vice President Charles G. Dawes. Seemingly stunned by the suddenness of what was transpiring, none of the legislators responded. "With no objection, the resolution is agreed to," Dawes said. Not a single senator moved from his seat as Dawes signed an arrest warrant that the committee had prepared.

As soon as Dawes gave it to the sergeant at arms to serve, pandemonium erupted as reporters rushed from the press gallery to the phones outside. "Order!" one senator called to no avail. Followed by a growing swarm of newsmen, the sergeant at arms and a deputy marched to the Stewarts' suite at the nearby Willard Hotel. With the deputy shouldering the hotel room door closed against the onrushing crush of reporters, the sergeant at arms served Stewart with the warrant ordering him to appear at the bar of the Senate the following day. Emerging a few minutes later, he told the newsmen that "Colonel Stewart was calm and cool" when served. Without a dissenting vote, the Senate had authorized Stewart's arrest. In the meantime, the oilman was to be confined to his suite in the Willard Hotel under guard.

Harry Sinclair had defied Walsh and the committee and had gotten off relatively easily. He had received a two-month sentence for contempt but still hadn't served a day. His lawyers were appealing the decision. Walsh and his colleagues were determined that Stewart wasn't going to wiggle off the hook. Even rich, powerful oilmen couldn't defy the U.S. Senate. "I think that the time has come when the dignity of the Senate of the United States ought to be recognized . . . and that it is no trifling affair to defy its authority, however high the recusant witness may be," Walsh said. On that issue, at least, members of both parties agreed.

Over the next few days, Walsh and Stewart, two old warhorses, sparred with each other. Stewart's lawyers responded to the warrant by getting their client a writ of habeas corpus relieving him of appearing before the Senate bar. Walsh immediately countered with a resolution seeking prosecution of Stewart for contempt of the Senate. Walsh asked for a special counsel to pursue the case.

Walsh had the entire Senate on his side in this battle, Republicans as well as members of his own party. Without a single dissenting vote, Walsh's resolution was passed and a special counsel was appointed, Republican George Wickersham. The former attorney general in the Taft cabinet, Wickersham had successfully prosecuted Mal Daugherty, the former attorney general's brother, for contempt in a bribery case. As for Stewart, Wickersham told reporters he needed several weeks to study the matter.

In the meantime, Walsh wrote Secretary of the Treasury Andrew Mellon, asking if Stewart, Sinclair, and the others who had profited from the Continental deal shouldn't have to pay income taxes. None had been collected to date, he reminded Mellon. With what some would recognize as Walsh's droll sarcasm, he also asked Mellon what recommendations the secretary might offer to avoid a repetition of the Continental scandal. He didn't expect a response, certainly not in an election year.

43

DIRTY BONDS, CLEAN CASH

O nce the committee hearings got under way, Walsh began working directly with Thomas Moran's team of Secret Service agents, the operatives who had served Pomerene and Roberts so well. Their mission for the revived Public Lands and Surveys Committee hearing was to track the Continental Liberty bonds that hadn't gone to Albert Fall. And they needed to move quickly. The bonds all had numbered coupons that could be traced after they were cashed in. However, Treasury, which served as a repository for these coupons, was legally obliged to destroy them after five years. That deadline was fast approaching.

By mid-February, the agents had traced many of the bonds to the Chase National Bank. In November and December of 1923, about $300,000 had been deposited in the Republican National Committee account at Chase, most of it in Continental Liberty bonds. The serial numbers matched up. None of this money had been declared by the RNC.

What was the Republican National Committee doing with bonds that had been the by-product of a crooked oil deal, bonds that had been used to bribe a cabinet member? Former RNC chairman Will Hays, still head of the Motion Picture Producers and Distributors Association of America, volunteered to appear before the committee on March 1 to explain. Four years earlier when he questioned Hays, Walsh had uncharacteristically given him a free pass. At the time, Walsh had known that Hays owned a large block of Sinclair stock. Privately, Hays had assured Walsh that his holdings were personal and had nothing to do with Harry Sinclair or politics. As a result, Walsh hadn't pressed the matter. He had since learned that Hays had lied to him. Hays had been Sinclair's man from the start, a director of one of his companies since the early 1920s and a Sinclair attorney. It had been Hays, Walsh now knew, who had coauthored Fall's famous letter claiming the $100,000 he received had been a loan from Ned McLean. Walsh also now knew about the meeting between Hays and former committee chairman Edwin Ladd, who had died in June 1925.

Hays had come to Washington to set the record straight, he told reporters. In a prepared statement, he told the committee he had needed to raise money to pay off a remaining RNC deficit of $1.2 million from the 1920 elections. Among those he had tapped for funds was Sinclair. In November 1923, Sinclair had given Hays $260,000 in Liberty bonds. At the time, as Walsh was quick to interject, the Senate was investigating the Teapot leases. Harry Sinclair needed political allies as never before. Hays, Walsh believed, had "blackjacked" Sinclair for the contributions. In return, the Republicans had done their best to derail the investigation and keep Sinclair out of the line of fire.

Why hadn't Hays mentioned this contribution in 1924? Walsh demanded. "I was not asked about it," Hays responded. Hays told the committee that he had met Sinclair in New York, where he'd received a package containing the $260,000 in bonds. He hadn't been asked for a receipt, nor had he given one. What had he done with the bonds? He had given them to four men, all of whom were active in the RNC: T. Coleman du Pont, former treasurer of the national committee; John T. Pratt, a wealthy New Yorker; John W. Weeks, Harding's secretary of war; and Fred Upham of Chicago, treasurer of the RNC in 1923. And what had they done with them? Walsh demanded. At this point, Hays's answers became elusive. He wasn't entirely sure what had been done with the bonds. The recipients were to use them to raise money. How, specifically? Walsh demanded. Hays couldn't really remember.

As it developed, du Pont, who had been treasurer of the RNC, received bonds worth $75,000; Pratt got $50,000; Weeks received

$25,000; and Upham got $60,000 worth and sold them to various rich Chicagoans for cash.

In what one reporter characterized as "his fiery, machine gun style," Walsh would ask one question before Hays had finished the last. Hays wasn't accustomed to being addressed so rudely. This, after all, was the man in charge of imposing the movie industry's draconian censorship code, of rooting out the drug fiends and sodomites in Hollywood. Hays had the backing of big studio heads—Jack Warner, Louis B. Mayer— the Roman Catholic Church, and many of America's most powerful conservative politicians. Here Walsh was treating him like some—some *felon.*

Hays squirmed in his seat and at one point bit his lower lip so hard that it began to bleed. From the Secret Service agents, Walsh knew one of the four recipients had been Fred Upham of Chicago, treasurer of the RNC. Upham, the Treasury operatives reported, had distributed $60,000 in bonds to rich Chicagoans such as William Wrigley Jr. in ex- change for like amounts of cash. "Did Mr. Upham take those bonds and distribute them around to various people in the city of Chicago, in amounts of from $1,000 to $10,000, and did not those people take the bonds out into the market and sell them . . . and then pretend to make contributions to the Republican campaign fund?" Walsh asked.

"Certainly, not to my knowledge," Hays responded.

Despite Hays's evasiveness, it was clear to those following the hear- ings that the former RNC chairman had laundered the Continental bonds, plain and simple; he'd given them to wealthy party backers who had kept the bonds and given like amounts of cash to the RNC. The cash was untraceable, the bonds weren't. "It was simply a way of doctor- ing the party accounts," a writer for *The New York Times* explained. Sen- ator T. H. Caraway put it more bluntly. Hays, he said, was "a fence . . . who knew that certain goods were stolen goods and was trying to help the thief find a market for them."

When Hays finally stepped down, even his allies were embarrassed for him. He had come across on the stand as spineless. Walsh dismissed him as a "pathetic little man."

44

ANDY

On February 19, a week after Hays's testimony, Walsh received a memorandum from the Secret Service team that promised further sensations. Hays had given a sizable portion of the Continental bonds to a prominent Republican named John Pratt. Pratt had since died, but one of the Treasury agents, M. P. Bolin Jr., had discovered scribbled notations in Pratt's files indicating that Pratt had passed along these same bonds to at least two other individuals. On Saturday morning, the cashier who had handled Pratt's estate appeared before the committee and was asked to examine Pratt's notations with the aid of a large magnifying glass Senator Nye provided. "One of them reads 'Weeks,'" the cashier said. Weeks was quickly identified as the late John W. Weeks, secretary of war under Harding.

"What is the next one?" Senator Nye asked.

"I am trying to read it," the accountant said, handing the slip of paper back to Nye. "See if that is 'Candy.'"

"Might it not be Andy?" Nye asked.

"Possibly," the cashier responded. Nye then asked him to venture as to the identity of "Andy." When the man said he had no idea, the onlookers in the hearing room broke out in laughter. Seemingly everybody in the room except for the cashier knew "Andy" was Andrew Mellon, the secretary of the Treasury and arguably the most powerful man in Washington. That Mellon, who many believed was the greatest Treasury secretary since Alexander Hamilton, may have had links to the Continental deal set off another shock wave in the press. As Treasury secretary the seventy-two-year-old Mellon was the architect of the economic boom that had spanned much of the decade. Since Mellon had taken office, he'd given $3.5 billion back to the rich in the form of Treasury refunds, tax rebates, and remissions and abatements. He had all but eliminated corporate taxes so that money could "trickle down" to workers in the form of more jobs.

The Democrats viewed his policies as reactionary. In the past four years, Mellon and Walsh had clashed repeatedly. Recently, Walsh had gone after Mellon for encouraging monopoly interests and attempts to undermine federal regulatory agencies. At best, Walsh believed, Mellon's efforts here represented a conflict of interest. Among his many holdings, Mellon controlled the Aluminum Company of America, which was constantly being charged with Sherman antitrust violations. He also had substantial oil holdings, including a controlling interest in Gulf Oil. Walsh had also frequently chided Mellon and the president for all but ignoring the ongoing Teapot investigations. Mellon had countered, criticizing what he termed "government by investigation."

With the discovery of the Pratt notations, Walsh invited Mellon to testify. "Invite" was the operative word. Mellon was not someone you ordered to do anything. He also subpoenaed Hays to take the witness stand for a third time. Both were scheduled to appear on March 13. Well before the hearings began, reporters and visitors crowded into the minority caucus room. For Washingtonians in attendance such as Daisy Harriman—her romance with Walsh had morphed into friendship—and Alice Longworth Roosevelt, this was political theater of the highest order, a confrontation between the man many believed gave Coolidge his marching orders and one of the nation's most important Democrats, the fearless and tenacious bane of Big Oil. Only three days earlier, Walsh had agreed to seek the party's presidential nomination.

Whippet thin, with an impressive mustache and pinched features—one reporter likened him to an elegant greyhound—Mellon arrived early in order to pose for photographers. As Mellon was being placed under oath by chairman Nye, Hays entered the hearings, creating a stir in the back of the room. Mellon began by explaining that in November

1923, Hays had called him to say he had sent Mellon $50,000 approximately ($1 million today) in Liberty bonds and was coming to Washington to discuss the matter with him. There the former RNC chairman asked Mellon to take the bonds and made a donation for the same amount to help eliminate party debt.

That the former RNC chairman had approached the most important man in the Coolidge administration to ask that he launder illicit campaign funds was a staggering revelation, yet Mellon downplayed it as trivial. "I objected to doing so because I would be making a subscription that was not what it was reported to be," he explained.

"Did Hays tell you where he got the bonds?" Walsh asked.

"Oh, from Sinclair," Mellon conceded.

Walsh reminded him that the oil lease investigation had begun a month before Hays had sent him the bonds.

"That may be," Mellon replied. "I can't follow all these investigations. I have troubles of my own and much work to do."

Paul Anderson, who was covering the hearings that he had started, looked at another reporter in disbelief. Mellon had been offered bonds from Harry Sinclair at a time when Sinclair was the target of the biggest political scandal in American history, a scandal in which hundreds of millions of dollars' worth of government-controlled oil had been co-opted illegally by a couple of greedy oilmen. *And the secretary of the Treasury had been too preoccupied to notice!*

Nye asked why Mellon had not come forth sooner and informed the committee about the bonds. "It was an incidental thing," Mellon said. "What purpose would that have served?" The questioning of the secretary continued for an hour or so, with Mellon taking the position that he was far too caught up in the heady task of keeping the American economy on course to trouble with some unseemly political imbroglio. Walsh finally excused him. "I think all members of this committee will agree that your attitude in this matter was entirely creditable," he said. Anderson and a reporter for the *Baltimore Sun* again exchanged quizzical glances. The normally relentless Walsh had let Mellon sail through the hearings without the slightest censure and then praised him for appearing!

Hays followed Mellon into the witness chair. Even to spectators in the rear of the room, it was clear from the outset there was a palpable animosity between the witness and Walsh. Even when he was frustrated or angry with a witness, Walsh had usually managed to keep his emotions in check. With Hays, however, he made no attempt to conceal his disdain. In turn, Hays was nervous but far more combative then he had been during his last appearance. Walsh had bulldogged him earlier. Now Hays was ready to fight back.

"Do you care to tell the committee why you didn't tell it about this [giving the bonds to Mellon] when you were last on the stand?" Walsh began. Hays explained that he believed the whole matter of Sinclair's bonds was "entirely irrelevant." Irrelevant? Walsh repeated the word as if it left a bad taste in his mouth. "If you attempted to bribe a public official with such bonds and he rejected you, won't you admit that should be disclosed?" he asked.

"That's an unfair question," Hays countered, jumping out of his seat.

"Sit down. Sit down," Walsh ordered.

For the ensuing hour, the give-and-take was ferocious. Walsh went back over Hays's testimony in his first two appearances, zeroing in on specific instances where the former cabinet member had clearly lied or skirted the truth. He pointed out that RNC records for the period in question showed no contributions from Sinclair. Throughout the cross-examination, Hays kept bounding from his seat like some hair-triggered jack-in-the-box and charging that Walsh was being unfair. At one point, Walsh gestured so violently for Hays to remain seated that his glasses flew off. After two hours of this, Hays was finally excused and left rather hurriedly. He was on his way to have dinner at the White House. President Coolidge liked to eat early.

45

FORTY-EIGHT HOURS

After Robert Stewart refused to respond to the oil committee's questions, Walsh appealed to John D. Rockefeller Jr. for help. Rockefeller's father, the wizened eighty-eight-year-old John D. Rockefeller Sr., had created the country's most feared and powerful monopoly, Standard Oil. This corporate trust—"the Octopus," as muckraker Ida Tarbell characterized it—refined and controlled almost 90 percent of the nation's oil until it was broken up in 1911.

A billion-dollar corporation, Standard Oil of Indiana was the largest and most successful remnant of the old Standard Oil empire. Thanks to Stewart, its chairman, the company had become a money machine, generating enormous profits and dividends. Fifty-three and a strict Baptist, Rockefeller Jr., reportedly now the world's richest man, was its largest individual stockholder. Family members and various family-backed institutions, including the Rockefeller Institute, which Junior headed, also controlled enormous amounts of Standard stock. Even so, Rockefeller, unlike his father, had never been active in the oil business. Likely he hadn't the slightest knowledge of Continental Trading. Walsh had summoned him to Washington in hopes that his testimony—and the headlines his appearance was bound to produce—would put added pressure on Stewart to testify.

Rockefeller seemingly was sympathetic. He responded in a letter to Walsh on February 8, 1928: "I have seen Colonel Stewart and have told him in person what I said to him in my letter of January 24th which you have a copy, namely that in my judgment the public interest demands that the fullest possible light be thrown under investigation by the senate committee."

Stewart, who'd had Rockefeller Sr.'s ear for more than twenty-five years, wasn't swayed in the least by the younger Rockefeller's appeal. He told Junior that he wouldn't testify even if not doing so meant jail. The shareholders could have his resignation if they liked. Of course, they would have to vote him out, which Stewart knew was highly unlikely. His company had recently paid out the highest dividends in Standard's history. In fact, the younger Rockefeller collected more than $2 million annually from his Standard Oil of Indiana stock dividends; his family and Rockefeller-backed institutions like the University of Chicago received millions more.

Flanked by several of his lawyers, who pushed ahead through the waiting reporters, photographers, and spectators outside, Rockefeller arrived at the Senate Office Building on February 12 and went directly to Walsh's office. There Walsh spent half an hour briefing him on the investigation and how Sinclair, Blackmer, O'Neil, and likely Stewart each pocketed about three-quarters of a million dollars in the fraudulent Continental transaction—at the expense of their own companies and shareholders, among them the Rockefellers. In asserting that he knew nothing about the Continental deal, Stewart had clearly perjured himself, Walsh believed.

Stewart, Walsh explained, was Sinclair's silent partner in Teapot. He told Junior how, like Sinclair, Stewart and Harry Blackmer had visited Fall at Three Rivers during the winter of 1921. Not long after, the Harding administration dropped a major lawsuit against Standard Oil of Indiana. It was certainly possible that Stewart used his share of the Continental jackpot to bribe Fall, he said, as had Sinclair. In other words, the chairman of Standard Oil of Indiana was very possibly a crook.

Once he and Walsh made their way into the jammed hearing room, Rockefeller conceded to the committee that until now he hadn't understood the details of the Continental deal. "You didn't question Colonel Stewart about them?" Walsh asked. Colonel Stewart had been unwilling to discuss the matter other than to say "that neither he nor his company had done anything improper," Rockefeller said. He "was bitterly disappointed" that Stewart had risked a jail sentence to withhold testimony before the committee, but at the same time he expressed "the utmost confidence in Stewart's integrity." Unfortunately, Rockefeller couldn't shed any new light on the Continental matter. Nor was there much more he could do to pressure Stewart, he conceded. Walsh, Nye, and the others thanked him profusely for his testimony and support. With two policemen running interference, Nye and Rockefeller, looking every bit the American aristocrat in his gray cutaway coat, went outside to pose for newsreel cameras. Walsh declined to join them. Rockefeller's endorsement of Stewart's integrity stuck in his craw. Worse, the Standard Oil of Indiana stockholders reelected Stewart chairman two weeks later with nary a negative word from Junior. Privately, Walsh stressed that he had been bitterly disappointed with "Junior's miserable failure to meet the standard of business of which he preaches."

ROCKEFELLER'S APPEARANCE at least infused some new energy into the hearings. Walsh, who had seemingly lost his prosecutorial edge in recent weeks, especially in questioning Mellon, had Moran's operatives renew their investigations by checking the financial records of banks with which Stewart and Standard Oil of Indiana did business. On March 1, Walsh contacted Continental National Bank and Trust in Chicago directly, asking for records of any deposits by Stewart between 1922 and 1924 in excess of $50,000 in Liberty bonds. Meanwhile, Walsh and his colleagues concentrated on the political fallout from the Continental Trading conspiracy. Hays had admitted giving bonds to Mellon and half a dozen other prominent Republicans, but had others been involved? How far did the conspiracy extend?

Throughout the remainder of February and March, Walsh was swamped with tips and leads regarding the disposition of the remaining bonds. Many clearly came from cranks, conspiracy theorists, and opportunists seeking travel money and a per diem to come to Washington and testify; a smaller number came from seemingly knowledgeable sources—among them established businessmen, government workers, lawyers, reporters, and newspaper editors. Harding's "one-horse newspaper" had been paid for with Continental bonds, the nationally known newspaper editor William Allen White suggested in a letter to Walsh. "My dear Senator," White wrote Walsh on March 14, 1928. "Did you ever think that big lot of Liberty Bonds found in Harding's estate . . . might have come there by way of the Continental Jackpot?" It was White who had previously advanced the scenario that the late president had been innocent of any wrongdoing, a too trusting soul who had been duped by his so-called friends. Now, the Kansan was having second thoughts.

A. E. Humphreys, whose crude oil Continental had acquired, had blown a sizable hole in his skull with a shotgun in May 1927 at his home in Denver. The Denver coroner ruled the death accidental, but several of Humphreys's former employees as well as former navy secretary Josephus Daniels wrote Walsh claiming the death was likely a suicide: "A gentleman told me yesterday that a deal was made for the sale of thirty million barrels of oil by a Charleston, West Virginia oil man [Humphreys], who killed himself long ago. This gentleman said that it was believed in Charleston that he got some of the divide with Hays and the rest."

I KNOW A. E. HUMPHREYS TOOK HIS LIFE BROODING OVER THIS AF-FAIR, one of Humphreys's former managers, A. A. King, wired Walsh on February 11, 1928. HUMPHREYS WOULD NEVER HAVE TAKEN HIS LIFE IF IT HAD NOT BEEN TO SHIELD SOME MEN OF AFFAIRS, AND OTH-ERS THAT HAVE A DYING BOND BETWEEN THEMSELVES TO ACT IN ONE ACCORD.

Boies Penrose, the Pennsylvania political boss who backed Harding's nomination, had died not long after the 1920 Republican convention. The executors of his will had discovered just under $250,000 in cash in one of his safe-deposit boxes. This was believed to have come from Jake Hamon—payment for Penrose's lining up the Pennsylvania delegation behind Harding. But the committee had also heard rumors that the safe-deposit box contained Liberty bonds. On March 14, 1928, Walsh wrote a government official in Philadelphia asking him to examine the inventory of Penrose's estate to see if his assets included any of the Continental spoils.

To the extent that time and his resources allowed, Walsh and his small staff tried to follow through on these and other leads, but the committee was rapidly running out of time, and many of the witnesses, plus Jake Hamon, Penrose, Harding, Jess Smith, Humphreys, and all four of the Republican bigwigs to whom Hays had given Sinclair's Liberty bonds, were dead. Hamon and possibly Smith had been murdered. Gaston Means, whose credibility was highly suspect, later claimed he had killed Smith on behalf of Daugherty. Means was also spreading stories that Harding had been murdered and would later write a book on the subject.

And, of course, many of those connected to the Continental deal, such as Blackmer and O'Neil, who remained out of the country, were afflicted with memory loss, or flat out wouldn't talk. "It seems exceedingly strange that those witnesses who have not yet fled to Europe either have faulty memories or are dead," chairman Nye noted.

Like Walsh, Nye was following through on various leads. He had sent a staff member to Hays's hometown of Sullivan, Indiana, to check out rumors that Hays had laundered Continental bonds through local banks there. But neither Nye's nor Walsh's investigative efforts were paying off. Penrose's financial records seemed to have disappeared, vanished into the bureaucratic ether. The Hardings? Walsh's investigators discovered that the estates of the late president and Florence Harding, who died a little over a year after her husband, together included about $380,000 in Liberty bonds from the sale of the *Star*. Problem was the serial numbers didn't jibe with those from the initial $3 million Continental lot. Of course, these bonds could have come from additional Continental funds. Of the $8.25 million Sinclair and his associates had made in the Continental purchase, more than $5 million was completely unaccounted for.

The committee had seemingly reached a dead end, but in early April 1928, just as the investigation was winding down, the Treasury agents made an important discovery. Moran cabled Walsh at once. In 1922 and 1923, Robert Stewart had deposited $38,000 in Liberty bond coupons in his personal bank account. And, yes, in this instance, the serial numbers matched those from the mysterious missing batch of Continental bonds. In another forty-eight hours, Walsh would later learn, those coupons would have been destroyed.

46

ACQUITTAL, REVELATION

One by one, the all-male jury in Harry Sinclair's conspiracy trial filed back into the courtroom and took their places in the jury box. Crowded with reporters and spectators, the room was silent except for the audible sobs of Sinclair's wife, Elizabeth. These last six years had exacted a heavy toll on him and his family. Since the Teapot investigations began in 1922, Sinclair had appeared before eleven congressional committees, given 175,000 words in testimony, and been the subject of four civil and three criminal cases. This was the fourth. Already the oilman was facing a six-month jail sentence for criminal contempt for jury shadowing. Add on another three months for refusing to answer questions posed by the oil committee. If this case went against him, Harry Sinclair would be looking at an extended stay in the Dickensian confines of the District of Columbia Jail and Asylum.

Fortunately for Sinclair, this most recent trial had been swift. More important, from the outset it had seemingly gone Sinclair's way. Sinclair and Fall had been slated to be tried together, but Fall remained in New Mexico, too ill to travel. Consequently, Sinclair had been tried independently. The trial had begun on April 2. At the outset the judge, Justice Jennings Bailey, made it clear that expediency was of the utmost importance. He selected the jury himself in just a few hours and then had them locked up for the duration of the trial. There would be no tampering with these jurors. Bailey also established narrow rules of evidence, excluding any evidence that did not relate directly to the question of whether Sinclair had given Fall $233,000 for the purpose of defrauding the government. As a result, the special counsel, Owen Roberts and Atlee Pomerene, were hamstrung to the extent that they could not inform the jurors that the U.S. Supreme Court had already canceled the Teapot leases as being fraudulent; that the bonds given to Fall had come from the profits of an illegitimate transaction; that M. T. Everhart, Fall's son-in-law, had avoided testifying on three separate occasions by pleading self-incrimination; and that Sinclair was under two separate indictments for contempt.

For the defense, the star witness was Everhart. No longer shielded by the Fifth Amendment, Everhart, with help from Sinclair's lawyers, had found a way to explain away all those bonds and cash he'd received on Fall's behalf from Sinclair. In actuality, Sinclair and his late attorney, J. W. Zevely, had been buying a one-third share of Three Rivers, intending to turn it into a hunting club, Everhart claimed. In fact—a detail that had slipped his mind when he testified before the oil committee—Sinclair had given Everhart $1,200 expressly to develop pack trails into the nearby Sierra Blanca mountains so that the oilman, Zevely, and their guests might more readily access big game. Martin Littleton, Sinclair's portly, white-haired attorney, gave the closing argument. Suave and unflappable, Littleton explained that Sinclair and Zevely had simply wanted a little sport. True, there was no deed, no lease, no record of the purchase, but this had been a handshake agreement. This had been not a bribe, but an up-and-up business transaction among friends.

From all the long nights at poker tables, Harry Sinclair had become something of an expert at reading people, but he couldn't "read" the twelve laborers, mechanics, and merchants adjudging his fate. The jurors were out less than two hours before reaching their decision. "Ashen pale," Harry Ford Sinclair rose from the counsel table as the twelve men took their places in the jury box.

"What's your verdict, Mr. Foreman?" Judge Bailey asked.

"Not guilty," the jury foreman replied after what seemed an interminable pause.

A collective sigh echoed through the courtroom. Seemingly dumbfounded, Pomerene and Roberts sat in silence. The beaming defendant was suddenly being congratulated by counsel and supporters. On hearing the verdict, his wife broke down and had to be taken out into the corridor by friends. Someone administered smelling salts as Sinclair was making his way to her. He called for a doctor, but Elizabeth Sinclair held up her hand to indicate she was all right, then collapsed into her husband's arms. Flanked by his legal team and supporting his wife, Sinclair pushed through the crowds outside in the late April sunshine, pausing a moment to give a statement to reporters. He had been confident from the beginning that he would be exonerated, Sinclair said. He hadn't acted unethically or corruptly. And then the Sinclairs started back to their apartment at the Carlton Hotel. Their ordeal was over, at least for now.

At the michigan avenue headquarters of Standard Oil of Indiana, the company's chairman had been waiting anxiously for word of the jury's decision. As soon as the call came from Washington that Sinclair had been acquitted, Robert Stewart summoned his seven directors to the boardroom. After the men—all had their offices in the Standard building—had assembled, Stewart and Roy Barnett, the company's tax officer, led them directly to Stewart's safe. As the directors gathered around expectantly, Barnett opened the safe door, extracting half a dozen thick parcels. These he placed on a conference table. Stewart opened one and produced a $1,000 bond, holding it up so that each of the Standard directors could get a good look. In total, the safe contained $759,500 in Continental Liberty bonds, the colonel said, his share of the Continental take. After seven years the $3 million from the Continental deal had been accounted for.

47

RICH MAN'S JUSTICE

At the news of Sinclair's acquittal and Stewart's revelation, the Senate's outrage went well beyond the usual political posturing. "Disgusting and discouraging," Senator Nye said of the acquittal. "Why, everybody in the United States and even the Supreme Court knows he is guilty," Senator Norris of Nebraska declared of Sinclair. "He has too much money to be convicted. We ought to pass a law now to the effect that no man worth a hundred million dollars should ever be tried for any crime." It was Stewart, however, who drew the most fervent vitriol. Even loyal Republicans seemed genuinely angered at Stewart's actions.

Under oath, the Standard Oil of Indiana chief declared he'd never heard of the Continental Trading Company, had nothing to do with the distribution of any Liberty bonds. Then he'd clammed up, claiming that the U.S. Senate didn't have the authority to question him. With Stewart's subsequent admission that the mystery bonds had been gathering dust all these years in his safe, it was clear he had deliberately kept his involvement in Continental under wraps until Sinclair's conspiracy trial concluded. His testimony might well have tipped the balance against Sinclair. Stewart had refused to testify "for the purpose of frustrating justice to aid his partner in crime," Carter Glass, the patrician Virginia Democrat, charged.

Eager now to extricate himself from pending contempt charges, Stewart reappeared voluntarily before the committee on April 24, three days after Sinclair's acquittal. He now wanted to be utterly candid, the colonel explained. He was eager to disclose all the facts in an effort to clear his good name. The committee went on the attack as soon as the beefy former Rough Rider settled into the witness chair. "Not since the flaming days of four years ago when the revelations of the Teapot Dome scandal were coming thick and fast has an oil operator been flayed on the Senate floor as Stewart was," wrote the Associated Press reporter covering the hearings.

In contrast, Stewart seemed entirely at ease, the combativeness that had marked his previous appearance gone. He conceded that he had received the bonds from the Canadian Osler, but he insisted he never knew their source. He'd never heard of Continental Trading. He'd arranged for the bonds to be put in a trust fund with an eye to eventually turning them over to the company. He'd locked them away in his safe and pretty much forgot all about them. What about the $38,000 in coupons he'd pocketed in 1923? Yes, he'd cashed in those bonds but had replaced them with other government issues for the same amount. Actually, he'd come out $4 short in the transaction, he noted with a chuckle. It was an inside joke. Why had he stopped cashing the coupons in 1924, the year the Teapot investigation was under way? He had simply wanted to avoid any untoward publicity. There had been all kinds of stories in the newspapers. Had he talked about the bonds with Sinclair? Walsh asked. Stewart had no problem recalling that five years earlier he'd come up $4 short in a bond swap, but talk with Sinclair about the bonds . . . ? He really couldn't remember, though he and Sinclair did have frequent conversations regarding the business of the various companies in which they each had an interest. How could he not have known about Continental Trading when he, Sinclair, Blackmer, and O'Neil had purchased Humphreys's oil through Continental? Walsh pressed. "I didn't know, and I didn't care," Sinclair said.

"What do you think John D. Rockefeller Jr. would think about your putting the bonds in a trust fund?" queried Senator Bronson Cutting, a New Mexico Republican.

"I don't know, and I don't care," Stewart said again.

After three and a half hours, Stewart was excused. Pausing at the top of the Senate steps, he took a moment to wave triumphantly to reporters and spectators before being whisked away to Union Station to catch the next train back to Chicago.

HARRY SINCLAIR WAS called back before the committee for yet another appearance the following day. Buoyed by his recent acquittal, he seemed to be enjoying himself. "Sinclair's answers were so loaded with memory lapses, denials, evasions and outright lies that one wonders . . . why the Senators . . . continued to fence with him," a Walsh biographer noted. Sinclair was the last witness to testify in the Continental hearings. "The committee is about winding up its inquiry into the Teapot Dome matters, and I feel that it has got to the bottom of the affair," Walsh wrote a reporter. As the acknowledged, if unofficial, committee head, Walsh was again asked to submit a report to the Senate summing up the Continental inquiry.

The Public Lands and Surveys Committee, he wrote, had revealed Continental as "a contemptible private steal. The speculations of trusted officers of great industrial houses, pilfering from their own companies, robbing their own stockholders, the share of the booty coming to one of the freebooters serving . . . as the price of perfidy as a member of the President's cabinet." Hays, Sinclair, and Stewart he excoriated. But it was the former attorney general and the Ohio Gang that earned his most severe censure. "The associates of [Harry] Daugherty [were] caught red-handed in the most stupendous piece of thievery known to our annals, or perhaps to those of any other country." Walsh concluded with a final accounting: "The expense of the inquiry . . . has resulted in the recovery of $2,000,000 with the prospect of getting as much more, has [to date] been $14,165." At a brief meeting on Saturday morning, May 31, the committee held its final session. The Senate had ended its official investigation of Teapot Dome and Continental Trading, yet Walsh had unfinished business with Robert Stewart. "He will be lucky if he does not take up his residence eventually in the common jail of the District," Walsh told a friend before the hearings closed.

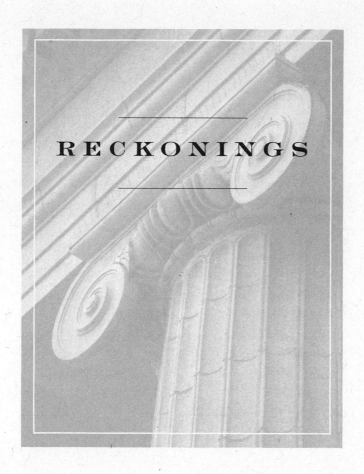

RECKONINGS

48

ROBERT STEWART

Amid the neighboring speakeasies and bawdy houses, John D. Rockefeller Jr.'s town house on Manhattan's West 54th Street was an oasis of temperance and piety. Frequently, Rockefeller began his day with a Bible study class conducted by a visiting Baptist bishop or prayer meeting, but on the morning of April 25, his concerns were of a secular nature. The morning papers all carried accounts of Colonel Robert Stewart's appearance before Walsh's committee on their front pages. In his testimony, Stewart exhibited the same defiance and arrogance he had displayed in the past, but what struck Rockefeller was Stewart's response to Senator Cutting's question "What do you think John D. Rockefeller Jr. would think about your putting the bonds in a trust fund?" "I don't know, and I don't care," Stewart had responded.

Rockefeller had asked Stewart about the bonds, respectfully requested that the Standard Oil of Indiana chairman testify before the committee. In response, Stewart had told him effectively to mind his own business. Still, Rockefeller had publicly supported him, attesting to his unassailable integrity. Now this slap in the face. *I don't know, and I don't care.* Perhaps the colonel believed that Rockefeller, the dutiful, devout Christian, would simply turn the other cheek. If so, he had badly miscalculated. Walsh and Nye forwarded Rockefeller the official transcript of Stewart's testimony two days later to Rockefeller's offices at 26 Broadway, doubtless hoping to light a fire under Junior. That same afternoon after reviewing the transcript, Rockefeller and Thomas Debevoise, Rockefeller's senior counsel and right-hand man, drew up a letter asking for Stewart's resignation as Standard's chairman. Rockefeller said "he had lost confidence in Stewart's leadership." When Stewart failed to respond, Rockefeller released a statement to the press on May 9 reiterating his demands. This wasn't going to go away.

Walsh was encouraged. Finally, young Rockefeller was showing some of his old man's spine. "It's reassuring to know that the public is not indifferent to transgressions such as those disclosed," Walsh said in a statement congratulating Rockefeller for his stand. "It is gratifying that the business world is waking up to the enormity of the offenses revealed by the committee."

STEWART NEVER WENT to prison. He hired Frank J. Hogan, Big Oil's best friend, to defend him. Hogan got Stewart acquitted on the contempt charges arising from his refusal to answer Walsh's questions. "Justice has been done," Hogan said after the jury's decision was announced on July 25, 1928. "It is time the Walshes, Nyes, and Norrises should learn that prosecutions of this kind cannot prevail."

Walsh wasn't done, however. Rockefeller Jr. had asked for Stewart's resignation. Working behind the scenes, Walsh was determined to see that he got it. Of course, Stewart was determined to fight back with every resource at his command. "If the Rockefellers want a fight, I'll show them how to fight," he said.

Time magazine portrayed the two combatants as prizefighters. Junior was fifty-four years old, five feet ten inches tall, and he weighed in at 170. He kept fit by playing squash and working out in his private gymnasium. Sixty-two, the six-foot-one-inch Stewart topped 240 pounds and got his exercise playing golf. "These two able-bodied men have clashed in what, if ever there was one, is a Battle of the Century," *Time* noted somewhat breathlessly. "It involves tycoons from coast to coast, quiet old estates, many a small John Stockholder, thousands of employees, Wall Street, La Salle Street and a department of the U.S. Government."

Actually, the two foes left most of the fighting to their lawyers, underlings, and public relations people, all of whom were charged with garnering as many shareholder votes or proxies for their bosses as quickly as possible. At the outset, Stewart was seemingly in a strong position. In 1928, Standard of Indiana was the largest producer of gas in the United States. It was enormously successful, with profits for the year amounting to about $80 million, or approximately $9 a share. With this kind of track record, Sinclair thought he was golden, and the bookmakers agreed, making Stewart an early two-to-one favorite. Even the elder Rockefeller, now nudging ninety, was rumored to be siding with Stewart in this contest.

While Stewart had his employees, who feared they'd lose their jobs if their chairman was replaced, and many a John Stockholder behind him, Junior had much of the old money, the institutional money, and, of course, his family's fortune backing him. Junior owned 14.2 percent of the Standard Oil of Indiana stock. That along with his father's shares— assuming the old man backed him—those of the Rockefeller Foundation, the General Education Board, which young Rockefeller had created in 1903 to aid education in the United States, and other Rockefeller-affiliated foundations came to a little over 30 percent of all the company's 9,160,000 shares. Junior needed more votes, more proxies, as did Stewart.

Each time a major shareholder committed to one side or the other, the newspapers and business magazines touted the results as though they were election ballots. The Sun Life Insurance Co. of Montreal gave 44,000 proxies to Stewart; Dartmouth College sent 2,360 shares to Rockefeller; one of Standard Oil's major stockholders, S.H.B. Payne, however, came out for Stewart; the San Francisco banker Peter Giannini offered proxies for his 32,000 shares to Rockefeller. Rockefeller's team was headed up by Winthrop Aldrich, who happened to be Junior's brother-in-law and the son of the late senator Nelson Aldrich, one of John Rockefeller Sr.'s intimates.

Walsh got involved early, recommending to Junior that Standard of Indiana's stockholders sue Stewart. "I stated to him [Rockefeller] it is quite immaterial whether Stewart personally profited by the transaction or whether he participated in the obviously corrupt purpose of the creation of the Continental Trading Company," he said. "He clearly failed in his duty to the shareholders of his company in consenting to pay $1.75 for oil which it had already contracted to get at $1.50."

Later, as the inevitable showdown neared, Walsh responded to letters from Standard Oil of Indiana shareholders saying that Rockefeller should call Stewart to account for the interest he withheld from the company from his share of the Continental booty. JOHN D. JR. BACKED BY WALSH'S LETTER was a February 3, 1929, *Washington Post* headline. Several weeks later, Aldrich sent out a seventy-two-page letter on Junior's behalf to all shareholders detailing Stewart's connection with Harry Sinclair in the Teapot–Salt Creek deal. It included a transcript of Stewart's testimony before the Walsh committee and closed citing the U.S. Supreme Court decision that Continental Trading had been created for some illegal purpose. Walsh's fingerprints were all over the document. Stewart immediately responded that this was "a cunningly drawn document . . . nothing less than dastardly libel."

THE STANDARD OIL of Indiana annual meeting was held on March 7, 1929, at the Whiting Community Center, Whiting, Indiana. "The entire financial community was on edge to see who would prevail," said an Associated Press reporter of the gathering at which the ballots regarding Stewart's proposed ouster would be tallied.

Whiting was in the heart of the Calumet industrial region, where Standard Oil of Indiana owned and operated the world's largest gasoline refinery. Stewart and his crew chose to drive down from Standard's Chicago headquarters. Rockefeller's team took the train from Chicago. The nonconfrontational younger Rockefeller hadn't come along. Instead he'd sailed for Egypt. "I sincerely hope that Mr. Rockefeller is having a very nice time on his trip abroad," Stewart said. This reminded a reporter of what one of Teddy Roosevelt's enemies said when he left for Africa on a hunting trip: "I hope a lion bites him," as reported in the January 28, 1929, issue of *Time*.

There were approximately 2,500 shareholders at the meeting, plus another 50 or so reporters. Seats were so hard to come by that Karl August Bickel, president of United Press, had to buy shares of Standard Oil of Indiana five minutes before the market closed the previous day to gain admission. Stewart began by vigorously defending his record. The company was more prosperous than at any time during its history, he reminded the attendees. Then the voting results were announced. It wasn't even close. Almost 8.5 million votes had been cast, 6 million by proxy. Stewart had fewer than 2.9 million, the Rockefeller group 5.5 million, including those of John Sr. "John D. Rockefeller Jr. won the biggest fight of his business career today," wrote the United Press reporter covering the meeting. After eleven years as chairman of Standard Oil of Indiana, Robert Stewart was out—fired. Of course, he wouldn't go without a paycheck for long. The newspapers were already running stories saying he was going to partner up with Harry Sinclair. If so, he'd have to wait until "Sinco" got out of jail.

49

HARRY SINCLAIR

On a misty, early May night in 1929, a black limousine pulled into the driveway of the District of Columbia Jail & Asylum. Constructed in 1872, the prison was situated on the southeast corner of East Capitol Street, a grim, brick, three-story structure. Several dozen newsmen and photographers lined both sides of the driveway, the photographers holding flashlights for illumination. It was 8:45 p.m., and Harry Sinclair had arrived to begin serving a ninety-day sentence for contempt of the U.S. Senate.

Sinclair was accompanied by his brother A. W. Sinclair and one of his attorneys, G. T. Sanford. After Sinclair's chauffeur opened the limousine door, the three men emerged. Sinclair, visibly nervous and flushed, his light gray soft hat pulled down low so that the brim covered his eyes, slipped briefly on the wet pavement but stopped himself from falling. With the chauffeur toting the two black suitcases containing the clothes Sinclair would wear for the duration of his stay, the group waited briefly for the prison's heavy barred door to be opened. Awaiting them was a United States marshal named Snyder.

"I am glad to see you, Mr. Sinclair," Snyder said.

"How do you do, Mr. Snyder," Sinclair responded.

Snyder then introduced the prison's newest guest to Major W. L. Peake, the superintendent, who led Sinclair into his office to spell out the house rules. Not to worry, Sinclair said. He intended to be a model prisoner. "I don't suppose you're used to getting up as early as we do here," Peake said.

"What time?" Sinclair asked.

"Five forty-five."

"Oh well, I guess I'll get accustomed to the routine in several days."

After filling out a prison card—his "jail jacket"—and being given a number, 10,520, Sinclair was led to the east wing of the jail by the chief of the guards, a Captain Ratherdale. The accommodating clerk carried Sinclair's bags. In the dormitory where all the short-termers, the so-called bull gang, and prison clerks slept barracks style, he was assigned cot number 62 all the way at the end of the room.

Wearing silk pajamas—not exactly standard prison issue—Sinclair sat up most of the night smoking, unable to sleep amid the cacophony of sixty petty thieves, pickpockets, bootleggers, and other assorted small-time criminals snoring through the night. At breakfast he sat next to a Syrian bookie, Nick Keart. Of course, Keart knew Sinclair's identity. By now, everybody in the prison knew who Sinclair was thanks to the prison grapevine. "Mr. Sinclair, I've taken a lot of bets on your horses and I've made a lot more on my own, and I've always wanted to meet you, but I'm sorry it had to be in jail," Keart said.

At this, Sinclair—"the Master of Rancocas," *Time* magazine had called him—slapped Keart on the back. "Don't worry about that, young fellow! We all get bad breaks. My colors will still be flying when this thing is over."

After breakfast, Major Peake assigned Sinclair to the prison pharmacy, where he was to serve as the prison pharmacist, and introduced him to the prison physician, Dr. Morris Hyman, and the blond, pretty prison nurse, Mary Kathleen Wright. "These are your bosses," Peake said. Sinclair nodded and smiled.

This wasn't going to be so bad, certainly better than being sent to the district workhouse at Occoquan, Virginia. Sinclair was soon moved to a private cell adjacent to the pharmacy. For the next ninety days, he slept, read, listened to the radio, received visitors who invariably brought him the Cuban cigars he favored, and no doubt availed himself of the pharmacy's ample medicinal liquor supply. In the pharmacy, Sinclair put in his eight hours a day distributing pills to the sick and the infirm, much as he had done thirty-five years earlier back in Lawrence, Kansas.

ON JUNE 10, Sinclair got some bad news. The U.S. Supreme Court had sustained his six-month sentence for contempt of court—this was the jury-tampering case. It also upheld a four-month sentence the trial judge had given Henry Mason Day and a fine of $1,000 to be paid by Sherman Burns. His father, Billy Burns, had been sentenced to fifteen days, but the Supreme Court overruled the trial judge, clearing the elder Burns of the charges.

At least Day and his old friend Sinclair would serve in the same facility. Day said he had no problem serving the four months out of loyalty to his boss. The sun rose and set on Harry Sinclair, Day told reporters. Day's wife, the mezzo-soprano in France, was less sanguine, however. On the day Burns was sentenced, she filed for divorce.

AFTER SERVING ALMOST seven months, Harry Sinclair emerged from the District of Columbia prison on November 21 a free man. As always, he was dapperly dressed—a pinstripe suit, a gray slouch hat, and highly polished brown shoes—and looked as robust as ever. After saying good-bye to Superintendent Peake and asserting that he'd been "railroaded to jail in violation of common sense and common fairness," he posed for twenty or so cameramen before being whisked off to a downtown hotel. There his wife, Elizabeth, who had suffered a nervous breakdown during his incarceration, was awaiting him. The following day, the Sinclairs retreated to the Rancocas stock farm in New Jersey.

A month later at the annual gridiron dinner in Washington, an evening where the president joins members of the press for fun and frolic, a portly man waving a fake pistol chased a second man through the audience. "That's Harry Sinclair pursuing the man who said you could not put $100 million in jail," announced the master of ceremonies. This brought a laugh from Herbert Hoover, Harding and

Coolidge's former commerce secretary. Hoover had succeeded Coolidge as president.

Surely Sinclair didn't mind a little ribbing. Welcomed back from prison enthusiastically by his board and shareholders, he went on to make several more fortunes before dying at his home in Pasadena, California, in 1956. He was eighty.

50

NED DOHENY

At 2:00 a.m. on Sunday, February 17, 1929, Leslie T. White, detective and material evidence expert with the Los Angeles Police Department, got a call from Lucien Wheeler, chief inspector investigator for the Los Angeles District Attorney's Office. "Les, young Doheny has just been murdered," Wheeler said. "Get out to their Beverly Hills home as soon as possible."

"You mean E. L. Doheny's son?"

"The same. I'll meet you there."

The younger Dohenys lived in an estate called Greystone, having recently moved there after Ned's father bought four hundred acres in Beverly Hills. As a gift to his son and daughter-in-law, the elder Doheny commissioned the well-known architect Gordon B. Kaufmann to design and build a fifty-five-room, forty-six-thousand-square-foot estate on a knoll on this property above Doheny Drive. It featured a huge stable, kennels, its own fire station, riding trails, a two-bedroom gatehouse, formal gardens, a sixty-foot swimming pool, several greenhouses, badminton and tennis courts, and an eight-foot-high waterfall that cascaded into an artificial lake adorned with white water lilies.

The interior: a thirty-seat movie theater, a two-lane bowling alley, a gymnasium, a walk-in fur and jewelry vault, a temperature-controlled wine cellar, servants' quarters to accommodate a staff of fifteen, hand-carved oak banisters, balustrades, and rafters, a grand hall with black-and-white inlaid marble floors, and a billiards room that retracted into the wall in the highly unlikely case the Prohibition agents were on the prowl.

There was nothing its equal south of San Simeon.

THE SECURITY AT Greystone was the best money could buy. The young Dohenys' children had been the targets of several failed kidnapping attempts. Then, with all the publicity surrounding Teapot, the walled-in compound provided a sanctuary from snoops, reporters, and quacks. Normally there were several private security guards on duty, but on White's arrival, he found the place surrounded by a cordon of guards and private detectives, some of whom momentarily refused him admission when his car pulled up to the great iron entrance gate. "It would have been simpler to crash Buckingham Palace," he later noted.

Inside, White encountered the young L.A. district attorney Burton Fitts talking to Chief Wheeler. Wheeler led White to the crime scene, one of the Dohenys' luxurious guest room suites on the ground floor. Wearing silk bathrobe, pajamas, and slippers, young Doheny lay flat on his back in a pool of blood a few feet from the bottom of the bed, the sheets of which had been turned down, the pillows fluffed. To his left, a wooden chair had been turned over. To his right, a few feet from his extended right arm, was a highball glass. "There was a bullet hole through his [Doheny's] skull from ear to ear," White later said. "Blood was criss-crossed in a crazy pattern over his finely chiseled face."

In the doorway of an adjacent room there was a second corpse. Hugh Plunkett lay on his stomach, spread-eagle, his head turned the opposite direction from Doheny's body. He too had been shot through the skull, the mortal wound leaving a smudge of blood on the ivory-colored wall and fragments of brain on the carpet. Wheeler told White to examine the physical evidence in an attempt to reconstruct what had happened. There apparently hadn't been any eyewitnesses to the crime.

After fingerprinting both victims, White rolled Plunkett over, discovering a still warm Beasely model .45-caliber Colt revolver (that he learned belonged to the Dohenys) wedged under his chest. White wrapped the pistol to preserve any prints and collected other evidence, including the whiskey bottle and the two glasses from which Doheny and Plunkett had been drinking. All this he intended to examine at his crime laboratory, but first he joined Wheeler and Fitts in talking to everyone who'd been at Greystone that night—family members, household staff, and Dr. E. C. Fishbaugh, the high-society doctor who tended to the Dohenys' medical needs. While attending a comedy at the Hollywood Playhouse, Fishbaugh had been urgently summoned to the theater office to take a call from his maid. She told him to go to Greystone immediately.

Arriving just before 11:00 p.m., Fishbaugh was met by Lucy Doheny at the mansion's main entrance. She led him to the guest room where Hugh and Ned had been talking. As they approached, Fishbaugh said, Hugh came out, brandishing the Colt in his right hand. After ordering Fishbaugh to leave the house, Hugh backed into the guest room, slamming the door behind him. A moment later, Fishbaugh and Lucy heard a single shot. Plunkett, the doctor said, shot himself through his brain. Though Fishbaugh reached the body only seconds after the shot was fired, Plunkett had died instantly.

An hour later, old man Doheny arrived from his home on Chester Place. Seeing his son's body, Doheny collapsed. "My boy," he cried, sobbing. He held one of Ned's hands until he was finally helped up from the floor.

THERE WERE TWO disparate versions of why Hugh Plunkett had visited Ned Doheny on the night of the murder and what his state of mind was at the time. In the story that the Dohenys put out and the one that was largely accepted by the mainstream press, Hugh Plunkett was a whack job, barking-at-the-moon crazy. Dr. Fishbaugh had diagnosed Hugh as subject to twitching spells and a lack of self-control. For his own good, the Dohenys had been trying to have him committed to an asylum for several months.

In fact, earlier that evening, Lucy and Ned had visited Hugh in his apartment at 636 Cochran Avenue in an attempt to get him to commit himself. Hugh angrily refused, after which Lucy and Ned left and ended up going to a movie. Soon after they got home, Hugh, who spent almost as much time at the Dohenys' as he did in his own place, showed up, appearing agitated and surprising Lucy and Ned in their master bedroom, where they had dressed for bed and were talking. Ned took Hugh downstairs to the guest suite, poured them both a drink, and tried to talk him down from his nervous state, even pulling down the sheets in case Hugh wanted to stay over. When Hugh failed to calm down, Ned decided enough was enough and put in an emergency call to Dr. Fishbaugh to lock up Hugh, consent or no.

In the unauthorized version, Hugh was perfectly sane. His ex-wife, Marian Hall Plunkett, said he was sane, though maybe a little highstrung. His sister claimed he hadn't been acting abnormally prior to the shootings. The only ones who claimed Hugh was loony were the Doheny bunch. The reason: At the time of the murder, the Dohenys and Albert Fall were scheduled to be tried for bribery, Doheny for giving, Fall for receiving. Fall was to be tried first. His being found guilty would, of course, make it all the more difficult for Doheny to get off.

The Fall trial hinged on the testimony of Ned Doheny and Plunkett, both of whom had collected the money and delivered it to the then interior secretary. "Obviously, if diagnosed as psychotic and residing in a sanatorium, Plunkett could not be called upon to testify about the bribe to Fall," a Doheny biographer said. "And even if he were out of the institution, the testimony of a man with mental problems would lack credibility. In any case, Plunkett was being put under tremendous pressure by the senior Doheny who wanted him out of the way."

If we accept theory B, Hugh had come calling on Sunday night to tell Ned that despite whatever leverage the Dohenys were applying, he wasn't going to commit himself voluntarily.

WHAT STRUCK WHITE as odd about the case initially was that all those questioned—Fishbaugh, Lucy Doheny, the servants—told essentially the same story down to the smallest details. "The testimony dovetailed with remarkable accuracy," he later wrote.

Visiting the morgue later with Wheeler to examine the corpses, White noted powder burns around the bullet hole in Doheny's head, proving the Colt was fired only inches from the entrance wound. Plunkett's wound lacked powder burns, which would indicate that Plunkett hadn't shot himself. In addition, from the trajectory of the bullet that killed Doheny, Ned had to be sitting in a chair when he was shot. If Plunkett had been the one to pull the trigger, he'd have to have been kneeling when he fired or had to have shot from the hip. Plunkett also had a half-finished cigarette in his left hand "in such a way that it would have been impossible for him to have opened the door and threatened witnesses as they so testified," White concluded. "He had the gun in his right hand, by their story." And Plunkett hadn't been wearing gloves, which begged one obvious question: Why hadn't White found any fingerprints on the gun? Someone clearly had wiped the Colt .45 clean.

White spent the rest of the night developing photographs, working up the fingerprints he'd found on the whiskey bottle and glasses, and evaluating the remaining evidence he'd collected. On Monday at 10:00 a.m., on Wheeler's instructions, he met with Fitts. "Mr. Fitts," he told the DA, "Chief Wheeler instructed me to bring this report straight to you. I don't believe Hugh Plunkett killed Doheny and then committed suicide—at least it could not have happened in the manner described by the witnesses. The physical facts and the testimony of the witnesses do not jibe. I understand, too, that some people believe that the Doheny family is too influential to tamper with."

"There isn't a man in the United States that's big enough to stop me from conducting a criminal investigation," Fitts responded. "What did you find?" After White enumerated the discrepancies he'd uncovered, Fitts asked if Plunkett hadn't killed Doheny, who had.

"I can't tell you at this time," White said. "My job is merely to show you we haven't found the truth—as yet."

Rising from his chair, Fitts said, "We'll damn sure find that out." Later that day, he announced to the press he was launching a sweeping investigation into the Doheny murder. It was likely one of the shortest murder investigations in history. On February 19, Fitts held a press conference to say that the inquiry into the murder-suicide was officially closed. The madman Plunkett had murdered his friend of seventeen years, end of story. White was naturally surprised and disappointed, but then he was new to the department, new to how things were done in Los Angeles. "The new turn of events in the case caused a twenty-four-hour sensation, then it was dead . . . *dead*," he later wrote.

Those who didn't buy the story that Plunkett was the killer proffered all kinds of theories: Lucy had caught her husband and Hugh in flagrante delicto and shot them both. If so, she'd have to have been handy with a large, powerful pistol. An intruder had done it—highly unlikely given that Greystone was only slightly less secure than Fort

Knox. The shooting had been the result of a lovers' quarrel between Ned and Plunkett.

The most likely scenario was offered up by Raymond Chandler in his third novel, *The High Window*. Chandler had been in the oil business in Los Angeles until he drank himself out of a job in 1932. He may have known the Dohenys. Certainly he knew of them. Likely he also had met White, who resigned as an investigator for the DA's office the same year Chandler got fired and began writing pulp mystery stories at the same time Chandler's own writing career got started. At any rate, here's Chandler's Philip Marlowe discussing the Doheny (Cassidy) case with a Los Angeles detective named Breeze.

"Don't forget this is a murder case, Marlowe."

"I'm not. But don't you forget I've been around this town a long time, more than fifteen years. I've seen a lot of murder cases come and go. Some have been solved, some couldn't be solved, and some could have been solved that were not solved. And one or two or three of them have been solved wrong. Somebody was paid to take a rap, and the chances are it was known or strongly suspected. And winked at. But skip that. It happens, but not often. Consider a case like the Cassidy case. I guess you remember it, don't you?"

Breeze looked at his watch. "I'm tired," he said. "Let's forget the Cassidy case. Let's stick to the Phillips case."

I shook my head. "I'm going to make a point, and it's an important point. Just look at the Cassidy case. Cassidy was a very rich man, a multimillionaire. He had a grown-up son. One night the cops were called to his home and young Cassidy was on his back on the floor with blood all over his face and a bullet hole in the side of his head. His secretary was lying on his back in an adjoining bathroom, with his head against the second bathroom door, leading to a hall, and a cigarette burned out between the fingers of his left hand, just a short burned-out stub that had scorched the skin between his fingers. A gun was lying by his right hand. He was shot in the head, not a contact wound. A lot of drinking had been done. Four hours had elapsed since the deaths and the family doctor had been there for three of them. Now, what did you do with the Cassidy case?"

Breeze sighed. "Murder and suicide during a drinking spree. The secretary went haywire and shot young Cassidy. I read it in the papers or something. Is that what you want me to say?"

"You read it in the papers," I said, "but it wasn't so. What's more you knew it wasn't so and the D.A. knew it wasn't so and the D.A.'s investigators were pulled off the case within a matter of hours. There was no inquest. But every crime reporter in town and every cop on every homicide detail knew it was Cassidy that did the shooting, that it was Cassidy that was crazy drunk, that it was the secretary who tried to handle him and couldn't and at last tried to get away from him, but wasn't quick enough."

51

ALBERT FALL

The jury in Albert Fall's bribery case, eight women and four men, marched back into the courtroom to announce their verdict. They had been out for twenty-four hours. Four days earlier on October 22, 1929, Fall's defense counsel, Frank Hogan, whose fee was being paid by Doheny on his friend's behalf, had delivered an impassioned four-hour summation of his defense, lashing out at the government's handling of the case. For all the eloquence of his closure, however, Hogan wouldn't let Fall testify that he in fact had been offered an executive position with Doheny and had volunteered to repay the loan from his salary. Such a disclosure, Hogan feared, would make it look as though Doheny were indeed trying to influence Fall. With Doheny's trial coming up next, that information could be damaging, though of course it might have helped Fall's case.

Fall also caught another bad break when, much to Hogan's chagrin, the judge, William Hitz, had allowed as admissible the $269,000 Fall had received from Harry Sinclair, even though this trial dealt specifically with the money the former interior secretary had been given by Doheny. Hogan had urged that Fall, who during the trial was wheelchair bound, spitting up blood, and suffering from viral pneumonia, be returned promptly to the salubrious climate of southern New Mexico.

At one point, after repeated delays because of Fall's condition, Judge Hitz directed Sterling Ruffin, physician to the late president Wilson, to examine the ailing man. Ruffin had been present when Fall had so rudely barged into President Wilson's bedroom at the White House to confront him regarding the kidnapping of an American diplomat in Mexico. According to his biographer, Fall told friends that, for personal reasons, this was the one physician in the entire United States whom he would not permit to enter his sickroom.

Judge Hitz wasn't sympathetic to Fall's health concerns. He tartly instructed the jurors, "You have nothing to do whatsoever with the sunshine of New Mexico. . . . You are here to decide the case on the evidence and nothing else."

Which they did. "Guilty," responded the jury foreman, Thomas E. Norris. At this, the sixty-eight-year-old Fall, the first cabinet member in U.S. history ever to be convicted of a felony, slumped forward in his wheelchair. Sitting near him, seventy-three-year-old Ed Doheny put his hands over his ears as if to deny what he'd just heard and began to cry. He then raised a fist and shouted, "It's that damn court!" Emma Fall rushed to her husband's side, threw her arms around him, and also sobbed as he embraced her silently. Both of Fall's daughters, Alexina Chase and Jouett Elliot, leaned forward in their seats and wept. Not accustomed to losing, Frank Hogan told anyone who would listen that Fall had been "robbed of his constitutional rights by the judge's charge."

Mark Thompson, one of Fall's lawyers and an old friend, passed out cold and lay on the courtroom floor for ten minutes before being revived. After taking all this in, a character witness who had appeared on Fall's behalf, Robert Geronimo, son of the famous chief Geronimo, declared he'd "had enough" of Washington and departed the same afternoon to rejoin his people in New Mexico. The conviction meant that Albert Fall could spend up to three years in prison and be liable for a $300,000 fine.

FALL WAS SENTENCED to a year in prison and ordered to pay a $100,000 fine, the amount he'd gotten from Doheny. On July 15, 1930, a week before Fall was scheduled to begin his term, political leaders from both parties in New Mexico, including Senator Bronson Cutting, tried to gain a presidential pardon for the former interior secretary. President

Hoover, who as Harding's secretary of commerce had sat in on all the cabinet meetings regarding Teapot, turned them down in a manner that Cutting described as vindictive.

Fall served nine months and nine days at the New Mexico State Prison in Santa Fe. In the meantime, he and Emma had lost the Three Rivers ranch and were nearly bankrupt, "having lost everything in the world since the government persecution . . . started," wrote Emma in an appeal for help to Andrew Mellon, who over the years had become a family friend. There's no record Mellon ever responded.

After Fall's release, he and Emma lived on his small pension from his service in the Spanish-American War and the salary Emma drew from managing a Mexican restaurant in El Paso. He hadn't the money to repay the $100,000 he'd been fined. Fall spent the remaining years of his life in and out of hospitals. On November 30, 1944, he died in his sleep in the Hotel Dieu Hospital in El Paso, a forgotten man.

Emma preceded him in death by a year.

52

EDWARD L. DOHENY

In defending Ed Doheny in the last of the criminal trials relating to the oil scandals, Frank Hogan was at the very top of his game. Five months after Albert Fall was convicted in this same courtroom and before the same judge, William Hitz, the million-dollar lawyer all but summoned in the Vatican to canonize his client on the spot. Doheny, Hogan told the jury of nine men and three women in his closing argument, was a great patriot, a man who had pulled himself up by his bootstraps, helping old friends along the way, a loving husband, and a doting father. "Do you believe this man is a crook?" he asked the jury, pointing at the seventy-three-year-old California oilman. "If he's a crook, then convict him. But can you believe that his mind was so corrupt that he conceived bribery and that he had fallen so low that he selected his own son, whom a few years before he had given to the navy, as the instrument of his bribery?"

Hogan then cranked it up one more notch. "Ned Doheny says to you from the grave that which in life he said from this very witness stand. The indictment charges that young Doheny was a briber. Can you believe that? Can you believe that a man who a few years ago had offered his only son to his country had fallen so low that he took him, the expected solace of his old age, and made him into an instrument of bribery? It isn't human to believe that."

Of course it wasn't. The jury took only an hour to vote for acquittal. "Thank you, and God bless you!" Hogan shouted when he heard the decision. He pounded Doheny on the back while Estelle was trying to give him a hug. Even some of the jury members—one in particular, Emory H. English—were in tears. Doheny, his own cheeks damp with tears of gratitude, walked to the jury box to shake his hand. In New Mexico, Albert Fall understandably expressed puzzlement that he could be convicted of taking a bribe while the man who had given it to him had gotten off scot-free.

The Doheny clan—Edward and Estelle, Lucy and the five grand-children—remained in Washington a few days so that Doheny could get some much needed rest. Before leaving, the old man had a Rolls-Royce delivered to Hogan's home in Washington on Sheridan Circle. He also presented the attorney and his team with a bonus check, in Hogan's case a rumored second $1 million. The Dohenys departed by train, arriving on March 30, 1930, at Union Station in Los Angeles, where they were mobbed by several hundred employees and well-wishers.

A broken man, Doheny lived another five years, the last three of which he was bedridden. He died on September 8, 1935, at the Do-henys' Chester Place compound. Estelle, the fervent Catholic—she had converted in 1918—invited two bishops, a dozen or so monsignors, and fifty priests to the funeral at St. Vincent's Church in Los Angeles. The former long-distance operator with the dulcet voice spent her remaining years supporting Catholic charities and amassing one of the world's great rare book collections. She died of heart disease on October 30, 1958.

THOMAS J. WALSH

Early on the morning of March 2, 1933, Señora Mina Perez Chaumont de Truffin, the wife of Senator Thomas J. Walsh, awoke in the drawing room she shared with her new husband on the Atlantic Coast Line to find the seventy-three-year-old Montanan doubled over in pain. Walsh rose from his berth, staggered over to his bride's bunk, and collapsed on the floor of a heart attack some eighteen miles south of Rocky Mount, North Carolina. Mina Walsh later said she tried unsuccessfully several times to lift him, then began screaming for help.

By the time the train reached the Rocky Mount station, the senator was dead.

Walsh and Truffin, the wealthy widow of Regino Truffin and a member of one of Cuba's most prominent families, had known each other for several years. They'd been married on the Truffin family estate, Finca Mina, on February 24 after Walsh flew in on Pan Am's morning plane from Miami. After a brief honeymoon in Daytona Beach, they headed back to Washington, where Walsh was to become attorney general in Franklin Delano Roosevelt's new cabinet. It was not a job he particularly wanted. Roosevelt had beaten out Walsh for the 1932

Democratic nomination. According to his old friend Burton Wheeler, Walsh was not high on Roosevelt. He agreed to take the attorney general post only after Roosevelt assured Walsh he'd appoint him to the U.S. Supreme Court at first opportunity.

At Rocky Mount, Walsh's body was removed from the train and embalmed at a local funeral home in preparation for the casket to be sent on to Washington on a later train. Meanwhile, the hysterical widow was taken to the home of a well-known attorney and given a sedative by a doctor who accompanied her. When she'd calmed down, she explained to the doctor in halting English, her hands pressed against her stomach, that her late husband had complained of stomach pains in Daytona Beach.

Accompanied by his widow, Walsh's body arrived the next morning in Washington aboard the *Florida Limited.* A throng of silent mourners looked on as the silver bronze casket was removed from the train and carried out to a waiting hearse. A good portion of the U.S. Senate was present, including Burton Wheeler, John Kendrick of Wyoming, and David I. Walsh (no relation) of Massachusetts. James Roosevelt represented his father. From the Mayflower Hotel where they were staying, awaiting the swearing-in ceremony the next morning, the president-elect and Eleanor Roosevelt announced they planned to call on the widow after the inauguration.

Among the family members at Union Station were Walsh's brother John; his only daughter, Genevieve Gudger; her husband, U.S. navy captain Charles Gudger; Walsh's granddaughter, Ellen; a sister, Sally Walsh; and a nephew, John Wattawa. When Mina Walsh, the widow, came off the train, clearly near collapse, Genevieve Gudger embraced her and, with John Walsh, led her out of Union Station to one of the waiting cars.

Appropriately, the funeral, a Catholic ceremony, was held in the Senate chamber where Walsh had served for twenty years. The family members lined the front row a few feet from the flower-banked bier surrounding the coffin, the heavily veiled widow seated directly at the head of the coffin. Immediately behind them sat Franklin Roosevelt, president now, his hands crossed in his lap, his head half-bowed. Eleanor Roosevelt looked on from the presidential gallery. Grouped behind the president were a congressional contingent led by former vice president Charles Curtis of Kansas; most senior military officers and the diplomatic corps in their mourning vestments; and a robed Chief Justice Charles Evans Hughes and the U.S. Supreme Court, whose members, ironically, now included Owen Roberts, a Coolidge appointee.

The eulogy was brief, just as Walsh, who valued the currency of language, likely would have wanted. "The beloved senator from Montana deserves a eulogy but needs none," said Archbishop Michael J. Curley of Baltimore, a longtime friend. "He loved and served his God—he loved and served his fellow man. National fame did not spoil him. Pride did not grip him. Humility grounded in self-knowledge saved him from the ruin wrought in the heart of a man by foolish egotism. . . . He served his country. The nation knows it and today gives ample recognition of that in a way in which the memory of few men has been honored."

Afterward, Walsh's body was taken back to Montana in a special Northern Pacific funeral car, the casket accompanied by Walsh's family members and Senators Wheeler, Kendrick, Thomas Schall of Minnesota, and Lynn Frazier of North Dakota. Senator Walsh's widow had suffered a nervous breakdown and hadn't been permitted by doctors to make the trip.

On its last leg of the journey from Chicago west, the cortege train passed through Wisconsin, where Walsh's parents, both Irish immigrants, had settled almost eighty years earlier, where Walsh had taught in one-room, woodstove-warmed country schools to earn his law school tuition. Traversing North Dakota, where Walsh had initially practiced law, the train crossed into Montana on the evening of March 8, passing through Glendive, Miles City, Bighorn, and Custer and the vast empty reaches of the eastern part of the state.

At each station, crowds gathered to pay their respects. At Billings, the train stopped long enough to pick up one of Walsh's cousins and allow admirers and friends to extend their sympathies to the family. From Billings in the predawn light, the train swung north to Helena, where Walsh was to be buried. It was here in this one-time mining camp, Last Chance Gulch, encircled by mountains that Walsh said "stand like sentries around the town," that he had settled on the west side of town in a modest home with his new wife, Elinor, and made a name for himself fighting the copper kings, before going into politics.

Elinor Walsh was buried here at Resurrection Cemetery. On March 9, with much of Helena's citizenry and members of the Walsh family looking on, Tom Walsh was buried beside her.

ACKNOWLEDGMENTS

There are a number of people to whom I am deeply indebted for their support on this book: most of all, my agent, Charlotte Sheedy; my editor, Will Murphy; Nancy Shockley, the best researcher with whom I have ever worked; Michael McCartney; David Feinberg; Lea Beresford; Meredith Kaffel; Nancy McCartney, for her diligence and honesty in reading draft after draft; the staff of the New York Society Library; and the staff at New Mexico State University. Bless you all.

NOTES

ABBREVIATIONS

The New York Times (*NYT*)
The Washington Post (*WP*)
Los Angeles Times (*LAT*)
Library of Congress, Manuscript Division (LOC)
Albert B. Fall Family Papers, New Mexico State University Library,
    Archives, and Special Collections Department (NMS)

I. A REVERSAL OF FORTUNE

Accounts of Jake Hamon's shooting appeared in many national and regional newspapers, including the *Kansas City Star* and the *Wichita Daily Times*. Clara's story of being seduced and dominated by Jake Hamon and their subsequent relationship came primarily from an interview she conducted with Sam Blair, a correspondent with Universal Service and the *Chicago Herald and Examiner*. After the shooting, Blair followed Clara to Mexico and interviewed her in Chihuahua. Jake's plans to make his son president of the United States were detailed in an *NYT* interview on 5/2/24 with Hamon's widow. The quote by Jake, "Clara, you hit me . . ." and his subsequent stay at the Hardy clinic were reported by the *WP* and numerous other papers. The information that Hamon had to reunite with his wife before he could have the Interior job was disclosed to Thomas Walsh through myriad sources, including Tiffin Gilmore, Department of State, Ohio (Gilmore to Walsh, 3/21/1924, LOC). Harding's "Too bad he had to be taken out" comes from Frances Russell, p. 422.

2. BREAKFAST OF CHAMPIONS

Much of the information for this chapter comes from Daugherty's *Inside Story.* The story of Hamon's attempt to bribe Gore appeared in *WP,* 8/6/20.

3. CONVENTION

Hamon's visit to the Harding campaign headquarters in Indianapolis, his meeting with Jess Smith and Howard Mannington at the Deshler Hotel in Columbus, Ohio, and his initial contributions to the Harding campaign were detailed by Smith's former wife, Roxy Stinson, in her appearance before the Wheeler Committee in 1924. *Inside Story* also details much of what went on at the convention. Hamon's role in securing the Republican nomination for Harding was detailed by Bill Nichols in a March 14, 1921, interview he gave to a United Press correspondent. At the time, Nichols was testifying at the trial of Clara Hamon for the murder of her paramour. When Nichols started to talk about the 1920 Republican convention on the witness stand, the judge stopped him and ordered him to step down. Bruce Bliven's August 1965 story in *American Heritage,* "Tempest over Teapot," provides a lively account of the convention, which Bliven covered. Perhaps the most thorough account of the convention and the dealings of Daugherty, Hamon, Penrose, and King on Harding's behalf appears in Frances Russell's *The Shadow of Blooming Grove.* Florence Harding's substantial role at the convention and later in Harding's campaign is brought out in *Inside Story* and Carl Sferrazza Anthony's *Florence Harding: The First Lady, the Jazz Age and the Death of America's Most Scandalous President.* Finally, Leonard Wood Jr. wrote a statement in 1924 explaining how oil interests had assured Wood the presidency in exchange for giving Hamon the Interior post. Wood's statement was published by the Associated Press on 3/8/24. The amount Sinclair paid to take over a floor at the Blackstone Hotel was reported to Walsh by *Denver Post* reporter D. F. Stackelbeck (Stackelbeck to Walsh, 1/24/24, LOC). Nan Britton's dalliances with Harding during the convention are detailed in *The President's Daughter.*

4. THE PRIZE

Daniel Yergin's *The Prize* remains the definitive history of the oil industry.

George Otis Smith's warning that America was running out of oil appeared in *NYT,* 1/7/20. The account of the postconvention gathering at the Daughertys' cabin in Washington Court House was drawn from Roxy Stinson's testimony before the Wheeler Committee.

5. A STAR OF A FELLOW

There have been a number of books about Albert Fall, the best of which is *Tempest over Teapot Dome* by David H. Stratton. Gordon R. Owen's *The Two Alberts* also provides valuable insights into Fall's early years and political dealings in New Mexico. Evalyn Walsh McLean knew Fall well and described his frontier persona in *Queen of Diamonds*.

6. THE FRONT PORCH CAMPAIGN

Frances Russell provides a comprehensive account of the Harding campaign, while John Morello's *Selling the President, 1920* is an incisive and thorough account of the extensive and largely unheralded role advertising king Albert D. Lasker played in putting Harding over and cleaning up the personal messes he'd left behind. Much of the correspondence between Fall, Harding, and others comes from the Walsh papers at the LOC or the Albert Fall Family Papers, NMS. The information about Jim Sloan comes from Britton's book but is also drawn from a 3/30/24 report written by a Secret Service agent identified only a "H-21" (LOC).

7. THE CAMPAIGN TRAIL

Both Carl Sferrazza Anthony and Evalyn Walsh McLean describe the cross-country train tour. Frances Russell is the primary source for the information on the Oklahoma City banquet.

8. FRIENDS OF JAKE HAMON

The material here is drawn from the testimony in Clara Hamon's trial. Hamon's request to ask Harding to take care of his friends was first revealed in Doheny's letter to Fall offering Harding the use of his yacht is in NMS, 11/3/21. The quote regarding Fall's return to Washington with the Harding cabinet slated appeared in several newspapers, including the *Bridgeport Telegram*, 2/3/21.

9. ACQUITTAL

The dialogue here comes from the trial testimony as reported by the numerous correspondents in attendance, one of whom was Clara Hamon. She was in the unique position of covering her own trial.

10. FATAL DISTRACTIONS

Frances Russell provides a lively portrait of Harding's early days in the White House. Nan Britton describes her early trysts with the new president in *The President's Daughter*. Evalyn Walsh McLean offers up some lively details, including the Nannie Duke anecdote. Gaston Means is the sole source of the dead showgirl story, which he relates in *The Strange Death of President Harding*.

11. TROUBLE AHEAD

Burl Noogle's *Teapot Dome: Oil and Politics in the 1920s* is the best source regarding Fall's attempt to roll back the conservation efforts that had been put in place by Teddy Roosevelt, Gifford Pinchot, and others.

12. THE OHIO GANG

As one of its senior members, Means provides a comprehensive (if self-serving) assessment of how the gang operated. Werner and Starr examine the interrelationships of the gang members and their individual functions. Charles L. Mee Jr.'s *The Ohio Gang* briskly chronicles the gang's activities, while Roxy Stinson, Jess Smith's former wife, revealed much about the gang in her testimony before the Wheeler hearings.

13. ROCKEFELLER OF THE WEST

The two best books on Doheny are Davis's *Dark Side of Fortune* and La Botz's *Edward L. Doheny: Petroleum, Power, and Politics in the United States and Mexico*.

14. BACK IN THE DAY

Doheny's efforts to develop the Tampico fields and the role of U.S. oil interests in trying to undercut Mexican leaders who were unsympathetic to their interests were chronicled in the 7/12/19 and 12/22/26 issues of *The Nation*. A veteran of the Tampico fields, Dan Williams vividly described his experiences during this period in *WP*, 1/5/47. Frank Seaver's work in Mexico on Doheny's behalf is the focus of "Frank Roger Seaver" by Lieutenant Colonel Norman S. Marshall, California Center for Military History.

15. POWER GRAB

Most of the information pertaining to Fall's efforts to take over the reserves came out in the Walsh hearings, which were covered on an almost daily basis by *NYT*, *WP*, and other papers. Stratton is also a key source here.

16. SURE THING

The details of what went on at the Vanderbilt came out in the Senate investigation of Continental Trading Co. Sinclair's techniques for finding oil were explained by Tulsa University professor Norman Hyne in a 2004 interview broadcast on *Sunflower Journeys*, KTWU Channel 11, Topeka, Kansas. Sinclair's high-stakes betting with Arnold Rothstein and his losses in the Black Sox scandal can be found in Eliot Asinof's *Eight Men Out*.

17. BLACK BAG

The source for information regarding Ned Doheny's preferential treatment in the U.S. Navy comes primarily from Major Norman Marshall's "The Forgotten Bagman of Teapot Dome." Fall detailed the terms of his employment agreement with Doheny in several documents and letters that are included in the Albert Fall Family Papers. Much of the information about Ned and Lucy Doheny's active social life is drawn from the *LAT*. Werner and Starr's *Teapot Dome* is the source for much of the information regarding the Dohenys' dealings with Robinson and Fall.

18. ALL ROADS LEAD TO THREE RIVERS

Stratton's *Tempest over Teapot Dome* and Fall's own papers, including the seventy-five-page report Fall wrote Harding justifying the leases, are important sources here. The source for the fight in the schoolhouse is Stackelbeck in a 1/24/24 letter to Walsh (LOC).

19. UNFINISHED BUSINESS

Wallace's threat to blow the whistle on Fall comes from Noogle's *Teapot Dome*. Fall's efforts to pressure Ambrose were drawn primarily from Werner and Starr. Jess Smith's complaints that he and Daugherty had been excluded from a $33 million deal were related by Roxy Stinson. The La Follette investigation was widely covered in the press, while the details of Sinclair's payoff to Fall's son-in-law M. T. Everhart were brought out in the Continental investigation during Walsh's interrogation of Fall's son-in-law.

20. A DOG'S BREAKFAST

The story of Lasker's visit to the White House to warn Harding about Walter Teagle's concerns about the oil leases comes from Morello, *Selling the President.* J. Leonard Bates's *Senator Thomas J. Walsh of Montana* provides a well-researched account of Walsh's life and career. Though a committed Republican, Mark Sullivan also profiles Walsh admiringly in *Our Times.* Walsh's papers in the LOC deal primarily with his career and include extensive correspondence dealing with his investigation of both the Teapot scandal and related Continental Trading scandals. Most of the major newspapers and magazines of the day also profiled Walsh, who appeared on the May 4, 1925, cover of *Time.*

21. THE BEST-LAID PLANS

The Fall-backed takeover of Navajo land by the oil interests was exposed by Newspaper Enterprise Association (NEA) Service writer Rodney Dutcher in a 1/27/33 article that ran in numerous papers. E. K. Gaylord, editor of the Oklahoma Publishing Company, first alerted Walsh to Doheny's Alaskan ambitions in a 1/25/24 letter to Walsh (LOC). The *Alaskan Dispatch* wrote of Doheny's visit to Kachemak Bay on 8/11/24.

22. NAPOLEON AND THE DUTCHMAN

There are three primary sources for this chapter: Gene Fowler's *Timberline: A Story of Bonfils and Tammen,* which presents a lively portrait of the *Denver Post* owners for whom he worked; the correspondence between D. F. Stackelbeck and Walsh in the LOC; and the correspondence between Fall and M. D. McEniry, the Department of the Interior's man in Denver. The information regarding Bonfils as a user of criminals to investigate potential blackmail victims came from a Secret Service agent named C. A. Betts in a report he filed to his superior, an agent named Adams. Another book on the history of the *Denver Post, Thunder in the Rockies,* focuses extensively on the Bonfils-Tammen era.

23. SUMMER OF THEIR DISCONTENT

Nan's visit to Harding in the White House comes from *The President's Daughter.* Means is the primary source on the book-burning incident. The details of Fall sending in the U.S. Marines to Teapot came out in the hearings.

24. SHAKEDOWN

The McEniry, Fall, and Hearst correspondence can be found in NMS. Schuyler gave his account of the $1 million payoff in various press interviews. The alternative account in which Harding approved of the payoff came from Miguel Otero (Otero to Walsh, 2/14/24, NMS). Some of the information Otero reported was corroborated by Fowler, namely that Bonfils went along on the Alaskan trip as the *Post*'s correspondent, without filing a word of copy; that Bonfils presented Florence with a sealskin coat before the trip and later was invited to cruise on a naval vessel by Denby.

25. THE UNRAVELING

Mrs. Poindexter's letters were the topic of several articles in *WP* beginning 1/29/23. Smith's claim "They're going to get me" was mentioned in the Senate by J. Thomas Heflin (*Congressional Record*, 69th Cong., 2nd sess.). In *Queen of Diamonds*, Evalyn Walsh McLean described Smith's frantic call to her the night before he died and being told by her son that he was dead.

26. DEPARTURE

The details of the Alaskan trip come from Anthony, Russell, and the extensive press coverage the Hardings received during the cross-country journey. The details about Brush buying the *Star* for an inflated price came out in the Continental hearings, as did Ungerleider's dealings with the president. Emma Fall's "delightful evening" letter resides in the Ohio Historical Society. Harding's approval of Fall's Russian trip is described by Stratton. Harding's uncomfortable horseback excursion through Zion National Park is recounted by Russell. The conversation between Hoover and Harding involving a great scandal appeared in Murray's *The Harding Era*. The Hardings' discussion with Pierce is related in Pierce's memoir, *Memoirs and Times of Walter Pierce*.

27. COOLIDGE

The account of Coolidge learning about Harding's death comes from several sources, including *The Autobiography of Calvin Coolidge*. Robert H. Ferrell's *The Presidency of Calvin Coolidge* is the source for much of the information on the Boston police strike and Coolidge's early days in the White House.

28. GETTING READY

The "crooked deal" anecdote comes from Wheeler's oral history. That Walsh congratulated Fall on his taking over the Interior position is noted by Stratton. The correspondence between Walsh and Kendrick and Walsh and Daniels can be found in Walsh's papers in the LOC.

29. TWO MASTERS

Stratton again was the main source on Fall's retirement plans. Zevely's visit and the details of the Russian trip came out in the Teapot hearings. NEA service writer Rodney Dutcher was the journalist who knew Day and profiled him in a 6/21/29 article that appeared in numerous newspapers. Mohammad Gholi Majd was the main source on Sinclair's failed efforts in Persia and the murder of Imbrie.

30. OPENING ROUNDS

The information for this chapter comes from the records of the Teapot hearings and from Fall's correspondence with McEniry. Margaret Leslie Davis provides a lively description of Doheny's first appearance before the Walsh Committee. J. Leonard Bates describes Walsh's friendship with Doheny. The Beall letter to Walsh can be found among the Walsh Papers, as can the Whipple telegram and Walsh's correspondence with Stackelbeck.

31. THE CRUSADER

Magee and his battles with Fall and the corrupt elements in New Mexico are detailed in the *Albuquerque Tribune* "About Us" section of its website. Magee's papers are at the University of New Mexico in Albuquerque. Taylor Branch profiled Magee in *Blowing the Whistle*. Incidentally, Magee went on to invent the parking meter.

32. THE CRACK-UP

The telegrams between Fall and Chase are included in Walsh's papers, as are Fall's wire to Mellon and his wire to McKinney. Stratton and Davis are sources for this chapter, though much of the information comes directly from the hearings.

33. THE PALM BEACH STORY

Walsh made a detailed report to the Committee on Public Lands and Surveys regarding his meeting with McLean and his attempt to question Fall upon his return from Florida. Daisy Harriman was long one of the most prominent women in Washington. In her book *From Pinafores to Politics,* she mentions her meetings with Walsh at the San Francisco convention. H. L. Mencken in *Thirty-five Years* describes Walsh hiding from Harriman. McLean's use of code names and telegrams was widely reported in the press and probed in detail during the Teapot hearings.

34. TRUE CONFESSIONS

Bates and Stratton provide the basic information for this chapter. Fall's acknowledgment of the consequences of confessing Doheny was his money source appears in a document Fall wrote on 1/21/29 (NMS). Stratton quotes it more fully. Walsh wrote of Doheny turning down his business proposal on 12/24/22 (LOC).

35. DAMAGE CONTROL

The information about Hays's collecting bonds from Sinclair and then laundering them through influential Republicans came out in the Continental hearings. La Botz is a good source for Doheny's maneuverings in Mexico. McCoy also writes about the events on the *Mayflower,* but the principal source for this segment is Werner and Starr.

36. THE CONSPIRACY

Both *WP* and *NYT* had reporters aboard the *President Harding* and covered Sinclair's arrival. Walsh's pique at not being consulted by Coolidge regarding the appointment of the special prosecutors and his concerns about Roberts and Pomerene's abilities to take on the legal teams of Doheny and Sinclair were reported by Bates. The story of the Washington, D.C., Police Department's stationing a detective at the hearing appeared in *WP* (1/26/24).

37. THE REDHEAD, THE RADICAL, AND THE ATTORNEY GENERAL

Wheeler's role in getting Roxy to testify and Walsh's defense of Wheeler are taken primarily from *Yankee from the West.* Bates is also a source here, as are a number of newspapers, including the *Helena Daily Independent.*

38. STATE OF DENIAL

The account of the Roberts-Walsh meeting appears in Werner and Starr, as does the story of the special counsel visiting Coolidge. The correspondence between Thomas Moran, Walsh, and Roberts comes from the LOC and Werner and Starr. The details of the Continental Trading scam came out in the hearings. *NYT* provided extensive coverage of the 1924 Democratic convention. Edward Ranson's "A Snarling Roughhouse" best captures the raucous event, however. Walsh's wire to Frank Walsh about illegal campaign funds being used in the Montana election was reported in several newspapers, including the *Lincoln State Journal* (10/24/24). The Dohenys' difficulties regarding the L.A. harbormaster bribe came from *LAT.* Hogan's "rich client" quote appeared in *Time* (3/11/35). Walsh heard about Sinclair's attempts to "get to" Judge Kennedy from a number of sources, including Joseph O'Mahoney, city editor of the *Cheyenne State Leader* and later a U.S. senator from Wyoming.

39. THE UNSEEN HAND

The information on Paul Anderson and the decision to reopen the hearings comes largely from Bates, Lambeth, and a profile of Anderson that appeared in the *St. Louis Post-Dispatch* (12/14/2003).

40. A BRIBE AS BIG AS THE RITZ

Almost all of the information here appeared in *WP.* Burns's previous efforts to bribe a juror appeared in the *Decatur Review* (11/11/27). Werner and Starr also describe how Sinclair and Burns's team were apprehended.

41. THE LINK

The information for this chapter is drawn from the hearing records and from Bates.

42. ABOVE THE LAW

Bates and the hearings records are the sources here. Walsh's quote about the "recusant witness" appeared in the *Congressional Record* (2/4/28).

43. DIRTY BONDS, CLEAN CASH

The testimony primarily of Will Hays brought to light how the bond laundering operated. Senator Caraway described Hays as "a fence . . . who knew that certain goods were stolen goods and was trying to help the thief find a market for them."

44. ANDY

This is drawn directly from the hearings.

45. FORTY-EIGHT HOURS

John D. Rockefeller Jr. wrote Walsh about his concerns regarding Stewart on 2/8/28. Walsh wrote A. E. Bowers about Junior's miserable failure on 2/8/21. Both letters are in the LOC. The Daniels letter about Humphreys's suicide was written to Walsh on 3/22/28. King wrote Walsh twice about Humphreys's suicide, on 2/11/28 and 2/24/28. These letters are also in the LOC.

46. ACQUITTAL, REVELATION

See *WP* (4/22/28) for the most thorough account of Sinclair's acquittal. Stewart would later inform the Committee on Public Lands and Surveys about his presenting the missing Liberty bonds to his unsuspecting board.

47. RICH MAN'S JUSTICE

Stewart's second appearance before the committee proved far more enlightening than the first. Most of the material regarding Walsh's reaction to Stewart comes from Bates.

48. ROBERT STEWART

Time gave enormous play to the Stewart-Rockefeller battle, milking it for all it was worth.

49. HARRY SINCLAIR

Time, WP, and the *Charleston* (West Virginia) *Daily Mail* covered the Sinclair internment most closely; in fact, the Charleston paper had an anonymous correspondent inside the jail writing about the favorable treatment the oilman was receiving. Sinclair, like A. E. Humphreys, had been born in West Virginia, which may explain the paper's interest in the oilman.

50. NED DOHENY

Leslie White was the primary detective on the Ned Doheny–Hugh Plunkett case and wrote about it in *Me, Detective*. Davis gives an evenhanded account of the killing in *Dark Side*. Chandler's "take" on the tragedy comes to us via Robert Moss.

51. ALBERT FALL

Stratton, *WP*, and *Time* were the principal sources for the Fall trial.

52. EDWARD L. DOHENY

Davis's account is the basis for this chapter.

53. THOMAS J. WALSH

An Associated Press reporter wrote about Walsh's body being taken off the train at Rocky Mount. *NYT* and *WP* gave extensive coverage to his funeral, while the Montana papers, notably the *Helena Daily Independent*, wrote about his return to Montana and the burial next to his first wife. Bates, of course, also deals with this material.

BIBLIOGRAPHY

BOOKS AND ARTICLES

Listed below are the books and articles and additional research resources I have drawn from for this book. The Teapot Dome documents, covering all of the major aspects of the scandal, including testimony, grand jury material, briefs, evidence, correspondence, hearings, and archival records, are available from Lexis in microfilm. In addition, The New York Times *and* The Washington Post *carried almost daily accounts of the hearings, while information on regional developments pertaining to the Teapot scandal can be accessed through Newspaperarchive.com, which has digitized the contents of more than two hundred newspapers.* The New Republic, The Nation, *and* Time *covered the scandal closely, though from distinctly different vantage points. Their archives are also available online.*

Adams, Samuel H. *Incredible Era.* Boston: Houghton Mifflin Co., 1939.

Allen, Frederick Lewis. *Only Yesterday.* New York: Harper & Row, 1931.

Anthony, Carl Sferrazza. *Florence Harding: The First Lady, the Jazz Age and the Death of America's Most Scandalous President.* New York: William Morrow, 1998.

Asinof, Eliot. *Eight Men Out: The Black Sox and The 1919 World Series.* Minneapolis: Tandem Library, 1999.

Bates, J. Leonard. *Senator Thomas J. Walsh of Montana.* Urbana and Chicago: University of Illinois Press, 1999.

Beals, Carlton. *Mexico: An Interpretation.* New York: B. W. Huebsch, 1934.

Bliven, Bruce. "Tempest over Teapot Dome." *American Heritage,* August 1965.

Britton, Nan. *The President's Daughter.* New York: Elizabeth Ann Guild, Inc., 1927.

Caesar, Gene. *Incredible Detective: The Biography of William J. Burns.* Englewood Cliffs, N.J.: Prentice-Hall, Inc., 1968.

Coolidge, Calvin. *The Autobiography of Calvin Coolidge.* Honolulu: University Press of the Pacific, 2004.

Daugherty, Harry M., with Thomas Dixon. *The Inside Story of the Harding Tragedy.* New York: Churchill Co., 1932.

Davis, Margaret Leslie. *Dark Side of Fortune.* Berkeley and Los Angeles: University of California Press, 1998.

Dean, John W. *Warren G. Harding.* New York: Times Books, 2004.

Ferrell, Robert H. *The Presidency of Calvin Coolidge.* Lawrence: University Press of Kansas, 1998.

Fowler, Gene. *Timberline: A Story of Bonfils and Tammen.* Garden City, N.Y.: Garden City Publishing, 1933.

Harriman, J. Borden. *From Pinafores to Politics.* New York: Henry Holt & Co., 1923.

Hosokawa, Bill. *Thunder in the Rockies.* New York: William Morrow & Co., 1975.

La Botz, Dan. *Edward L. Doheny: Petroleum, Power, and Politics in the United States and Mexico.* New York: Praeger, 1991.

Lambeth, Edmund B. "The Lost Career of Paul Y. Anderson." *Journalism Quarterly* 60 (1983).

Majd, Mohammad Gholi. *Oil and the Killing of the American Consul in Tehran.* Lanham, Md.: University Press of America, 2006.

Marshall, Norman S. "The Forgotten Bagman of Teapot Dome Edward 'Ned' Laurence Doheny Jr." California Center for Military History, Sacramento, Calif. (www.militarymuseum.org/Doheny. htm), 1998.

Marshall, Norman S. "Frank Roger Seaver: A Hero's Life." California Center for Military History, Sacramento, Calif. (www.militarymuseum.org/Seaver.htm), 1999.

McCoy, Donald R. *Calvin Coolidge: The Quiet President.* New York: Macmillan, 1967.

McLean, Evalyn Walsh. *Father Struck It Rich.* Boston: Little, Brown & Co., 1936.

McLean, Evalyn Walsh. *Queen of Diamonds: The Fabled Legacy of Evalyn Walsh McLean.* Franklin, Tenn.: Hillsboro Press, 2000.

Means, Gaston B. *The Strange Death of President Harding.* New York: Guild Publishing Co., 1936.

Meer, Charles L., Jr. *The Ohio Gang: The World of Warren G. Harding.* New York: M. Evans, 1981.

Mencken, H. L. *Thirty-five Years of Newspaper Work: A Memoir.* Baltimore and London: Johns Hopkins University Press, 1996.

Morello, John A. *Selling the President, 1920.* Westport, Conn.: Praeger Publishers, 2001.

Moss, Robert L. "Cracking the Cassidy Case, Criticism and Scholarship." Raymond Chandler website. http://home.comcast.net/~mossrobert/

Murray, Robert K. *The Harding Era: Warren G. Harding and His Administration.* Minneapolis: University of Minnesota Press, 1969.

Noogle, Burl. *Teapot Dome: Oil and Politics in the 1920s.* New York: Norton, 1962.

Owen, Gordon R. *The Two Alberts: Fountain and Fall.* Las Cruces, N.M.: Yucca Tree Press, 1996.

Peters, Charles, and Taylor Branch (eds.). *Blowing the Whistle: Dissent in the Public Interest.* New York: Praeger Publishers, 1972.

Pierce, Walter Marcus. *Memoirs and Times of Walter Pierce.* Portland: Oregon Historical Society, 1981.

Ranson, Edward A. "Snarling Roughhouse: The Democratic Convention of 1924." *History Today,* July 1994.

Russell, Frances. *The Shadow of Blooming Grove: Warren G. Harding in His Times.* New York: McGraw-Hill Book Company, 1968.

Sinclair, Andrew. *The Available Man.* New York: Macmillan, 1965.

Stratton, David H. *Tempest over Teapot Dome: The Story of Albert B. Fall.* Norman: University of Oklahoma Press, 1998.

Sullivan, Mark. *Our Times: The Twenties, Vol. VI.* New York: Scribner's, 1935.

Werner, M. R., and John Starr. *Teapot Dome.* New York: Viking Press, 1959.

Wheeler, Burton L. *Yankee from the West.* Garden City, N.Y.: Doubleday & Co., Inc., 1962.

White, Leslie T. *Me, Detective.* New York: Harcourt, 1936.

Yergin, Daniel. *The Prize: The Epic Quest for Oil, Money and Power.* New York: Simon & Schuster, 1992.

PAPERS AND COLLECTIONS

Albert B. Fall Family Papers, New Mexico State University Library, Archives, and Special Collections Department.

General Records of the Department of Justice, National Archives, Washington, D.C.

Carl C. Magee Papers, 1873–1946, University of New Mexico, Albuquerque, N.M.

Records of the U.S. Secret Service, the National Archives, Washington, D.C.

The Reminiscences of Senator Burton K. Wheeler, 1981, Oral History Research Office, Columbia University.

Thomas J. Walsh Papers, Library of Congress, Manuscript Division, Washington, D.C.

INDEX

Agriculture Department, U.S., 66, 105–6
Alaska, 66, 119, 120–22, 139, 140, 145–51
Albuquerque Morning Journal, 46–48, 49, 126,
   146, 175, 177–78, 179
Ambrose, Arthur, 106–7, 133–34
Anderson, Paul Y., 259–61, 262, 279
attorney general, U.S.: Daugherty
   appointment as, 30, 56, 60–61, 63; and
   leasing of naval reserves, 29, 30, 107; Stone
   as, 253; Walsh as, 316–17

Blackmer, Harry M.: and Bonfils-Tammen
   allegations, 136, 137; and Continental
   Trading, 243, 282, 285, 290; and criminal
   conspiracy case, 263; flight of, 220, 252,
   285; and La Follette committee, 136;
   Midwest Refining sale by, 103–4, 170; and
   Rockefeller-Walsh meeting, 282; and Salt
   Creek fields, 103; and Sinclair-Bonfils
   payoff, 139; and special prosecutors, 252;
   Standard Oil of Indiana deal with, 103–4,
   170; and Teapot Dome hearings, 170; at
   Three Rivers Ranch meetings, 103–4, 136,
   137, 225, 282; and Vanderbilt Hotel
   meeting, 92, 243, 252
Bonfils, Frederick: Alaska trip of, 139, 140,
   148; as crusading newspaperman, 137;
   Denby trip with, 221; Fall views about, 138,
   140; Florence Harding gift from, 140, 148;
   and Harding, 136, 139, 140, 148; and

Lenroot resignation, 222; and marines at
   Teapot Dome, 135; personal and
   professional background of, 123–24;
   pseudonyms of, 124; secret agents of, 125,
   136, 175–76; Shaffer rivalry with, 128; and
   Sinclair, 127, 128–29, 135–37, 139–41, 148,
   149, 170, 176, 178, 220–21, 225, 226; and
   Stack allegations, 123, 126–27, 128, 129;
   Tammen partnership with, 123, 125; Teapot
   Dome testimony of, 220–21, 226. See also
   Denver Post
Britton, Nan: child of, 15, 25, 39, 130; diary
   of, 130; and elections of 1920, 15–16, 18,
   22, 25, 26, 39, 42, 43; Harding's relationship
   with, 15–16, 18, 22, 25, 63–64, 130
Buena Vista (California) Petroleum Reserve,
   29, 96, 161, 202, 239
Bureau of Investigation, 64, 70, 71, 72, 192,
   232, 238, 241, 263, 264
Bureau of Mines, U.S., 84, 102, 107, 115, 170
burnings, of papers and records, 131, 158, 239
Burns, W. Sherman, 264, 265, 269, 302
Burns, William "Billy": appointed head of
   Bureau of Investigation, 70; and Chandler
   book, 131; and criminal conspiracy case,
   263–64, 265, 269; and Daugherty, 70, 71,
   230; and H Street house death, 64;
   headquarters of, 265; jury tampering by,
   263–64, 265, 269; and Ohio Gang, 70, 72;
   prison sentence for, 302; resignation of, 235;

Doheny, Edward L. (*cont'd*)
and Pearl Harbor project, 96, 109; personal
and professional background of, 74–77, 78;
profits of, 106–7, 174, 202; Republican
comments about, 207; as "Rockefeller of the
West," 74; and special prosecutors, 219,
239, 249–50, 251, 261; and Supreme Court
appeal, 255; and Teapot Dome hearings, 75,
173–74, 193, 194, 195, 199, 201–5, 209,
212–13; testimonies of, 173–74, 202–5, 209,
212–13; and transfer of naval reserves to
Interior Department, 87, 88; and Vanderbilt
Hotel meeting, 89, 92; and Walsh, 117,
173–74, 193, 194, 201–2, 205, 211; and
Wheeler resolution, 229

elections of 1920: campaign contributions for,
12, 14, 18–19, 20, 24, 25, 42–43, 55, 91,
175, 185, 207–8, 212, 220, 225, 226, 227,
275; campaign during, 4, 9, 10, 11, 12–13,
34, 35, 36–44, 49, 50–51; Democratic
convention for, 36; and oil industry, 27–29,
50, 91, 220; Republican convention for, 4, 9,
10, 14–26, 71, 251, 284; and Stinson
testimony, 234; vote in, 51; and Walsh
conspiracy theory, 235; women as voters in,
37
elections: of **1884**, 16; of **1896**, 37; of **1912**,
117, 188, 189; of **1916**, 11, 160; of **1918**, 32,
47, 226; of **1920**, 170; of **1924**, 147, 159,
170, 174, 207, 213, 224, 231, 240–41,
244–48; of **1928**, 260, 273, 278; of **1932**,
316–17; cost of, 170
Elk Hills (California) Petroleum Reserve:
Doheny interest in, 87, 88, 94, 96, 230; and
Doheny "loan" to Fall, 94; Doheny profits
from, 202; and expansion of Fall
responsibilities, 66, 67; official
announcement of Fall-Doheny deal
concerning, 109; as part of naval oil
reserves, 29; and Roosevelt Jr., 85; signing
of Doheny contract concerning, 111, 161;
and special prosecutors investigation, 239,
250, 251; Supreme Court ruling about, 255;
and Teapot Dome scandal as political issue,
224; and transfer of naval reserves to
Interior Department, 87, 88
Everhart, Mahlon T., 111–12, 241–43,
252–53, 259, 263, 266, 267–68, 287

Fall, Albert Bacon: appearance of, 48, 190;
appointment/confirmation as interior
secretary of, 53, 54–55, 56, 60, 61, 87–88,
161; conviction and fine of, 312–13;

criminal prosecutions/trials of, 34, 248,
262–65, 286, 307, 311–12; criticisms of,
105–6, 120; death of children of, 32, 46,
203; death of, 313; Democrat pressures
concerning, 209; and Doheny acquittal,
315; early career of, 85–86; and elections of
1918, 32, 47; and elections of 1920, 34, 35,
43–44, 45, 49; enemies of, 32, 35, 46; as "fall
guy," 186; financial affairs of, 47–48, 78,
87–88, 93–94, 96, 97, 98–99, 100–101, 106,
109, 110, 111–12, 115, 126, 136, 161, 165,
172–73, 175, 176, 179, 181, 185–86,
241–44, 252, 275, 313; health of, 45, 181,
182, 183–84, 185, 190, 196, 199–200, 214,
262–63, 265, 286, 311–12; indictment of,
248, 271; lawyers for, 311; letter to Teapot
Dome hearings from, 184, 185–86, 187,
275; and media, 206; as Mexican Affairs
subcommittee chair, 80, 81–82; personality
of, 31–32, 46, 48, 172, 192; poker parties of,
62, 219–20; professional background of, 34;
pseudonyms of, 190, 192; refuses to testify,
252, 263; Republican comments about, 207;
reputation/image of, 31–32, 120, 200;
Russian trip of, 164–68; as senator, 31, 80,
81–82, 87; surveillance of, 197; views about
politics of, 34; views about Teapot Dome
hearings of, 174–75; and Walsh, 196. *See
also* Interior, Secretary of; *specific person or
topic*
Fall, Emma, 32, 34, 55, 148, 164, 168, 183,
190, 194, 200, 262, 312, 313
Fifth Amendment, 214, 226, 242, 252, 267,
287
Finney, Edward C., 108–9, 110, 111
Fitts, Burton, 305, 306, 308
Forbes, Charles R., 70–71, 143
Foreign Relations Committee, U.S. Senate,
33, 43–44, 80, 81–82
Forest Service, U.S., 66, 67–68, 105–6, 122
Foster, Thomas B., 241–42, 243
Four Corners area, 119–20
Frankfurter, Felix, 235–36, 254

Geological Survey, U.S., 28, 84, 115
Gulf Oil, 27, 278

H Street house, 63, 64
Hamon, Clara Smith, 3–4, 5, 6–7, 51, 52, 53,
57–59, 91
Hamon, Jake: ambitions of, 4, 5, 11, 13;
campaign contributions of, 42, 55, 175;
Clara's relationship with, 3–4, 6, 57–58;
Daugherty dealings with, 9, 10, 12–13,

ABOUT THE AUTHOR

LATON MCCARTNEY is an award-winning author whose work has appeared in numerous national publications. He is the author of *Friends in High Places: The Bechtel Story—The Most Secret Corporation and How It Engineered the World,* and *Across the Great Divide: Robert Stuart and the Discovery of the Oregon Trail.* He and his wife, Nancy, divide their time between Manhattan and Wyoming.

ABOUT THE TYPE

This book was set in Caslon, a typeface first designed in 1722 by William Caslon. Its widespread use by most English printers in the early eighteenth century soon supplanted the Dutch typefaces that had formerly prevailed. The roman is considered a "workhorse" typeface due to its pleasant, open appearance, while the italic is exceedingly decorative.